RESOURCE-BASED LEARNING

Resource-Based Learning

NORMAN BESWICK

Course Tutor in Education and Library Studies,
Loughborough University of Technology

HEINEMANN EDUCATIONAL BOOKS

LONDON

Heinemann Educational Books Ltd
LONDON EDINBURGH MELBOURNE AUCKLAND
TORONTO SINGAPORE HONG KONG KUALA LUMPUR
IBADAN NAIROBI JOHANNESBURG
LUSAKA NEW DELHI KINGSTON

ISBN 0 435 80077 9

First published 1977

SO 10451 £6.50 7.79

Published by
Heinemann Educational Books Ltd
48 Charles Street, London W1X 8AH
Printed in Great Britain by
Cox & Wyman Ltd,
London, Fakenham and Reading

Contents

Foreword

Linking theory with practice is one of the central purposes of the *Heinemann Organization in Schools Series*. Norman Beswick has already demonstrated in an earlier study in the series, *Organizing Resources*, that he can helpfully look in detail behind the ready educational platitude and help schools work out for themselves what really are the practical implications. In *Resource-Based Learning* he makes a major contribution to the study of curriculum in schools by relating the needs of the pupil learning by 'his own direct confrontation with a learning resource or set of resources' to the professional skills of media producer, librarian, and teacher, and to the organizational context in which they work. His concept of the 'three professions together' is worked out in convincing detail in a way that allows schools to see the full implications of using resource-based learning as an element in the curriculum.

Like other books in the series, we have a number of different readers in mind. Obviously all teachers concerned with curriculum planning, but especially Heads of Department, anyone concerned with educational media production, and librarians, headteachers and senior staff responsible for leading discussion in schools, for making decisions, and for implementing them, will find this vital reading in relation to a consideration of a school's curriculum. Too often considerations have stopped at classroom method, and have not followed through the requirements in terms of the professional skills and organizational support required.

The *Heinemann Organization in Schools Series* has been devised as a whole, so that the central philosophy and every aspect of the planning and running of a school will be methodically covered. However, each book has been written by a different author and from a different point of view out of his or her own observation, experience, and conviction. Since each book is written to stand on its own, there is inevitably some overlapping between volumes, and certain topics appear in more than one book. *Resource-Based Learning* takes its place as an integrating volume, built on Mr Beswick's unique knowledge and experience, and showing us how learning method, professional approaches, curriculum planning, and school organization are related to each other.

MICHAEL MARLAND

Preface: What do we mean by resource-based learning?

'Resource-based learning' is a term with a variety of meanings, and in these pages practically all of them will be intended and relevant. Some people use the term to mean learning that is closely sequenced, teacher-directed, and programmed; others use it for very open-ended work based on enquiry and discovery techniques, with a considerable element of student choice. As a blanket term, 'resource-based learning' thus covers a wide spectrum of possibilities and modes, according to the temperament and professional decision of the teacher and the circumstances of the subject matter, class and school.

Essential to all variants, however, is the assumption that the student will learn from his own direct confrontation, individually or in a group, with a learning resource or set of resources, and activities connected with them, rather than from conventional exposition by the teacher. He may work in a classroom, in a laboratory, in a library, in a separate 'resource area', or outside the school altogether, exploring the environment with some particular task or problem in mind. In all cases he will be active, whether proceeding through a series of planned steps or making his own decisions in a problem-solving predicament.

It is not presupposed that this is the only type of learning experience he has; resource-based learning is normally regarded as one element to be added to the variety of school life, rather than as a substitute for all that has been traditionally offered. The teacher is not replaced, but given a further strategy to employ. There have been instances, to be sure, in the UK and overseas, where dramatic revolutions have taken place, and these pages will be hospitable to such boldness and interested in the results, but our discussion here does not start from the assumption that all previous methods of teaching and learning are to be overthrown. We shall note that some styles of resource-based work have been very widely employed in many British primary schools (for ages 5–11) for many years, but this does not necessarily imply the prescription of primary methods for secondary schools, nor should it be taken to assume that all sixth forms must adopt the 'integrated day'.

What is however assumed and argued is that the introduction of resource-based learning depends upon, and occasions, important changes in the organization of schools and educational services, many of them more widely beneficial, and that in particular it must necessarily alter our attitudes towards the two 'ancillary' professions of media producer and librarian.

This conclusion was underlined by the experience of the Schools Council Resource Centre Project 1970–3. The immediate stimulus for the setting up of that project was the organization problem faced by curriculum development teams in the creation of new learning resources to accompany their new schemes; in particular there were problems which fell directly into the area of the organization of recorded knowledge. The Schools Council's recognition that this was a matter which it was suitable to refer to the University of London Institute of Education Library was a noteworthy breakthrough in teacher–librarian relations. The project rapidly found that schools' problems over information retrieval were matched by their need for maximum help in materials creation, and in the list of 'the five resource centre skills' in *Working Paper 43* an important item was 'the skills of the resources producer'. The discussion of these problems in the context of the schools visited, and in the project's second phase, that of the six pilot schools intensively studied, brought to light many problems and a variety of solutions, at a time when the development of resource-based learning in England and Wales (and elsewhere) was rapidly increasing. Within the limitations of the project guidelines and the Schools Council's own areas of interest, these questions were reported and discussed further in *Organizing Resources: Six Case Studies*, the project's final report, which was published in 1975 in this present series.

Resource centre problems are not confined to schools, nor are the developments from which they arise peculiar to this country. The British experience must be seen in the context of a world-wide movement, which in some countries began rather earlier, and from which we have much to learn. Some of the overseas trends will be discussed in subsequent pages, and the relevance of the British contribution towards what is an international experiment should then be easier to assess. But that contribution ought not to be underestimated. We have lacked the funds which have been made available to some (but not all) schools in the United States, but we have been able to demonstrate in some of our institutions what can be achieved by re-organizing the spending of capitation accounts only average by British standards. We lack a national education

system in which curriculum is imposed by ministerial fiat, but this
has enabled many imaginative teachers to demonstrate the success
of experiments that might never have begun had official approval
been necessary. We have no populations for whom schools can be
established for the first time, but we have a school system undergoing
intensive change under unusual pressures (including drastic economic pruning). And although our schools have mostly lacked the
trained and established ancillary specialists so common in trans-
atlantic circles, we may have had less of the demarcation disputes
and jockeying for power that have sometimes accompanied innovation in that context. The contribution of teacher, media producer
and librarian can be considered afresh with a minimum of position-
striking and attidunizing. This book hopes to make a contribution to
that discussion.

*　　*　　*

We shall begin by looking at the context in which the developments
to be analysed have arisen. It is a common characteristic of writers
on educational topics to remark on the novel times in which we live,
the changed circumstances that we face, and the new methods we
must use to cope with our predicament. Indeed, a person who knew
teachers only from the literature of education might conclude that
they existed in a white heat of perpetual innovation; he would
probably be disconcerted by first acquaintance with the weary conservatism of many a staffroom. The more education changes, the
more they doggedly remain the same: and yet great changes there
have been and will be still, and many creative teachers have made
outstanding contributions quite outside the normal call of duty and
promotion-seeking. These changes have been accompanied, and in
some cases occasioned, by changes in other related areas of activity.
One of these, communications technology, is popularly understood
to be in perpetual revolution, and a writer has to work hard to
avoid repetition of cliché and ill-examined half-truth. Librarianship,
on the other hand, does not in the popular mind call up a trendy
image, and teachers and media producers alike have sometimes been
startled at the comparative equanimity with which that profession,
at its best, has accommodated itself to their demands and even on
occasion anticipated them.

Our backroom scholar, receiving experience through print alone,
would notice signals of change in the altering emphases of language
use. Until recently, the phrase 'audio-visual *aids*' told audiences that
the user thought in terms of adjuncts, appendages, useful decorative
flourishes, something additional but not absolutely essential; the
context showed that the 'aid' given was conceived in terms of the
teacher ('a teaching aid') rather than the learner. This has misled
generations of teachers, who have tended to look no further at a
term that presupposed type of use; but increasingly one now sees

the substitution 'audio-visual materials', a more neutral phrase implying something to be considered in its own right; and the British alternative 'resources' has more definite overtones of 'learning resources', something to be turned to in enquiry work by the learner, as well as used by the teacher in exposition.

Similarly in the USA the term 'instructional materials center' appeared in *Education Index* around 1944, when it meant a district centre from which audio-visual and other materials could be borrowed by schools for their use; succeeding decades saw a gradual shift, so that by the mid-1960s it became the accepted official designation for the multi-media school library, usually abbreviated to IMC. Signs are that 'media center' is now replacing it; not only is the term more euphonious, it represents yet again a shift of attention away from the direct intervention of the teacher towards a contemplation of the variety of communication media by both teacher and learner alike. (Purists will argue, of course, that one finds in these centres not 'media' but *examples of media*, or better, specific media items.)

Change is also signalled in the situations vacant pages, where advertisements for Heads of Resources in UK secondary schools still burgeon, even if the term does not yet rate a heading of its own in the *TES*. Moreover, in the early 1960s, a hapless government minister proposed 'teachers' aides', giving the impression that he was offering sub-professional alternatives to the employment of teachers. The howl of protest resounded through education offices for many years, making the employment of various types of skilled ancillary an occasion for LEA diplomacy and teachers' union suspicion. Today the Inner London Education Authority has invented the Media Resources Officer (as will be described), and devised for him a special training; many schools have leapt at the chance of employing him. Many colleges of art and technology now offer courses for educational media technicians of one kind or another, producing a steady stream of skilled and dedicated young people for whom all too few schools can at present afford places in their 'points system' but which very many of them covet. Equally, a recent survey by the Library Association revealed a sharp upwards trend in the number of chartered librarians at work in schools in England and Wales, on a full-time basis (some others are, very misguidedly, employed 'during term-time only'); and a variety of courses exists in universities, institutes of education and polytechnics which will result in the steady production of people dually and fully qualified as both teachers *and* librarians

Such signals, blandly described, do less than justice to the ferment underneath. As we shall see, changes within schools were not entirely capricious, nor were they doctrinaire, the result of a sharp swing of opinion towards the audio-visual propagandists or the School Library Association. They were forced by a combination of social changes and political developments, the maturing of educational opinion and the revelation of new insights into pupils and students. Equally, there were others ready to help at just the right time: media specialists with new simplicities of equipment and facilities for local production; librarians with an expertise that had suddenly become valuable, ready to undertake wider responsibilities and offer services in untraditional areas. The results were by no means entirely new. Old, discarded enterprises such as the Dalton Plan were dusted off and re-examined in new contexts and with new possibilities. Among many other things, what resulted was a new interest in, and fresh extensions of, the various facets of resource-based learning.

Acknowledgements

This book is the result of ten years' involvement with its specific subject, during which time I have met and discussed with many people from many lands who have shared their experiences and opinions and frequently shown me their work in action. Some of these people have been named and thanked in other publications of mine during these years, but I would particularly like to thank my friends at the Library School of the University of Wisconsin, Madison, for making it possible for me to earn my way across the Atlantic at regular intervals in such happy circumstances.

The three years of the Schools Council Resource Centre Project 1970–3 were a rich source of stimulus and information, and in saluting again Maurice Plaskow and the members of the consultative committee I would also like to praise those many schools, teachers, resources ancillaries and librarians whose unadvertised ventures into educational innovation (often at great cost to their own domestic activities) taught me, and I believe their pupils, so much.

Douglas Foskett and the library staff of the University of London Institute of Education Library have continued to be a major information source and one wishes for them a better building in which to continue their role as the major national education library service.

My own students at Loughborough University Department of Library and Information Studies have continued the debate and often kept my feet on the ground. Those from the developing countries have brought valuable information as well as hard questioning and I praise their enthusiasm. I hope this book will help those British students now qualifying as both teachers and librarians, at Loughborough and elsewhere.

Without my wife, who has read, criticized and re-read every page of this and my other work, and whose bibliographical searches have provided much of the source material (as well as checking the accuracy of their citation), I cannot imagine that anything at all would have been achieved. Her own MA studies in education, and her experience as a qualified teacher and (more recently) a chartered librarian, have been invaluable; every writer should have such a partner and I count myself greatly blessed. Chauvinists of either sex may however note: I did the typing.

N.W.B.
January 1976

PART ONE

Three Professions in a World of Change

Introduction

Resource-based learning is not an isolated phenomenon, a trick of the trade like voice production or colour printing, and its full implications are only now being understood and articulated. The present interest in it arose from a number of contributing circumstances, all leading in the direction of curriculum change. In the pages that follow we shall trace a few of the most interesting factors: changes in the nature and pattern of human knowledge, changes in human society and our understanding of its demands, changes in our understanding of students and the processes of learning. Equally noteworthy are changes in the communication media available to us, and the recognition of the multiplicity of ways in which they can be used for educational purposes; these have called into being new movements among teachers, articulating new doctrines in language borrowed from other disciplines, and new help from media creators.

One major learning resource has been with us for centuries; you hold an example in your hands at this moment, and there is a long and tested tradition of its organization in large collections for flexible information retrieval. Librarians have always tended to feel an affinity with proponents of individual and informal learning, and have a natural interest in promoting the fullest use of their own collections. Whatever their individual views about the financial, staffing and other problems attendant on widening the range of formats under their care, librarians as a profession have long recognized that the basic processes of information analysis and retrieval are the same whatever the type of material involved. They too have faced as a profession the problems of the knowledge explosion, and librarians working in educational institutions have also felt the full impact of the social and other changes bringing in a student clientele with very varied needs and expectations.

It is only recently that genuine discussion has been possible between teachers in general, media specialists both teaching and otherwise, and librarians, and the full implications of what might emerge from such discussion have not yet been completely realized. Yet the attempt to bring to our pupils and students a range of learning experiences that will genuinely match their personal needs as well as match the pressures that bear in on us from outside urgently requires that the discussions continue and lead to co-operative action.

Fortunately the 'resources movement' has always been about co-operation. Much of the impetus behind this has been economic, because interest in the resource-based mode has shown itself at a time of financial stringency. In such circumstances, resources organization has an important part to play. Just as important as spending extra money is to be sure we are using most effectively such money as we already receive; just as important as asking for extra staff is to make more thorough and perceptive use of the staff skills already available to us; just as important as the purchase of vast stocks of materials is the need to know everything about what we already have, and to organize it for maximum use – even if this means treading on departmental toes; a first priority before we begin to clamour for expensive production equipment is to share facilities and skills to better effect.

To do this requires more than simple co-operation; it requires understanding. We need to know one another's skills, contributions, standards and aspiration, and be clear in our minds what we should each do. More important still, we need to be clear about the nature of the educational movement in which we participate, about its origins, motives, mixed feelings, diverse strands and unexpected requirements. This first section therefore attempts to draw together some of the most notable aspects. It does not, and could not, attempt to be comprehensive; that would require a different book. For some readers, it may seem to be going over old and familiar ground; other readers may not find it so, and I believe we are in danger of forgetting some of the essential points. There are dangerous murmurings of turning tides and swinging pendulums. Successive sections will therefore look at recent trends within three groups of people whom we have categorized under broad headings. Teachers, media specialists and librarians have come a long way before meeting together, sometimes to their own surprise; but the paths, as I shall try to show, have often been going in similar directions before they joined.

1 Education and Change

New maps of knowledge

Schools and teachers all over the world have been caught up in more than a decade of re-appraisal, radical re-structuring and considerable curriculum revision. That it is not a limited, one-country phenomenon can be attested by the briefest of glances through the files of the appropriate educational periodicals, and prosperity or economic difficulty has not been an important factor. Many a teacher has longed for innovation to stay still – just for a year – while he and his colleagues gathered their breath and absorbed the lessons of the last lot of alterations. Official reports thud into administrators' in-trays and on to tables in schools and teachers' centres; changes of government bring new politicians reversing the decisions of the old ones and always involving change, re-structuring, new constraints and different difficulties; parental and other pressure groups campaign and lobby, and experimental projects with bewildering acronyms and surprising purposes seem to proliferate.

Among the many pressures for change in education is one that is now so commonplace we tend to overlook its implications. C. E. Beeby has described it cautiously as:

> ... the dramatic increase in the speed at which man is acquiring knowledge. Modern prophets tell us that, in some subjects, knowledge is doubling every ten years. Whether or not this is literally true I do not know – it is certainly not true of wisdom – but there is some justification for the view, now commonly expressed, that new ways of teaching, learning and understanding must be found if the new generation is not to be intellectually smothered beneath a mountain of facts. (Howson 1970:40.)

Dr Robert Hilliard, quoted by Alvin Toffler, puts it more forcefully:

> At the rate at which knowledge is growing, by the time the child born today graduates from college, the amount of knowledge in the world

will be four times as great. By the time the same child is fifty years old it will be thirty-two times as great, and 97 per cent of everything known in the world will have been learned since the time he was born. (Toffler 1971: 149.)

Toffler also quotes Lord James:

'I took my first degree in chemistry at Oxford in 1931.' Looking at the questions asked in chemistry exams at Oxford today, he concludes, 'I realize that not only can I not do them, but that I never *could* have done them, since at least two-thirds of the questions involve knowledge that simply did not exist when I graduated.' (Toffler 1971: 149.)

As Beeby implies, it hardly matters whether or not Dr Hilliard has got his figures exactly right, or whether Lord James had taken a meticulously exact sample. The phenomenon is unlikely to be disputed. The so-called 'knowledge explosion' is not simply the accumulation of more 'facts'. The discarding of aether and phlogiston, the discovery of quasars and strange particles, the unmasking of Piltdown Man and the re-assertion of continental drift are not isolated jigsaw pieces to be fitted in or taken out for replacement from a static puzzle, but elements in a constantly changing pattern of concepts and hypotheses that re-shape themselves and run off in different directions before our eyes. We are now beginning, I suspect, to forget this phenomenon again, but as Phenix put it:

The condition is not one of a quiet accumulation of information, but such a rapid expansion as to cause a shattering effect upon modern mentality. A revolution of quantity has taken place, demanding a wholly different orientation to learning. The gradual assimilation of a relatively fixed body of knowledge can no longer be the goal of education. (Phenix 1964: 304.)

New disciplines burgeon – who in 1931 could easily distinguish between ecology and ethology and explain their content? – often forming links between existing concepts and subject areas, lending point indeed to the proponents of inter-disciplinary studies. Dr Whitfield points to the nature of the problem as he sees it:

The problem is that there are so many potential components of varying substance and shape arising from the progressive differentiation of knowledge ... We can never return to the three 'subject' curricula of ancient Athens: reading and writing (serviceable and useful for life), gymnastics (for courage) and music (for pleasure). (Whitfield 1971: 9.)

Equally unsettling is the 'publications explosion', and again we have perhaps become so used to the phrase that we tend to overlook its import. But with scientific and technical literature mounting at 60 million pages a year (in over 2 million articles by 75,000 authors in 50 languages in approximately 35,000 periodicals), and sociological and humanities literature bulking not inconsiderably alongside, one can be pardoned for wishing to invest in forests and papermills. In 1960, European countries produced 100,000 book *titles* in just seven and a half months (before AD 1500 the norm was around 1,000 titles a *year*). Add to the question, 'What is there to know?' (to which the answer is already disturbing) the subsidiary question, 'How can I keep up to date?' and it will be seen that the average school 'specialist' can necessarily only keep up with the broadest of generalities, and this through the main medium of secondary and other sources. Toffler engagingly quotes Dr Emilio Segre, a physics Nobel prizewinner: 'On K-mesons alone, to wade through all the papers is an impossibility.' (Toffler 1971: 148.) K-mesons are, of course, a particularly awkward phenomenon to account for in current theory, and the literature is not likely to be small, but one doubts whether the problem is any easier in the Humanities: for instance, even for those coping with what, according to the Honours School at Oxford University, is the studiable part of English Language and Literature. True, this stops at around 1820, and thus slowly and inexorably recedes from us into a past when K-mesons were not even contemplated or missed; but publication on Shakespeare alone is colossal, and the relevant studies (in history, criticism, linguistics, politics, philosophy, psychology and all the many other aspects that determine what the phenomenon of Shakespeare can be said to mean for *us*) spread dauntingly outward.

It is unlikely that the average teacher sees the problem in quite the dramatic terms of Mr Toffler's book. This may be an insensitivity or over-complacency on his part, or it may be that he is just too overwhelmed by other problems we will examine later. However, schools are undoubtedly more ready than before to accept that much of what students currently learn may well be irrelevant or out-moded within as little as a decade or so, certainly within a third of a vocational lifetime. There is even the dreadful possibility that some of it is irrelevant already! We are beginning to see that we teach, not a series of revealed truths, but the latest of approximations along an ever-broadening and changing continuum. Many of these approximations gell together into new patterns of current importance; thus, Professor Bruner and his colleagues concluded that our whole concept of 'what it is to be human' had been significantly changed and clarified by developments in zoology, anthropology, psychology, sociology, linguistics, philosophy, and the study of myth, and thus they developed the famous 'Man: a course of study' complete with supporting materials in many formats.

Whitfield, of course, welcomes the 'knowledge explosion':

> . . . since it not only represents human progress (assuming that for rational man it is better in general to know than not to know) but it also embodies a maturing of the disciplines of knowledge. The maturing of a discipline involves the development of a distinctive structure of unifying ideas, a network of relationships and concepts from the bald facts; indeed, it is fair to comment that the factual burden of a discipline

varies inversely with its degree of maturity, and this can have immense pedagogical significance. (*op. cit.*: 8.)

This leads him to the eventual conclusion (but note the deceptively simple first word): 'All we now require is an adequate theory for selection, for establishing priorities, for determining . . . the knowledge of greatest importance and greatest utility.' (*op. cit.*: 9–10)

Certainly if knowledge patterns are expected to undergo continual change, then this itself becomes an element for consideration in curriculum planning. Morris and Howson signal this when they write:

Education is now seen to be as much concerned with 'what might be' as with 'what is' (or, alas, in some instances, with 'what was'!) . . . Although the future is inscrutable, no one any longer expects it to be like the present – still less like the past. The importance of imparting factual knowledge about 'what is' therefore tends to diminish with a growing belief in the impermanence of the present. 'Knowing' is less important than being equipped to 'find out for oneself'. (Howson 1970: 6.)

We find this interestingly exemplified in the American experience at the famous Woods Hole Conference in September 1959. Two earlier projects had already begun active curriculum development work, in physics and mathematics, and had taken a positively 'discipline-centred' approach, partly as a reaction to what were felt to be the excessively 'child-centred' tendencies of the previous two decades. At Woods Hole, too, it is notable that the problem of an up-to-date curriculum was seen essentially in terms of bringing together the creators of the new knowledge to consult with leading educators and learning psychologists. Jerome Bruner spoke of:

. . . the growing separation of first-rank scholars and scientists from the task of presenting their own subjects in primary and secondary schools . . . In consequence, school programs have often dealt inadequately or incorrectly with contemporary knowledge . . . (Bruner 1963: 3.)

This was to be put right at Woods Hole, and the result was widely influential, not only in the United States. One of the fascinations of Bruner's account (and indeed of the subsequent movement of his thought as successively laid out for us in later books) is the sensitive way in which an emergent 'learning to learn' theme is examined and spelled out in terms of the student's needs and responses and the teacher's task. Bruner stresses:

the development of an attitude toward learning and inquiry, toward guessing and hunches, toward the possibility of solving problems on one's own . . . To instill such attitudes by teaching requires something more than the mere presentation of fundamental ideas . . . an important ingredient is a sense of excitement about discovery – discovery of regularities of previously unrecognized relations and similarities between ideas, with a resulting sense of self-confidence in one's abilities. (*op. cit.*: 25.)

A noticeable feature of such thinking is that it sees the problem as consisting essentially of what we may call discontinuities between what is known and what is taught, and in a world where the rapid expansion of knowledge can be expected to continue. The student is to be led to see himself in the discovery mode, to form the basic concepts that enable him to discover, to understand the subject field as it currently is, and to understand some of the attitudes and approaches that will lead to further understanding and later changes of emphasis. The task of the teacher is no longer to purvey facts but to develop understanding, which includes the planning of experiences and tasks from which that understanding can grow. Intuition is to be stressed as much as analysis. As Peter Dow has said of 'Man: a course of study':

> As education turns increasingly to areas of human concern where questions abound and where answers are few and short-lived ... a style of thought which can be comfortable with the tentative hypothesis and the unanswered question will be increasingly necessary. Even schoolchildren must learn to live comfortably on the frontiers of human knowledge. (Dow 1971: 169.)

The concept of 'learning to learn' suggests that there is transference between one learning episode and another:

> Virtually all of the evidence of the last two decades on the nature of learning and transfer has indicated that, while the original theory of formal discipline was poorly stated in terms of the training of faculties, it is indeed a fact that massive general transfer can be achieved by appropriate learning, even to the degree that learning properly under optimum conditions leads one to 'learn how to learn'. (Bruner 1963: 6.)

This is, many teachers may feel, a phenomenon upon which it is unwise to rely in any given situation, desirable though the achievement may be and no matter how optimistic one is about the probability of its attainment. Friedlander, in a thoughtful article, has indicated his caution; his conclusion is that: 'the factor of judgement is crucial ... students need good teachers as much now, possibly more, than ever before' (Friedlander, 1965: 36). Bruner would no doubt agree; he has never suggested that the teacher's role is irrelevant or marginal, but that it is concerned primarily with leading the students to arrive at important insights by their own active, participatory work. The kind of 'learning by discovery' to which Bruner has continually returned is much more rigorous and intellectually respectable than the use of the same term by the flabbier progressivists and sub-Montessorians would suggest, and his work, whatever our reservations, has rightly been profoundly influential as a result.

One reservation, raised among others by Postman and Weingartner (1970), goes right to the heart of the teacher's dilemma in the context of the information explosion: what is it important to discover? They point out that in Bruner's method, students discover what is interesting to Bruner, the structures of established disciplines. This may not be the most important thing to them; the factor of the student's own motivation in discovery learning has to be faced. Thelen (1972) wonders if we have 'ground out students who can solve problems but who will for ever have to be guided by someone else'. (26) There may be a value in careful structuring in the early stages of a student's discovery career, but, as Rowntree comments:

> It can also be helping students towards a most unfortunate affective objective if it encourages the belief that 'others' must be relied on both to sanction the problems and to ratify the solutions. We are back to objectives, and the need for students to learn how to formulate their own. (Rowntree 1974: 96.)

This need to balance the responsibility and experience of the teacher against the need for any discovery process to be meaningful to the student is one we shall come up against frequently in this book. It is not simply a matter of content versus method; it must be accepted that 'covering the syllabus' takes longer with discovery methods. Rowntree quotes Coulson (1971) who compared the five hours taken to learn a scientific topic by discovery methods with the thirty minutes it had taken him to 'teach' it: 'But during the 4 or 5 hours, the discovery group had also gained experience of planning and carrying out experiments, making mistakes, rethinking their assumptions . . . Students learn what they do.' (Rowntree, 1974: 94)

Discovery methods were an important element in the UK in the Nuffield Science Projects, which sought not only to bring curricula in line with new knowledge, but also, as Coulson and Nyholm explained to chemistry teachers: 'to enable our pupils to make progress through their own efforts at investigation.' (Coulson and Nyholm 1966: 229)

L. C. Taylor put it this way:

> Thus, the content of a new Nuffield science course is certainly more closely connected with contemporary experience than what it replaces; but more important is the opportunity it provides for learning by the experimental method – for thinking like a scientist. (L. C. Taylor 1972: 20.)

Perhaps: but implementation is not a simple matter. The discontinuity between what is known, and taught, and learnt, extends to the available textbooks and other learning resources, and all curriculum renewal projects have found it necessary to produce vast quantities of learning materials to enable the new courses to operate. The Physical Science Study Committee, and the School Mathematics Study Group, in the USA, were actively producing such materials at the time of Woods Hole. The Nuffield Science and Nuffield Mathematics projects in the United Kingdom produced sufficient quantities of support materials to warrant the establishment of the

Resources for Learning Project with which Mr Taylor was associated. Woods Hole may have seemed to some to be disappointingly
divided about the new technology of education:

> The two extreme positions – stated in exaggerated form – were, first,
> that the teacher must be the sole and final arbiter of how to present a
> given subject and what devices to use, and, second, that the teacher
> should be explicator and commentator for prepared materials made
> available through films, television, teaching machines and the like.
> (Bruner 1963: 15.)

This is an area of disagreement we shall meet again in later
chapters. In practice, the much later 'Man: a course of study'
required an investment in both software and equipment that has
led many British education authorities to think twice.

Woods Hole and other curriculum development projects of this
period appeared to work on the assumption that knowledge of the
new knowledge plus skill in teaching were the two necessary elements
of the equation; all that might need to be added were the insights
and understanding of the learning psychologist. Bruner himself has
subsequently commented on the oversimplicity of this view, picking
out among other things the assumption that every student has
already been 'the beneficiary of the middle-class hidden curriculum
that taught them analytic skills and . . . the traditional intellectual
use of mind.' (Bruner 1971: 19.) The 1960s became a period of deep
and tumultous change in the USA, a time when it was perhaps
easier for the sciences to revise their curricula than the humanities
where issues were already becoming increasingly explosive. It was
clear even to the most conservative that if knowledge was in turmoil
and a determinant of educational change, so also was society. In
the United Kingdom, many of the most formative pressures of our
time have undoubtedly been social in origin, and in the developing
world it is social and national needs which above all else have
determined the drive toward innovation.

Whitfield's 'all we now require' therefore is only an initial clearing of the throat and writing down the words WHAT WE NEED
at the top of a sheet of paper. If we dwell too long on the explosion
of knowledge, formidable though it is, we shall overlook a multiplicity of other factors relating to the dilemma of schools in a world
that will not stay still.

New pressures from without

Educators, like everyone else, are strongly influenced by prevailing
mores and their own social and cultural standpoints, swayed by
pressures felt but not articulated, by assumptions never challenged
and biasses not recognized. Our present educational practices

cannot be understood except as the result of unco-ordinated responses to half-acknowledged pressures. Douglas Holly reminds us:

> Convention dictates the list of subjects which are recognized by secon-
> dary schools: history is included, archaeology usually is not; geography
> is taught universally but not sociology; classics is still relatively com-
> mon, philosophy or logic almost unknown; French is widely studied,
> German relatively rarely – and so on . . . To say that such a curriculum
> in the last quarter of the twentieth century is rationally derived would
> be to fly in the face of reason. (Holly 1974: 19–20.)

In examining social pressures on education, we cannot entirely
distance ourselves from what is being studied, and it must be recognized that there are some matters about which no consensus view
will be possible. Our society is divided, not only along familiar class
lines but also into regional, cultural, racial, religious and genera-
tional groupings with a variety of incompatible or at best only
half-compatible viewpoints and value systems. The customary
division of politics into 'left' and 'right', and an attempt to match
this by ranking the *Black Paper* school on one side and the educational 'progressivists' on the other greatly oversimplifies the complexity and also the richness of the situation.

For some indeed, the whole discussion of the knowledge explosion
so far has overlooked what for them is the most significant of all
facts: that any view of what constitutes knowledge must be entirely
relative to the individuals or groups who acknowledge or profess it.
For the group of educational sociologists forming the so-called
'phenomenological' school, associated with the University of London
Institute of Education and the contributors to M. F. D. Young's
Knowledge and control (1971), the 'objectivist' view of knowledge is to
be explicitly denied. For this group, the curriculum is socially
organized knowledge, and much of the writing about curriculum
studies is, in Young's words: 'more informative about the writer's
perspectives and beliefs, than about school curriculum' (Young
1971: 44). Knowledge is an active phenomenon embodied in
people; an individual's view of knowledge is 'existentially related to
his social structure', as Geoffrey Esland explains:

> It is important to emphasise that the cognitive tradition which forms
> an epistemology can exist only through a supporting community of
> people. Its members are co-producers of reality and the survival of this
> reality depends on its continuing plausibility to the community . . .
> this is of particular relevance to teachers and pupils who, through their
> joint action, form epistemic communities more or less supporting the
> cognitive structures which make up the educational culture. In other
> words, the changing forms and content of knowledge will have social-
> structural correlates. (Young 1971: 77–8.)

The criticism of conventional and positivist views of the educational scene is so radical and thorough-going that Young acknow-
ledges a problem for the teacher–reader:

The problem here is cultural relativism, where if all knowledge is a social and historical product, then we have no grounds for deciding the worth, truth or value of anything – something both as teachers and as ordinary men and women we have to do all the time . . . The second concern is with teachers who can read this relativism . . . as not so much redefining problems but 'undermining action' – their action, as teachers. (Young 1973: 210.)

The point is well taken, whether or not we decide the problem is unavoidable. None the less the group does represent a much wider uneasiness among many younger teachers about the validity of their role as knowledge purveyors. There has been a recognition that the pattern of knowledge may well change according to the situation of the observer, and that in many ways the teacher is best occupied not in presenting *his* knowledge but helping the learners to find theirs. This is a point we shall return to later in this section, and in subsequent chapters.

In selecting from the disparate elements of the knowledge explosion what to teach, or to teach first, or teach to whom, all teachers and administrators would feel they were looking for indications around them as well as drawing from past experience and the value systems they have come to represent. It is worth noting that many different responses have common factors relevant to us.

National governments, for instance, have made deliberate intervention into education for economic and other motives. Halsey and Floud noted: 'Education is a crucial type of investment for the exploitation of modern technology. This fact underlies recent educational development in all the major industrial societies.' Halsey, Floud and Anderson (1965:1). This was seen at its starkest in the USA, following the shock of Sputnik. Many Americans at that time genuinely believed with Peter Drucker (1959):

We know now that the Russian achievement does not rest on the Communist tenets of 'socialist ownership of productive resources' . . . The achievement rests squarely upon the tremendous concentration of resources, time and effort in producing an educated society. (Halsey and Floud 1965: 18.)

A great nation was convinced ('conned'?) that it must restore the balance and national morale by pouring money into its educational system. Among other things, money was made available in large quantities for the purchase of audio-visual equipment; and with or without conviction schools were not slow to cash in on the bonanza while it lasted. The boost given by this injection of funds to developments in educational technology is hard to underestimate. Few would claim that the money was always used as wisely as it might have been, and fewer still in America today would claim that the resultant changes in what actually takes place within schools have been as dramatic or as rapid as had been hoped. It is one thing to have money to spend in a hurry, and to make impressive proposals and establish organizational structures; it is quite another to re-shape curriculum, methodology and organization really *effectively*.

The biggest danger of such situations is disillusion and the sub-sequent backlash. Spending vast sums of money on education was going to put America back in the lead in the space race; but as interest in this goal diminished and other social problems emerged, it began to be questioned whether heavy federal spending on edu-cation was necessarily the best use of public money. Many ques-tioned, as we shall see later, whether the continued support of schools as they were was desirable at all.

British teachers will smile with insular superiority at the Sputnik episode. However, if we turn to simpler objectives, such as the preparation of pupils and students for the achievement of satisfac-tory vocational goals, we find that in modern social and industrial circumstances the dilemma of what to provide and how to plan is very considerable. As with the knowledge explosion, so with the pace of technological and social change – it runs away with us, turns sudden unexpected corners opening up alarming vistas that make all our previous decisions look foolish. We can at least learn from American attempts.

In 1972 OECD published the report of a fourteen-nation con-ference on 'The nature of the curriculum for the eighties and onwards', organized by the Centre for Educational Research and Innovation. However one views their conclusions, they offer as good a place as any to begin a survey of the perplexities of choice. The report commented:

> Inventions and techniques are radically altering most branches of industry and commerce ... it is impossible to anticipate what know-ledge or skills will ultimately be most useful to students ... All that is known for certain is that most people will be subject to rapid change within their working environment ... (CERI 1972: 12.)

After a brief genuflexion before the 'knowledge explosion' the conference asserted:

> Curricular renewal, which will of necessity be a continuous process, must therefore concentrate on students' attitudes to learning, and on techniques that will enable pupils to continue their education in adult life ... Whereas in the past teaching could be described as a process of communicating knowledge, of encouraging pupils to acquire prescribed information and of testing their success in doing so, it is now apparent that the urge to ask questions and the willingness and the ability to find answers is more important than the acquisition of factual knowledge. (*op. cit.*: 12.)

Specialization and depth came in for re-appraisal: 'ultimately, general education is likely to prove more important....' (*op. cit.*: 13)
Content, once again, is secondary to method and attitude: we are

to teach, not 'the facts' but the skills, problems and concepts 'behind the facts': 'The present shift from teaching for information to teaching for experience will continue; in consequence, problem-solving and problem-finding activities, both for individuals and groups, will assume a more central role.' (*op. cit.*: 27)

For Peterson, writing in the same year, the necessity to prepare the pupil for 'lifelong education' freed the secondary school from previous constraints:

> The more we assume, surely, that formal education does not end when the pupil leaves school, the more free we should be to respond to his actual interests of the moment in the knowledge that omissions can be made up at a later stage when their relevance has become apparent to him. (Peterson 1972: 3.)

This hints at a cafeteria-like concept of education, in which the learner takes up units and subject areas at his own choice and when he sees the need: a model which would perhaps be more acceptable if one were sure an appropriate dietician was there if called upon to give suitable guidance.

As we saw earlier, however, there are many subject areas where there can be no one truth or subject structure, but where opinion and individual value-judgements are necessarily predominant. In some, the learner will perhaps expect to be told what he must say or believe, and must learn that this is not how the subject works: in literature and the arts, for example, where the quality of the student's personal response and involvement is the crux. In others, such as religion, social studies, current affairs, 'humanities', what is at issue is the learner's personal orientation to the modern world, where we share fewer assumptions in common than ever before. How do we teach in areas of controversy?

The Nuffield/Schools Council Humanities Curriculum Project adopted an extreme posture of 'neutral chairmanship'. It was based on the five premises that controversial issues should be handled in the classroom with adolescents, that the teacher accepted the need to 'submit his teaching . . . to the criterion of neutrality', that the mode of enquiry should have discussion rather than instruction as its core, that the discussion should protect divergence of view among participants, and that the teacher as chairman of discussion should have responsibility for quality and standards of learning. Basis for the discussion was to be 'evidence', by which was primarily meant the HCP materials for each of the areas of enquiry chosen by the Project.

> Each collection includes both print and non-print materials. In printed form are: poems and songs; extracts from drama, novels and biography; letters, reports and articles; readings from the social sciences; maps, cartoons, questionnaires, graphs and tables; and advertisements. Non-print materials consist of approximately three hours of taped material,

some of which – mainly poems, letters and extracts from plays –
appears also in printed form: some folksongs and original material such
as interviews are on tape only. Details of recommended films . . . are
included in each handbook . . . (The Humanities Project 1970: 11).

Other forms of non-print material were available from time to
time or developed by other bodies. The immediate impression is of
a completely open society where very little can be automatically
assumed or taken for granted – except the value of 'open' discussion
itself. Some teachers attack this as an abdication of responsibility;
to others, it seems basic to the whole concept of education. The
extreme opposite is no doubt the parent in the American Bible belt
who complained, 'I don't want my child to be *asked* what is right
and wrong, I want him to be *told* it.' On the other hand, Douglas
Holly has shrewdly and disconcertingly commented: 'what is at
issue in the minds of the Humanities team . . . is *not* the criteria and
techniques of using and evaluating evidence but the technique of
rational, urbane, liberal, middle-class discussion . . .' (Holly 1974:
53).

It was the Humanities Curriculum Project which developed the
first ill-fated Race Pack, intended for use with children from 14 to
16 in an enquiry-and-discovery situation, with the teacher as usual
in the 'impartial chairman' role. When the Pack was rejected by the
Schools Council's steering committee, Mr Christopher Bagley indignantly defended it on the grounds that: 'detailed research . . .
shows that the use of the pack has beneficial effects on race relations
in the schools for which it has been used.' (Bagley 1972: 4) The
claim was evaluated by 'a special version of the Wilson-Patterson
conservatism scale . . . with expanded sub-scales measuring attitudes about race relations'. Whether or not the pack's rejection was
based on faithless doubt of this method of evaluating educational
effectiveness was never clear, but it is noteworthy that the main
objective, the modification of attitudes towards a socially acceptable
norm, was never in question. The chairmanship was, of course,
neutral, but the neutrality was a strategy towards a committed
purpose.

If the Nuffield Science Project (as M. F. D. Young has pointed
out) was directed towards the minority, those pupils undertaking
'O' level studies, much of the work of the Humanities Curriculum
Project and similar Schools Council ventures was directed towards
'leavers', those pupils staying on for an extra year because of the
raising of the school leaving age to 16: pupils by definition 'non-
academic', for whom extra effort was to be made, whose experience
of school work had typically been one of failure and discouragement
rather than success and reinforcement, and who generally saw it as
irrelevant to their interests and attainable ambitions. In a moment,
we must look briefly at this problem, and the oft-quoted relevance
of enquiry- and resource-based methods in relation to them. How-

ever the received liberal opinion that for such pupils a prolonged stay in school was beneficial and should therefore be compulsory has none the less been challenged, and not only from traditional right-wingers and discouraged teachers.

The rise of 'de-schooling' as a movement has given great publicity to sharp and radical questioning of many of our assumptions and institutions in education, and whatever one concludes at the end there can be little doubt that the movement struck a number of shrewd blows at complacency. De-schoolers trace much of our present malaise to institutionalization, which they claim has dulled and routinized our responses and led us to confuse form and content and what is supposed to happen with what is in fact the case. In the early 1960s, Paul Goodman suggested that in looking at what Americans call school drop-outs we were missing the point:

> What are they dropouts from? Is the schooling really good for them, or much good for anybody? . . . Is it the only means of education? Isn't it unlikely that any single type of social institution could fit almost every youngster up to the age of sixteen and beyond? (Goodman 1971: 19.)

Everett Reimer concluded that the school system was bad for everyone:

> Thus the poor are deprived both of motivation and of the resources which the school reserves for the privileged. The privileged, on the other hand, are taught to prefer the school's resources to their own and to give up self-motivated learning for the pleasures of being taught. (Reimer 1971: 33.)

De-schooling is essentially, of course, a movement on the side of the poor, the disadvantaged and the unsuccessful. True equality of educational provision is seen as economically unachievable, particularly in the developing countries. Ivan Illich concluded bluntly:

> Equal obligatory schooling must be recognized as at least economically unfeasible . . . The escalation of the schools is as destructive as the escalation of weapons . . . Everywhere in the world school costs have risen faster than enrolments and faster than the GNP; everywhere expenditures on school fall even further behind the expectations of parent, teacher and pupils . . . Rather than calling equal schooling temporarily unfeasible, we must recognize that it is, in principle, economically absurd, and that to attempt it is intellectually emasculating, socially polarizing and destructive of the credibility of the political system which promotes it. (Illich 1971: 9–10).

Illich and his supporters propose instead 'learning webs' or networks including:

1. Reference Services to Educational Objects – which facilitate access to things or processes used for formal learning . . .

2. Skill Exchanges – which permit persons to list their skills, the conditions under which they are willing to serve as models for others who want to learn these skills, and addresses at which they can be reached.
3. Peer-Matching – a communications network which permits persons to describe the learning activity in which they wish to engage, in the hope of finding a partner for the inquiry.
4. Reference Services to Educators-at-Large – who can be listed in a directory giving the addresses and self-descriptions of professionals, paraprofessionals and freelancers, along with conditions of access to their services. (*op. cit.*: 78–9.)

De-schoolers celebrate spontaneity, creativity, local participation and freedom from bureaucratic standardization. Many will question their blanket statements and accuse them of oversimplification, while acknowledging the generosity of their concern and the genuine warmth and imagination which is evident in their writings. Bruner has spoken of their 'new romanticism, salvation by spontaneity, disestablish the established schools', but has gone on to add that when asked his view, in 1970, of American education he was forced to say that as well as being in a state of crisis the educational system was:

. . . in effect our way of maintaining a class system – a group at the bottom. It crippled the capacity of children in the lowest socio-economic quarter of the population to participate at full power in society, and did so early and effectively. (Bruner 1972: xi.)

Rightly or wrongly, similar criticisms are levelled at the (very different) British school system, and not only in inner city areas, not in those counties which retain the selective system.

Most of us tend to be eclectic in our approach and take our insights from wherever they are to be found. Some of Illich's criticisms, for instance, would be applauded by teachers none the less happy to remain and work within the present system. The plan for 'learning webs' is one that, in a different form, has been the goal of many a teachers' centre warden, identifying skills, knowledge and resources within a neighbourhood which could be inducted quite informally into the schools; the new Devon project of the Exeter University Institute of Educational Regional Resource Centre has devoted much attention to the building up of networks on a friendly basis – though access will, of course, be through institutional channels in most cases, and the initial benefit will be to teachers not learners.

Illich and his colleagues look for changed attitudes towards authority. In fact such attitudes are already in flux. 'Participation' is a key element in contemporary management theory, and not only because of its inherent usefulness. All our major political parties in the United Kingdom show their awareness of the trend, stressing severally workers' control, workers' participation, widespread sharing of power, regional devolution of authority, and the like. (I willingly leave it to the reader himself to decide whether any or all of these trends are desirable, or sufficient, or well-considered.) Our students live in a world where the homeless form into action groups and take over derelict property, where consumer groups test impartially the claims of advertisers and official departments, where amenity groups campaign against airports and for playgrounds and crossings, and where unions and employers' associations show themselves prepared to take action up to and sometimes beyond the brink of disaster. They live in a world where the so-called 'experts' (and particularly the economists) have, to put it mildly, been singularly prone to error and failure; indeed, few give evidence of having the faintest idea what should be done to cope with most of our plight. For all these reasons, 'authority' is in question as perhaps never before.

Many pupils, too, recognize from their own observation a sharp differentiation between the values embodied in the school system and those in their own socio-cultural group. Pupils who see the main object of school as 'helping you get a good job at the end' see no relevance in the system to them if they are 'non-academic' pupils in areas of high unemployment – particularly if they are also black. What they need to know about the world can usually (they may feel) be learnt from practice and from television, and the quaint, old-fashioned and boring exercises offered in all too many schools are hardly calculated to alter that opinion. To assume that such pupils are beyond the reach of schools and teachers is unnecessarily defeatist, but the situation does require of teachers an act of imagination, of seeing oneself in the pupils' predicament, of isolating and identifying goals that would be recognized by them. Some teachers have articulated such goals in terms of subjects to be taught – car maintenance and football rather than English and Geography. This may in the first instance be how pupils themselves see the situation, but must be a very early and trivial first step. The alternative to alienation is involvement, not just an accepting involvement but an assertion, a demanding and deciding act, an annexation of a piece of the action, which participation requires. To be involved one must be able to take real decisions. Douglas Holly observes:

> ... no good teacher is happy with non-involvement, still less with ignorance of the possibilities. The contradiction facing teachers of working-class pupils especially is that quite frequently they rebel against freedom ... But if school learning is not to be 'schooled' learning it needs to involve the students not in the sense of 'motivation', a means to an end, but as an end in itself. Non-alienated learning requires the active participation of the learner; it is essentially self-realization. In this sense the curriculum is necessarily subservient to the student. (Holly 1974: 165, 168–9.)

Self-realization, moreover, means realization of the actual self, the warm, sweating, clumsy-thinking pupil himself and not some abstract idea, some perfectly ideal learner whose needs happen to fit one's own estimation of one's interests and teaching skills. 'Starting from where they are' means, quite unnervingly, what it says. Such students are not free, and need the teacher and the school if they are in any degree to realize their freedom. It is because of this (as Holly argues) that Illich and Reimer put forward an inadequate solution:

> By contrast the liberation proposed by Illich and Reimer would be a freedom to be dependent on others. For libertarians they seem curiously addicted to authority centres, the criteria for which cannot be questioned or discussed – authors, museum-keepers, networks of 'masters', 'professional advisers' and 'skill instructors'. For a schooled imagination they would seem to substitute a de-schooled credulity. (Holly 1974: 179–80.)

True participation requires participants, among them teachers. But such an approach to teaching and learning requires a considerable level of support for both teachers and learners, recognizing that last year's lesson-notes will rarely be adequate to so fluid a situation and so self-generated a search. We are led again, in all the aspects of our subject so far examined, to similar conclusions. We can usefully itemize them as follows:

1. Changing maps of knowledge mean that teachers will tend to lay more emphasis on basic concepts and methodology than on a pre-determined list of specific facts, important though some factual knowledge still is for concept formation itself.

2 The information and publications explosion make it more important than ever that students should learn how to find out: the basic methodology of research, whether in laboratory or library.

3 Rapid social and industrial change means that schools cannot easily predict the specific requirements of the future, particularly in connection with the preparation of the student for vocational goals. The student must therefore be prepared for subsequent re-training, and the 'lifelong education' concept. For the teacher this may have the advantage of lessening the pressure within the conventional school years to include particular subject knowledge, allowing more time for the development of skills and attitudes.

4 All these trends point to the need to encourage the student to develop as an independent learner and an autonomous enquirer, able to locate information, frame hypotheses, weigh the evidence, consider alternative viewpoints and arrive at conclusions. Moreover, this is true for all students, 'academic' or not.

5 The autonomous enquirer participates actively in his own education, and exemplifies the opposite of educational alienation; at a time (and within areas) of considerable scepticism of the claims of authority, such participation is a key objective for the teacher, but it involves the student's own ability within the system to make decisions meaningful to him.

In all these matters we see the importance of the teacher's role, but it is a changed role. He is much less the instructor and director, much more the collaborator and adviser. He no longer commands the instruction; instead he participates in the learning. He devises learning experiences, he selects and indicates learning resources, he discusses learning strategies, he helps to evaluate learning performance. In most of these roles, information- and communication-materials will be valuable to him, and he will wish to re-organize and create more. Resource-based learning, of one variety or another, is likely to be of increasing help to him as a means of student involvement in his own learning. His employment of the method is not predicated however by these considerations alone. Having spent quite a number of pages on the general macrocosm of information and society, we must now turn to the equally important insights we have been given into the nature of the clientele: students and pupils, the individual microcosm of the learner.

New insights into the learner

For schools to say, as the fashionable cant now is, 'we are concerned not so much with teaching as with learning', is not just an empty phrase, though it will give considerable irritation to those old stagers who had always thought that was what they were doing in any case. During the three years of the Schools Council Resource Centre Project it was commonplace to hear headmasters, teacher advisers and field officers claim that the development of individualized and resource-based methods had been stimulated by observation of 'how children learnt', though further questioning often revealed a variety of suggested views on the process in practice.

Some pointed, and with good reason, to the enormous variety and strength of the mass media of press, broadcasting and cinema, and their effects on the child's development of concepts and acquisition of attitudes. These will be discussed more fully in the next chapter, in relation to the development of new media themselves and the teachers, producers and consultants who have specialized in their educational applications.

Others pointed to the enormous variety of individual needs and abilities with which our schools and colleges were grappling, and to the many determinants of these differences that had been identified. Some are specifically environmental, relating to the social unit within which the child grew up or from his own recognition of the range of opportunity open to him; others are more individual, the physical and mental equipment which the child has (from whatever cause) to work with.

Finally we may also cite the studies into the developmental processes common to most learners at various stages and ages, with which the factors mentioned above must be permutated.

It seemed so easy in 1944. The selective system of secondary education in the United Kingdom had as its purpose, not merely 'secondary education for all', but the provision of a schooling fitted to the child's individual needs. The weakness was that these individual needs were to be met by an administratively tidy system based on as broad and unindividual a classification system as can be imagined, keyed to school types; Grammar, Secondary Technical, Secondary Modern and Educationally Sub-normal. Even without the social and political overtones of such a system, there was clearly room for question. In practice, it ran into trouble.

Some of the discussion of and pressure for (and against) the comprehensive principle has been what is called 'political', that is to say, arising out of deeply felt social beliefs and attitudes. But whether or not the comprehensive school in one form or other is the perfect answer to the problems it sets out to solve, it is important to recognize that some of these problems are specifically 'educational' in the narrow sense, arising from observation of the selection process in practice. Thus the comprehensive movement has wide support among teachers themselves (it has been official NUT policy for many years) and even teachers who were unconvinced have often been ready to consider its methods and achievements. (Benn and Simon 1970; Rubinstein and Simon 1969; Vernon 1957; Yates and Pidgeon 1957)

The merging of grammar and secondary modern schools during comprehensivization faced many former grammar teachers with the task of teaching for the first time pupils of average and below-average ability, and required all teachers to consider afresh the nature of the secondary curriculum and methodology. The general boost this gave to the curriculum development movement (whose broader roots we have already hinted at) was considerable. A further impetus came from those who were digesting the disturbing evidence that was coming to light on the effects of selection in another form – what was called 'streaming' in the UK and 'tracking' in the United States. In practice, unforeseen difficulties began to be reported.

Many of these difficulties were sufficiently similar to those arising from selection in general to cause some teachers to inveigh against any kind of 'labelling' of children. It was found that streaming tended to be self-perpetuating: that there was much less movement from one stream to another than might have been predicted: and that in some cases the 'lower streams' did much worse than expected. In fact, comparisons between the lower streams of grammar schools and the top streams of secondary modern schools sometimes seemed to indicate that pupils of comparable IQs achieved at a lower level in the former than the latter. A pupil 'branded as a failure' often reacted by losing the incentive to succeed. Furthermore, because under-achievement was so closely related to attitude and to the affective domain, lumping ill-motivated pupils together with a lot of other ill-motivated pupils simply tended to reinforce the problem. Teachers, moreover, tended to react by lowering their expectations. As Marburger (1963) puts it:

> The teacher who expects achievement, who has hope for the educability of his pupils indeed conveys this through every nuance and subtlety of his behaviour. The teacher who conveys hopelessness for the educability of his children usually does so without ever really verbalizing such an attitude – at least, in front of his pupils (p. 306.)

Such a hypothesis is strengthened by C. Burstall's (1970) study of French teaching in primary schools; schools where teachers positively believed that French could successfully be taught even to the slowest child recorded the best results with such children. Douglas Pidgeon (1970) in an NFER study has examined this factor in relation to streamed schools and drawn attention to its importance.

Such considerations have led some schools to reconsider their whole approach to differences of ability and performance, and to see what alternatives to streaming are available. If children take their attitudes from one another, there seems on the face of it every chance that the successful children may communicate their positive approaches to others, particularly as it is among such children that leadership potential in general is often found. In the formal class where the teacher operates by presentation and questioning it is very difficult indeed to be sure that one is carrying the slower children with one and at the same time fully absorbing the energies and perceptions of the brighter. In activity work, on the other hand, children can pursue tasks themselves at their own pace, working alone or with other children, but in the same classroom without 'labelling' or 'branding'.

The very expression, 'activity work', is redolent of the primary school where it has a long and respected history. The term recognizes that children are often most ready to learn when they are concerned with active tasks, rather than sitting passively and silently in rows under the teacher's verbal processing. The primary teacher recognizes that a child's intellectual development proceeds in stages related to his growth in other ways, and that although a child may make sudden spurts and breakthroughs in particular subjects and skills he will only consolidate these when he can reinforce them with other insights to which he is moving.

Activity work in the primary school concentrates on the child's development of concepts and skills, with a range of games, experiments, constructive and creative tasks, and problems to resolve verbally or numerically. The work is based squarely upon the child's own interests and attempts to build upon chance discoveries and events as well as broadly planned projects. In the process books are consulted, pictures and slides examined, music played, filmstrips

shown, maps drawn, models made, interviews recorded, and sometimes even 8mm movies are taken; moreover, everybody and everything is comprehensively and exhaustively measured. Long before
the 'resources'-boom in the secondary schools, primary schools were
busily and unselfconsciously employing 'resource-based learning'.

The older the child, the better he is supposed to be able to handle
abstract ideas and logical discussion, and to grasp subjects presented
in a more 'academic' way. But in fact the slow learner is often the
person for whom the repeated activities of primary schools have not
gone on long enough, reinforcing and emphasizing links and relationships insecurely grasped. The child whose success in purely
intellectual activity has only been average or less (which means most
children) is often better induced to flex mental muscles by active and
problem-solving methods which utilize his own purposive work. In
mixed ability classes, such pupils can be assigned learning tasks and
sequences geared to their particular needs, just as other children in
the same class can get to work on more advanced assignments, or
tasks better suited to their particular sets of talents and skills. Each
is able to contribute to the various activities of the class, to feel
valued as an individual and to see other children of very varying
abilities and natures also valued for their efforts and contributions.

No one concludes that secondary age children are to be taught by
primary age methods. The child who has grasped the bases of arithmetic may no longer be helped at all by Cuisenaire rods, and it
would be foolish to fill our comprehensive schools with sandpits and
places for water play. Moreover, the approach to 'individual difference' must not be an undercover replacement of the earlier
streaming: bright, interesting work for the very able, tediously
simple assignments for the very slow. As soon as the teacher's labelling tendencies come into play we are likely to see the same results,
the student responding to teacher's expectations which he consciously
or unconsciously absorbs, rather than to the full challenge of the
task and the interest of the question. Indeed, there is no reason to
assume that activity and resource-based methods are only for the
'slower' children and therefore unsuitable for the 'very gifted'. Bright
children are by no means a homogeneous group; a typical characteristic however is their aptitude for autonomous learning, and helping them to develop such abilities, especially in the area of enrichment education, can be an exciting challenge for the teacher (see,
for instance, Bridges 1969). Children learn at very different rates at
very different times, and previous classificatory patterns of 'ability'
more closely resemble the averages of widely scattered learning episodes than anything more usefully concrete.

Expository classroom teaching, when it is employed as the main
teaching/learning mode, must work under the assumption that
students will be able to learn at the same rate; if this is demonstrably
not so even within closely selected groups (such as those selected for

grammar school entrance) it is clearly even less the case with 'mixed ability classes'. Interestingly, this is even (as we shall see) postulated by the psychometric school itself, and the results of some experiments based upon its supposed findings. When we move from intelligence testing and its misuses and abuse, and look instead at some of the research into hypothesized personality types, we shall be struck by the follow-up studies which explore the ramifications of individual personality differences in a variety of situations, many of them educational.

Cattell has identified to his own satisfaction some fifteen basic personality factors, to which he has given his own neologistic terms to avoid confusion with expressions common in lay use. He has announced correlations between some of his factors and achievement in learning, and implies that this may often allow us to predict. Thus 'sizothymes' and 'desurgents' tend to have better vocabularies and grammatical skill than 'extraverts', although the latter do more talking. Up to about twelve years of age, 'affectothymia' correlates positively with school achievement, but among university students of equal intelligence it is 'sizothymes' who get better grades. Cattell asserts: 'Whereas it is very rare for any known *ability* to load an achievement performance negatively, personality factors are frequently good for one kind of achievement and bad for another.' (1965: 312)

Many teachers will regard such talk with suspicion, worried about the unfamiliar terminology, associating much of its talk of personality factors with such twilight areas as astrology and zodiacal signs. Certainly Cattell's work does not convince me that we have reached the stage he predicts, where teachers will turn happily to a Cattell-trained counsellor for guidance on how to teach Willy and Ahmad and what to expect from Jane and Fatima – even if it were desirable that we should. Yet other researchers, building either on Cattell or his contemporary Eysenck, have begun a search to see whether personality traits of one or other school of thought can be correlated with success in different educational modes, approaches and even media.

This may be important despite all our misgivings. Much experimental work (especially in audio-visual instruction) tends to measure comparative effectiveness of one medium against another, or one method against another, judged in terms of averaged performances of unsorted groups of children. Variables such as the attitudes and effectiveness of the teachers, and the attitudes and personality characteristics of the learners, are usually omitted from research parameters. Haney and Ullmer (1970) correctly questioned whether current measurements tested all that went on in (say) visual presentation; Leslie Briggs and his colleagues (1967) also criticized the major omission of data about the individual learner, adding that 'eventually this should be done'. (The devastating analysis by

Jamison, Suppes and Wells (1974) of the 'no significant difference'
findings that abound in research reports on AV media will be
examined in a later chapter.)

Some of the most interesting work here has been done by Amaria
and Leith, and the reader is recommended to follow up the literature for more references than are given below. For instance, by
matching pairs of children with similar abilities but dissimilar
personalities, they were able to show that differences in personality
called for different instructional methods. Their conclusion was blunt
and to the point: 'When the conditions of learning are good for many
children there are some for whom these same conditions are debili-
tating.' (Amaria and Leith 1969: 199)

In a separate study Leith stressed the differences in apparent
results when individual personality characteristics were included in
the experiment design (Leith 1969). At age 10, highly structured
and prompted materials were helpful to anxious children, but not
to non-anxious; at age 18, introverted students performed well on
materials which demanded tolerance of uncertainty, but extraverts
displayed the opposite tendency. Snow, Tiffin and Seibert (1965)
tested individual differences in relation to the effects of instructional
films; significant factors emerging included attitude toward the
medium, prior knowledge of the subject, 'ascendancy' and 'responsibility'. Snow and Saloman (1968) in a later general survey hypothesized that specific intellectual abilities, specific personality traits
and 'cognitive styles' were, in relation to each other, likely to provide
meaningful interaction, and that anxiety, attitude to authority, high
or low self-esteem, and such ability factors as spatial visualization,
would all be found to have an important place in the design and
choice of instructional styles and media.

Similar studies introducing personality differences into research
on programmed learning have also shown interesting results (Woodruff et al. 1966; Campeau 1965; Davis and Leith 1967). Equally
suggestive is the work of Sigel, Jarman and Hanesian (1967) which
sought to investigate 'styles of categorization and their intellectual
and personality correlates' in children between 4 and 5 years old;
correlations tended to be confirmed, and the whole study (which
included showing children sets of pictures and asking them to pick
two that were 'like each other' in some way) certainly reinforces the
suspicions of many teachers and librarians, that two individuals see
something quite different in the same item.

Many teachers, having waded through all this, will be tempted to
cry impatiently that it is all rather irrelevant, that we know already
that children are different from one another and that the good
teacher bears this in mind when planning the term's work. Yet what
happens in all too many classrooms at both school and university
level is based on the assumption that students will all learn equally
well from the same method of presentation. If we certainly all know

that they do not, how can this be? The converted ought not to scorn the help of others in establishing a truth which cannot be as self-evident as they feel.

Personality psychology is by no means a securely established discipline; there is a disquieting lack of unanimity as to whether the tests and results of one worker can be duplicated by another. P. E. Vernon, for instance, in an admirably clear discussion of the entire field (1964), inclines in the end to a friendly scepticism. Yet we need not credit personality psychology with a precision it does not yet have, to recognize that studies of this kind in an educational context can give us useful hints. It is undoubtedly true that in previous decades we have graded and labelled children on grossly over-simple measures and concepts, but this does not mean that we cannot make use of as much knowledge about learners as we can possibly get. We must recognize that IQ and aptitude tests give wholly insufficient data; that it is perilous to use such measurements for purely administrative purposes; that there are other tests which can be useful but which we must treat with a similar discretion; and that to study a living organism in isolation from its contexts and interactions is likely to lead to error. When we have said that, it is still true that the studies quoted above, and some others, give us further encouragement to seek to vary the traditional teaching pattern and introduce a multiplicity of learning avenues to match individual variety.

Other areas where testers and measurers have plied their trade have included the study of creativity. J. P. Guilford for several decades has studied what he regards as the various characteristics of creativity through factor analysis, tending to suggest that for some students this is a built-in personality characteristic. E. P. Torrance developed the Minnesota Tests of Creativity, both verbal and non-verbal, scoring the results for flexibility, fluency, originality and elaboration in a way the average teacher will find it difficult to replicate. A typical concept of writers and experimenters on creativity is that of 'divergent' and 'convergent' thinkers, and Liam Hudson (1966) suggested (on the basis of his studies of bright schoolboys in the Cambridge area) that about 30 per cent of schoolboys were divergers, an equal number convergers, and some 40 per cent 'all-rounders' able to deploy the techniques of both to some degree. What is suitable for one will presumably be less ideal for another, and Getzels and Jackson (1962) believe that divergent thinkers are often less acceptable to schoolteachers than are children with a bias towards convergent thinking or towards conformism.

Psychological and personality testing of this kind gives us, at best, partial knowledge, and its usefulness here has simply been to underline the wide variety to be expected in the average classroom. But a child's personality is not just an empty fact; it exists, and is formed, in dynamic relationship with other people, with immediate surroundings, and within a social context. Bruner's recognition of the dangers of assuming that every child had received the 'middle-class hidden curriculum' has already been quoted. Bernstein's widely influential studies of what he at one time referred to as 'language codes' suggested that children arrived at school with class-based differences of language which were significant enough to alter profoundly their attitudes towards and ability to make use of learning. In crude terms, 'middle-class' speakers use language to elaborate their meanings verbally, giving rise to an 'elaborated code', whereas 'working-class' speakers rely more heavily on context, gesture, intonation, facial expression and so on, giving rise to a 'restricted code'. There has been much argument as to how far this is true, just as there has been considerable debate in the United States about the supposed language codes of black ghetto children; Labov in particular has denied that the typical speech responses of the latter are necessarily as restricted or inexpressive as middle-class whites have commonly thought. Holly (1974), quoting Labov's work, attacks the conventional view that 'elaborated' middle-class discussion is necessarily more meaningful. What cannot be in contention is that important differences frequently exist, and that these arise not so much from individual genetic or 'personality' differences as from differences of situation and context. The world of possibilities open to a company director's son in Surrey does not in the least resemble that of the unemployed textile worker's son in Lancashire, and these differences affect not only the total community of which the child sees himself as a part but also his or her attitude towards the relevance of school and education.

To learn language skills is to learn to mean: but whose meaning? Growing up is learning to define oneself, but from a context of deprivation and discouragement many millions in Britain and America (and of course elsewhere) do not and cannot define themselves in terms of the meritocratic middle-class view of the educational and social ladder to success. The self-definition, bitter and cynical, includes an acceptance of educational failure and individual inadequacy: instead of 'I'm going to be a chartered accountant like Daddy' the half-recognition that 'anything I could do will be done by a machine anyway by the time I'm thirty'. To the boy hero of the film 'Kes', the world of school and work alike were irrelevancies to be endured as best one could; personal identity was only achieved in totally separate, non-utilitarian activities such as entering into a relationship with a proud, alien bird. For every pupil in our schools, the nature of 'meaning' is different and is a question of relationship. The expository lesson as the major teaching/learning mode is as out of place here as the teaching machine programme or the discussion under neutral chairmanship of topics dreamed up by 'them'.

John Holt put it simply (1964): 'Most children in school fail' (p. xv). The major message of his brilliant little book was that the child spends much of his time in school developing strategies of protection to cope with his failure. Instead one wants to present in school the opportunity for the child to make something more meaningful, to find 'his meaning' in active learning involving important elements of his own choice, guided, prompted, stimulated and provoked by the teacher. This is where psychologists, social critics and experienced curriculum builders find common ground, where the 'learning by discovery' urged by Montessori, Bruner and the Nuffield Science Projects alike links with the free-schoolers recognizing the importance of relevance and personal decision.

We come once again to the conclusion that the task for teachers and schools is to offer as wide a range of learning experiences and learning styles as can sensibly be managed, to match on the one hand the challenge of individual difference, and on the other hand the complexities of the modern world for which school is (at least in part) an attempt at preparation. If the learning is to be meaningful and valuable, it must induce an acceptance by the learner of the tasks and goals concerned, his or her personal involvement in the learning strategy, and an increasing participation in meaningful decision. The eventual goal must be the development of the learner's capacity for individual, self-chosen or autonomous learning, for the 'éducation permanente' required by the exigencies of a changing society.

In all of this, expository and directed teaching has its place, but it is a smaller place. The decline of the formal 'teacher' has been called for and predicted over many decades, and the Dalton Plan was a well-documented experiment along such lines. (It has recently been sympathetically discussed in L. C. Taylor's valuable *Resources for Learning*, 1971 and 1972.) But teachers have been rightly cautious of the widely trumpeted assertions of some of the more enthusiastic 'progressivists', recognizing that alongside enthusiasm, creativity and love must go intelligence, responsibility and care. Many well-intended experiments have collapsed for lack of adequate preparation, and from lack of adequate material support. In this regard, the development of new media of communication and record, and of reproduction, together with new methodologies of teaching and learning arising from them, is a significant new factor. Our problems have not been solved, but perhaps they have been made easier; meanwhile, the world of possibility and influence surrounding pupils and students is quite radically different, as the next chapter will explore.

Postscript to the above

Dr Neville Bennett's Lancaster University study, *Teaching styles and pupil progress* (Bennett 1976) appeared after the main text of the present book was completed. Bennett's team studied the academic progress of pupils in primary schools in northern England in relation to the teaching styles employed by the class teachers; a typology of such styles was distinguished, resulting in twelve categories along a continuum from 'formal' to 'informal'. The team also asked whether pupils of differing personality characteristics proceeded uniformly when taught by different approaches. The results indicated that 'formal' methods achieved better results than 'mixed' or 'informal' methods in the teaching of reading, number work *and* creative writing, within the limitations of Bennett's defined objectives; personality characteristics, as expected, played a part, but a lesser part. Analysis of pupil behaviour showed that, among other things, the children were busier and did more actual work in the formal situation, and this may be reckoned to have played some part in the final results.

The importance of this research is hard to over-estimate, despite the fact of its triumphant championing by publicists of the unattractive far right. The woollier-minded or over-optimistic 'progressivists' must certainly re-examine their practice and their assertions in the light of Dr Bennett's criticism. Nonetheless the study was effective precisely because it was limited, and it would be rash to extrapolate to other areas, other objectives and particularly other age-groups. The research team did not, and could not, give us the crucial data about teacher preparation and planning, nor about the quantity and disposition of resource materials, which would help us to meet some of the questions which instantly arise. Exponents of resource-based learning see the method as providing a necessary bridge from 'formal' towards 'informal', and one wants to ask about how the pupils in the informal classrooms were prepared for their informality. Meanwhile, Bennett has noted that the single most successful teacher in their sample was in the 'informal' camp – but that the work was apparently underpinned by careful preparatory planning and structure. Exactly!

2 Change in communication media

A new plurality of formats

Those who acquire it will . . . become forgetful . . . they will receive a quantity of information without proper instructions and . . . be a burden to society.

So, crushingly, spoke Socrates, and he was talking about the book, and the handwritten form at that. With Gutenberg came the fifteenth-century invention of printing and there, so far as educational technology was concerned, innovation stayed until the nineteenth century. From then onward the pace of change accelerated. Photography altered our entire concept of illustration; we could conceive of the apparently objective record, and thus recognize that some other forms of record included the recorder in unacceptable form. As we came upon the moving picture with its ability not only to entertain us but also to analyse what we could not easily see with the unaided eye, we began to recognize that we had new tools for discovery; we now knew *exactly* how a horse used its feet in galloping, what an explosion was like in slow motion, what a street looked like to the condensed eye of the time-lapse camera. Sound recording enabled us to repeat musical and other aural experiences, with profound effects upon the musical profession as well as on the range of cultural opportunity open to the ordinary person. The moving picture spoke, and sang, and acquired colour. Radio broadcasting introduced a new dimension of communication in the 1920s, and television brought a hint of novelty to the late 1930s without revealing the overwhelming impact it would have when fully developed in the 1950s and after. Electronic sound recording gave individuals the chance to bring a fleeting permanence to their radio listening and their own aural environment, and video recording did the same, rather more expensively, for the TV screen.

Yet these were not the only revolutions. It has been suggested that the arrival of mass education in Britain in the late nineteenth century was only possible because of the new use of esparto grass in machine-made paper, enabling mass production. Certainly much of the 'resources revolution' of the curriculum development teams of the later 1960s was only possible because of improved duplicating processes and the mass production of the stencil cutter. While the audio-visual media were in full development, the paperback was bringing the old-fashioned print format to a non-book-buying public. Microphotography brought new methods of book and periodical production, and data storage, that even now have surely not exhausted their usefulness in the mere saving of shelf-space. Media began to be used and issued together: filmstrips with booklets and records, slides with synchronized tapes, books with records and sometimes slides in a pocket, kits including a varied assemblage of formats in one box of goodies.

There is no sign that the revolution will stop: indeed, types of equipment become obsolescent so quickly that even the most fanatical audio-visual specialist must sometimes feel uncomfortable. In the last few years we have been promised (and in the UK have never actually been given) ready-made video programmes on *EVR*, requiring one set of equipment, and on videodisc, requiring another. In both cases the opportunities for specific data storage use, as well as full length programmes, have been emphasized by the promoters. The reverberations of the Super 8/Standard 8 controversy can still be detected; institutions were encouraged to invest in the new film equipment, but found that some manufacturers persisted in producing material only in the earlier format; the resultant collapse of confidence has not been easy to repair. Quadrophonic sound offers another potential example.

Futurologists however continue as confidently as ever to predict what we shall soon be doing, and it has been very easy for them to extrapolate from contemporary trends, possibilities and experimentation into an even more thoroughly machine-using future. The 1985 Committee of the National Conference of Professors of Educational Administration, for instance, took the best advice they could find from a wide variety of sources to produce the prophecies in *Educational futurism 1985*, published in Berkeley, California, in 1971. They decided that by 1985, the computer would be a 'commonly used tool' in education, both for computer-assisted instruction and for record-keeping:

> Practically all aspects of the curriculum will have been programmed into machine-usable form by 1985 . . . By 1985 the computer will also have assumed much of the burden of instructional classroom management, such as pupil progress reporting, attendance and general information keeping . . . The teacher will be able to place inputs such as pupil and instructional data into the school's computer via a remote input–output console in each classroom. The same console will enable the teacher to retrieve data or generate more meaningful reports almost

instantaneously. Other computer consoles will be reserved for pupils' use in drills, exercises and exploration experience. (NCPEA 1971: 49.)

This facility will be improved by the added capacities of laser storage devices, enabling an entire 20,000 volume library to be stored on a piece of nickel foil eight inches by ten inches (the same information would require ten miles of magnetic tape).

Holography ... may do to visual image reproduction what lasers will do to data storage and computers have done to data processing ... The projection of three-dimensional visual images will revitalize the 'audio-visual' education thrusts by 1985. (*op. cit.*: 51.)

The Professors looked unblinkingly at all possibilities; we may be glad that: 'It is highly improbable that by 1985 chemical gases will be released through the school ventilating systems to keep pupils and teachers, with or without their knowledge, alert during formal school sessions.' (*op. cit.*: 55)

This caution, and indeed the whole tone of their study, contrasts sharply with the unbridled enthusiasm of other futurologists of earlier periods, for instance Thomas Alva Edison in the New York *Dramatic Mirror* in 1913:

Books will soon be obsolete in the schools. Scholars will soon be instructed through the eye. It is possible to teach every branch of human knowledge with the motion picture. Our school system will be completely changed in ten years. (Quoted in Saettler 1968: 98.)

It did not happen: and yet the demise of the book, the transformation of the traditional classroom, and indeed the end of schools and colleges as we now know them, have all been forecast with an almost hilarious regularity throughout the century, with the results that we see around us.

What we do see is the tremendous transformation by the newer media of society, communication and recreational habits, a huge impact we have often been slow to recognize. At moments of great national importance perhaps three-quarters of the population will be watching the same event on screen; indeed, internationally exciting events such as a lunar landing or the funeral of an assassinated president get world-wide instantaneous coverage. We see war, famine, disaster, the scurrying of diplomats and the habits of exotic animals on our home screens; we are aware of patterns of life not our own, of alternatives of choice, habit and provision as well as of thought. We have the feeling of participation in events over which, for the most part, we have in fact very little, if any, control. We only discriminate between our mediated experiences by a conscious effort, finding ourselves watching comedy, beauty contests and international disasters from the same chair. The newsreader describes the starvation of tens of thousands whilst we automatically notice the colour of his tie and shirt, and comment on it.

For Marshall McLuhan and his followers, the proliferation of media as the extensions of our sensory system has an immense importance, and much effort has been expended in defining whether a particular medium is 'cold' or 'hot' and in declaring the unity of medium and message. McLuhan believes that writing fosters 'linear thinking': 'The fragmenting of activities, our habit of thinking in bits and parts – "specialism" – reflected the step-by-step departmentalizing process inherent in the technology of the alphabet . . .' (McLuhan and Fiore 1967: 44). By contrast, the electronic mass media of our contemporary society have made all things new, or rather, have returned us to the primordial situation:

> Ours is a brand-new world of allatonceness. 'Time' has ceased, 'space' has vanished. We now live in a *global* village . . . a simultaneous happening. We have begun again to structure the primordial feeling, the tribal emotions from which a few centuries of literacy divorced us. (*op. cit.*: 63.)

McLuhan's response was to write a series of books about the situation, but any suggestion that this might be reinforcing linear thinking is rapidly dispelled by the nature of his own prose.

McLuhan was enormously popular and apparently influential only a few years ago, since when it has been commonplace to pick out many of the absurdities and contradictions of his thought. Yet looking at many young people today, the targets of communication channels unknown to their grandparents, it is hard to believe that for all his showmanship McLuhan was entirely wrong. Once, what a child learned came partly from parents, partly from participation in local society, partly from practice, and much from teachers and schoolbooks; today, a large part of what a child knows comes directly from the mass media. A 5-year-old knows of famine in Asia before he comprehends what it is. Moreover, the young are able to surround themselves, via the transistor and the cassette recorder, with a total world of aural sensation which sometimes seems to replace a missing element in their emotional lives.

Whether or not McLuhan is wholly right, some things are indisputable. Our young people see and hear a very great deal of radio and television, together with movies and records, and these form an important element in their lives. They are accustomed to presentations that are professionally, even slickly, performed, and which make the average class lesson seem amateur, especially in the use of communication aids such as graphics, film clips and animated cartoons.

All this is often put forward to support the extended use of audio-visual and other media in schools and colleges: we are to use them because they are so ubiquitously there. Haney and Ullmer (1970) note that the modern American generation will have viewed, on average, 15,000 hours of television, attended 500 motion pictures and spent approximately 11,000 hours in class by the end of their school careers, and put this forward as a reason for using television and film very much more in the classroom. One can imagine some teachers using the same figures as evidence for using them less. McLuhan lambasted the print media for encouraging linear thinking, but it can be argued that this way of thought brought to mankind very substantial benefits which one is not confident would be matched by the uncriticized new tribalism. One does get the feeling, none the less, that many traditional teachers still think of film as being a classroom novelty useful to give their students a welcome treat: yet many students, watching the grey, flickering images uncertainly projected on to unsuitable screens by elderly and noisy equipment in stuffy ill-curtained rooms, may be forgiven for wanting a bit of first-rate formal teaching as a relief.

The glory of the audio-visual media is the contribution they bring to the teacher's communication skills. Pictures, still and moving, can inform and excite through the eye, making real and vivid what would take a tedium of words to describe; overhead projectors provide a more efficient, more stimulating and admirably repeatable blackboard; records and tapes enable words, music and sounds to be replayed at will; and all can be combined into patterns and programmes that do more than simply reinforce and enliven a lesson given in the traditional style.

Thus the so-called 'new media' are not new, even to education. Since the beginning of the century there have been dedicated enthusiasts among the teaching fraternity, promoting (often in millenarial language) the latest and sometimes the most expensive devices as they appeared. Saettler (1968) has admirably charted the development of audio-visual instruction in the United States, picking on the six years, 1918–24 as the key period when what was then called the 'visual instruction' movement properly emerged. The movement continued to grow and develop and to absorb new media as they came ton to the mrket.

Yet Saettler comments (1968: 193): 'the audiovisual instruction movement was a relatively late development of this century and emerged as a small, specialized movement almost completely separated from the mainstream of instructional technology.' A considerable research tradition was built up, and yet: 'this tradition has been confined largely to studies of the comparative effectiveness of conventional procedures and selected types of so-called visual or audiovisual media in attaining the same objectives.' Indeed, Saettler goes so far as to assert:

> ... it is clear from the historical development of the audiovisual movement that it has generally ignored psychological theory, stressing group presentation of materials without explicit regard for individual differences in learning ability (*op. cit.*: 194.)

In this they may have been not entirely alone, but it is a serious charge, and it would be a brave man who would assert that it could not be substantiated for the British audio-visual scene as well. An enormous amount of the talk and literature has centred upon gadgets and machinery, sometimes with a dismayingly naïve view of the learning process implicit therein. It has assumed 'the system as before', but with trimmings, and this can be seen in the very use of the phrase 'audio-visual *aids*', a term which presupposes a type of use, as an adjunct, an added extra, a novel way of doing the same thing. Non-enthusiasts, moreover, have sourly claimed for some decades that attention often centres on the glossiest, latest and most expensive format: film and closed-circuit television, rather than filmstrip, record or slide. The McNair Report noted in 1944 that Great Britain was:

> ... undoubtedly behind certain other countries in the use of the cinema for educational purposes ... there are also other important mechanical aids to teaching, such as the epidiascope, episcope, lantern and gramophone ... Television may also play a part in education in the future. (1944: 138.)

But when the journal *Visual Education* first appeared in Britain in 1950, it showed evidence of a great deal of worthy grassroots activity; the very first issue contained reviews of new materials written by local 'visual aids groups', a valuable feature that has been retained ever since. Interest in such LEA activities as the development of film libraries was also apparent, and politicans were echoing the claims of the AV campaigners in very similar language (see, for example, Gould, 1950).

Despite such claims, it is hard to avoid the conclusion that in both the USA and the UK, the audio-visual movement rarely came to grips with the need for an elaborated theory going beyond the use of audio-visual materials as decorative additions to the traditional lesson. A recent study concluded with the recognition that research had not yet identified any variant of the existing system that was *consistently* related to students' educational outcomes (Averch *et al*, 1972). Moreover, as Jamison, Suppes and Wells penetratingly noted:

> ... when highly stringent controls are imposed upon a study, the nature of the control tends to force the methods of presentation into such similar formats that one can only expect the 'no significant differences' that are in fact found. (1974: 36.)

As they went on to comment:

> ... there has been widespread disillusionment with where educational technology is today that results ... from the pattern of 'no significant difference' findings that we have reported in this paper. Furthermore, because technology has been primarily an add-on input to enrich the

student's experience, there are few, if any, examples one can point to where it has improved system productivity. (Technology has been more successful in providing an *alternative* to schools; successful examples here include the British Open University, the Bavarian Tellehallez, and the Japanese NHK's Secondary School of the Air.) (*op.cit.*: 57–58.)

None the less, the 1960s saw in fact the first significant signs of new and creative thinking; the context was the curriculum development movement, and the catalytic factor was programmed learning.

A new technology of education?

Saettler traces programmed learning back to Montessori, but for ordinary purposes it is to B. F. Skinner that we must turn for the initiation of the programmed learning movement as such. His famous call, reprinted in 1954, summoned us all to a new technology of instruction in much the same millenarial language as typified the audio-visual movement: 'There is a simple job to be done. The task can be stated in concrete terms. The necessary techniques are known. Nothing stands in the way but cultural inertia.' (Skinner 1954: 97) Based on his remarkable work with pigeons and other creatures, and upon the theory of stimulus-response and operant conditioning that developed from it, Skinner's belief was that quite simple and inexpensive equipment could be fashioned that would revolutionize education and render it more scientific. Subject-matter, in the Skinnerian teaching machine, was broken down into small steps which built upon one another into a great complexity, the student making successive responses and receiving the reinforcement of immediate confirmation at each stage. Very properly, it was enormously influential: it 'worked'.

More flexible systems developed as the movement grew, and Crowder's work with intrinsic or branching programmes, in which the learner's responses and mistakes are built into the sequence and determine subsequent steps, made greater concessions to individual differences among learners. This was, of course, correspondingly more difficult to prepare. Devising programmed sequences in general proved very much trickier for the average teacher than was perhaps originally predicted, and the variations in curricula and in the subject-matter taught in different establishments revealed as over-optimistic (certainly in the UK) some early prophecies, which saw great blocks of time in the average school taken up by individual work with teaching programmes. It is also interesting that, whereas Skinner and colleagues initially thought in terms of 'teaching machines', the vast majority of programmes have in fact been in book form, and there is little if any evidence to suggest that the machine has any important advantage.

Programmed learning made significant contributions to education, particularly in industrial and military training (where of course
motivation is fairly high and the units of information to be assimi-
lated are uncluttered by humanistic value judgements). It is by no
means a purely technical or scientific tool; the technique can be
used for teaching the differences between the Petrarchan and
Shakespearean sonnet forms. Recently, experimental work has investigated the use of the programmed technique in what is now
called computer-assisted learning, where the programmes are fed into
the computer; the machine can then, if the initial preparation has
been thorough enough, monitor the responses of a great many
students at a time, switching them to the appropriate branching
sequence as their responses demonstrate the need. Such developments, to make economic sense, require student numbers running
into tens of thousands, and a corresponding subtlety of initial
preparation.

There is a widespread impression among British schools at present
that 'the programmed learning fad is finished'. This must be a
result of the extravagant claims made at the movement's inception,
what Leith (1969) has described as the work of 'flamboyant cheer
leaders'. In fact programming is alive and well and still active as
one of many tools available to the good teacher. What is much less
clear is that it is the answer to all problems, or that it has even
solved the problems its proponents themselves recognized. To put it
no more strongly, it has not been proved beyond doubt that self-
paced learning is the most effective, and it is odd that a movement
claiming to 'individualize learning' has paid such scant attention to
individual personality and other differences among learners in its
practice. Much of the learning theory behind programmed learning
advocacy has been challenged as narrow and over-simple. Moreover,
as used in teaching machines or books, the method gave little scope
for the use of senses other than sight, or of other media, or of the
fruitful interaction between students and with teachers, which is the
main justification of classroom teaching. Many of the current experiments have been interesting and thought-provoking; none the less we
must beware of the tendency to enjoy the use of the latest expensive
and prestigious gadget and it is wise to remember Oettinger's warn-
ing in his devastating book:

> When we go into schools where computers are actually in use, we find
> them serving as expensive page turners, mimicking programmed
> instruction texts. Yes, computers have practically infinite branching
> capabilities, but this matters little when we are unable to foresee more
> than a very few of the more common possible learner responses.
> (1969: 50.)

There is still much that we do not know; J. Hartley in a thirty-
year survey ended shatteringly:

There is a complex job to be done. The task cannot be stated in concrete terms. The necessary techniques are not fully known. The equipment cannot always be easily provided. Other things – primarily our ignorance of the complexities of human learning – stand in the way, as well as cultural inertia. (Hartley 1974: 288.)

Yet programmed learning played a crucial role in directing attention to a new way forward. The feelings of many audio-visualists and other teachers were effectively summed up by Francis A. Cartier in 1964. Denying that people learned in precisely the same way as pigeons, Cartier insisted that the reason why a programme taught better than typical traditional methods was usually because of the latter's inadequately prepared design:

> As a programmer struggles over the fifth tedious revision of a 25-word frame, it is difficult to escape the conclusion that if he had worked this hard on every sentence of the textbooks he had written, these textbooks would probably teach as well as programmes .... The programmer has given us a production concept which will spread to every aspect of the teaching process. (Cartier 1964: 4.)

This proved to be a prophetic attitude. In the 1960s, the curriculum development tide carried all before it; programmed learners and audio-visual enthusiasts met in the general activity of re-thinking methods and re-designing curricula. Many of the concepts of systems analysis, useful in management theory as well as in computer technology, spilled over into adjacent areas. From the creative interaction, came the new concept, which came to be called Educational Technology.

In Great Britain the emergence of the new movement from the marriage of contributory movements was symbolized when, in 1967, the journal *Programmed Learning* added the three words *and Educational Technology* to its title. An editorial declared that the change of name signified a 'steady trend towards a wider outlook' and heralded the fact 'that teaching technology appears to be advancing on separate fronts and that these fronts could well be brought more closely together.' (p. 1) A similar process was occurring in the United States, though the term in use over there, 'instructional technology', is worth noting. There is scope for a thesis of sorts on the distinction between the Commission on Instructional Technology's definition: 'Instructional technology means the media born of the communications revolution which can be used for instructional purposes alongside the teacher, the textbook and the blackboard' (AVI, April 1970: 89); and the National Council for Educational Technology's definition, for the UK, of educational technology: 'the development, application and evaluation of systems, techniques and aids to improve the process of human learning.' (NCET 1974: 13) The American version still concentrates attention on the agent of instruction, whereas the British definition lays stress on what is to happen as a result – human learning.

It is a common complaint of educational technologists (self-styled) that people still think of them as 'something to do with machines', or 'audio-visual-aids people', and most books and articles on educational technology spend valuable space on definitions, especially when addressed to the lay reader. This problem stems partly from unresolved and sometimes unarticulated contradictions within the movement itself. Many who claim the title 'educational technologist' do not properly exemplifiy the true nature of the concept. Readers of the various chapters in Unwin (1969) will see a clear distinction made between what may be called education plus technology (where individuals try to find uses for available equipment) and the study of instructional methods and systems, which is what the true discipline of educational technology is properly concerned to encourage. Like many new disciplines, the manner of its explication is sometimes a barrier to understanding. When the concept is explained by some writers, educational technology:

> ... can best be viewed as a well-disciplined, systematic approach to education and training characterised by explicitness (particularly in regard to objectives), by sophisticated analysis and synthesis, by the utilisation of optimal decision making procedures and by rigorous empirical evaluation. (Davies and Hartley 1972: 1–2.)

One suspects that the language of this definition would alarm and antagonize many teachers in the average British school staffroom; no doubt this is unnecessary, but one welcomes the admirable simplicity of Derek Rowntree:

> ... educational technology is as wide as education itself: it is concerned with the design and evaluation of curricula and learning experiences and with the problems of implementing and renovating them. Essentially, it is a rational, problem-solving approach to education, a way of thinking sceptically and systematically about learning and teaching. (1974: 1.)

A look back at programmed learning shows how the concept began to arise. Programmers began to realize that the effectiveness of their work depended not so much on the particular format they had adopted as on the disciplined care with which their work was planned and executed. Rowntree again:

> Many programmers realized that they had been programming things that should never have been taught at all, or that should have been taught by some other method or combination of methods. More and more they saw the folly of setting out with a medium in search of a message ... This is where systems technology took over from the tools, and the change of emphasis may prove to have been programmed learning's greatest gift to education. (*op. cit.*: 4.)

The systems approach, as we saw, developed from cybernetics, management theory and computer technology, and crudely transferred from these areas of activity its use in education can be appalling. Applied sensibly and sensitively, however, it is a different story; as always in education, it depends how you do it.

The systems approach to educational technology involves four basic activities or stages:

1. The identification of objectives: what must the students learn?
2. The design of appropriate learning experiences: how will they learn it?
3. The evaluation of effectiveness in practice: how well did they learn it (also: how can I know whether they have learnt it or not)?
4. The improvement of the design for the next occasion.

This analytical structure can be applied much more widely, including the design of administrative structures; to think systematically and rationally about an educational system that has grown up (as we saw) in a wholly irrational and unplanned way can have disturbing and revolutionary effects. The application of systematic thinking to, for instance, the courses offered by the Open University has resulted in the production of syllabuses, learning methods and study materials which are not only of extremely high quality but are profoundly influencing the approach of teachers and administrators all over the world and at many levels of educational activity.

Educational technology is therefore offered as almost a synonym for systematic thinking in education. Rowntree says:

> . . . if educational technology is what educational technologists do, then educational technology is educational problem-solving . . . You may feel that this . . . is not very revolutionary. Nor is it, unless applied by someone brave enough to face up to all the disturbing hypotheses that can arise in the course of it. (*op. cit.*: 7.)

This is fine so long as we recognize how little we genuinely know about education, and how cautious therefore must be the claims that we are able to make. We lack, for instance, one agreed and unified learning theory. We lack general agreement on the formulation of objectives, and in many subject areas there is great dispute as to how far, if at all, we can test whether some quite crucial objectives have been achieved. We are far from being able to specify all the things that actually take place in a learning situation, and (as we saw earlier) we have little knowledge of the implications of individual difference for our work.

The argument on objectives is perhaps particularly noteworthy. Bloom's *Taxonomy*, for example, with its distinction between objectives in the cognitive and affective domains, has increasingly come under fire (see, for instance, the discussion in J. H. Gribble 1970). Lawrence Stenhouse (1970/1) has seriously doubted whether the articulation of behavioural objectives is practical in (for instance) the teaching of *Hamlet*:

The content of a work of art cannot be reduced to students' behaviours. Here, 'understanding' means to respond to or experience the concrete reality of a work of art. The response or experience is individual, though there are canons by which one can judge its appropriateness, by which one can discriminate understanding from misunderstanding. (Stenhouse 1970–1: 75.)

Many of Stenhouse's objections arise out of other people's over-simplifications, and it is of course true that we know very little of what actually goes on as a result of our work with students. As Stenhouse provocatively puts it: 'Planners might aim to break the hypothesis: "The effects of any curriculum differ in important ways from those expected by planners, experimenters and teachers".' (*op. cit.*: 82)

Professor Hirst (1973) none the less feels that Stenhouse takes too narrow a view of what is meant by 'outcomes', arising from the 'engineering approach' which he finds is encouraged by writers such as Tyler, for many years the key author in the field. Hirst admits that there is much difficulty ahead:

> ... our ignorance on a huge scale re-asserts itself. We simply do not know how to predict many of the outcomes of our actions ... Rational planning, as I have tried to outline it, is, if you like, an ideal, whose application necessitates conditions that will never be completely fulfilled. (1973: 22–3.)

These are useful cautions; like the programmed-learning advo-cates before them, there is a tendency among many in the educa-tional technology school to oversimplify, to brush aside difficulties, and to state as proven doctrines it will take many more years of experiment and experience to establish. Moreover, as Hirst has suggested, it is not by any means certain that more knowledge in itself would help; disagreement among supposed experts suggests that in fact we are comparing differing practices, differing values, differing approaches, and that in the end we shall come down to a series of judgements in which personal preferences will play their part.

For all that, the teacher can hardly be absolved from the attempt to clarify his own mind. If we can never be certain that we have stated every objective we might have, in the clearest form, and with the most practical means of testing whether it has been achieved, this does not mean that we abandon the attempt or that to try one's best under the circumstances is not a helpful activity. For what is the alternative? As Mager has truthfully (and unnervingly) said: 'If you are teaching skills that cannot be evaluated, you are in the awkward position of being unable to demonstrate that you are teach-ing anything at all.' (Mager 1962: 47) In fact the definition of objectives and the evaluation of progress is something which as teachers we do all the time; it simply happens to be true that many of us do it very amateurishly and very half-heartedly, indeed we do it badly.

One reason for insisting on such an analysis is our need (as Rowntree (1974) reminds us) to 'beware of implicit objectives'. What is the message of the medium? Our school system has its own inner logic which may not always be what we wish or proclaim, and the same goes for our methodologies. Harry Judge has commented on programmed learning that it:

> ... does assume ... that A knows fully and in advance what would be good for B to learn ... But the claims of programmes must be scrutinized carefully, not because they offer wrong answers but because they assume that there are answers. (Judge 1974: 67.)

Rowntree quotes Philip Jackson on the average school system and what it teaches the student: 'He learns to be passive and to acquiesce to the network of rules, regulations and routines in which he is embedded.' (Rowntree 1974: 40) He quotes Harold Taylor:

> The usual kind of education ... is designed to give answers to questions which nobody asked and to inhibit the student in discovering his own truth and insight. The lectures and texts do all that sort of thing for you. They provide a way in which the student can cover up his true self by finding a vocabulary acceptable to most people and a set of facts which are generally known among people generally considered to be generally educated. (Rowntree 1974: 40.)

Rowntree's general comment on all this is much to the point: 'The hidden curriculum marches on. If we don't specify the objectives we want, we'll have to put up with those we get.' (p. 41)

Educational technology and systems thinking is therefore a controversial approach involving elements of many previous educational trends and taking part in arguments beyond its own orbits. It does not give us answers, but a way of procedure. This is important to stress, because the tradition of over-selling still persists in some quarters and it is possible to find extravagantly foolish predictions and claims within the educational technology literature, which will be a considerable embarrassment to the many sensible and imaginative teachers who have applied the method and found it helpful to them. Educational technology is a theory and a set of hypotheses; it is a habit of mind, and a readily applicable methodology; it is far too early to claim for it that it has a large body of accepted practice. It is in fact a movement: a coming together of teachers whose common conviction it is that teaching up to now has been conducted in far too random and amateurish a fashion, based at best on a kind of inspired guesswork, and that it ought to be possible by putting our minds to it, and applying the sort of thinking that is successful in other fields, to do a better job than before. As such it holds the promise of much good.

The objection may be raised, 'If what we are talking about in educational technology is *not* the promotion of AV aids but the cultivation of a systematic problem-solving attitude, why is it that so many self-styled educational technologists did in fact emerge from the audio-visual movement or related areas, and why is it that so much educational technology literature is concerned with the applications of audio-visual formats of one kind or another to learning development?' This is a useful question to ask, for if all we are doing is applying systematic thinking, it may well be that the best answer to a specific teaching problem would be a straight lecture with blackboard illustration, or alternatively simply sending a student off to the library to find a book. Somehow one does not find very much in the various educational technology journals on these matters. Teachers and librarians cannot always resist the uneasy thought that they may be being given the soft sell: like demythologizing theologians laughing too heartily at our ideas of what religious doctrine involves, perhaps the educational technologist's bland 'all we are saying is' is simply the prelude to smuggling all the old gadgetry back again while our backs are turned?

One answer to this must be the effectiveness and value of audio-visual methods themselves. The facilities are here, they have an important role and when one is looking openmindedly and systematically at a teaching problem one cannot possibly ignore them. To say: 'Educational technology is not *about* audiovisual materials' is perfectly true, but we cannot suppose from this that it does not *include* them. What is astonishing is not that educational technology makes such important use of audio-visual facilities, but that other movements within education in the last quarter of the twentieth century still make so little use of them. It is the argument of this book that many of the reasons for this are organizational, and that a very considerable change in attitudes and practice results from taking up the administrative implications of all aspects of resource-based learning (audio-visual, print-form and other) and putting them to hand.

Meanwhile it should not be thought that no one is doing research into the uses of the printed book. In a report of an International Conference on Frontiers in Education, it was announced that Mr Michael Macdonald-Ross of the Open University was doing research into the efficacy of the printed word: 'a field where very little research had been done.' (Locke 1974: 121)

What, then, *is* educational technology, and what is an educational technologist? The term is used, even by its most literate apologists, in at least three separate senses, and often in the context of one article or policy document. Much of the misunderstanding surrounding the term and the subject, and the people who lay claim to its mystique, arises from this imprecision. 'Educational technology' in practice means one of three things:

1. The equipment and software of the audio-visual and computing industry which can be applied in education.

2. Such equipment and materials being used as an accompaniment to or in educational processes.

3. The systematic analysis and design of learning sequences, based on a careful examination of objectives and constraints, and utilizing a chosen selection from all available methods and resources according to their suitability; the systems approach to teaching and learning; a theory based upon this.

Any pronouncement about educational technology needs to be scrutinized with great care to ascertain what meaning is intended – the machines, the machines in use, or a methodology. Equally, an educational technologist can be one of several people:

1. A person who knows about the different audio-visual and programmed formats, how they work, how they can be repaired, or what in general they are capable of.

2. A person who can manufacture learning resources in reprographic, audio-visual, programmed or similar formats and is reasonably knowledgeable about their educational uses.

3. A teacher who has been away on a short course including elements of both these skills, and can therefore give useful general advice.

4. A teacher with considerable experience and further training, who has demonstrated his abilities as a design consultant for both curricula and materials.

5. A person who believes in and/or practises educational technology as a theory and methodology.

Because of the term's many meanings, and the confusion they therefore create, it is proposed in these pages to avoid them wherever possible. Resource-based learning, like resource-based teaching, can obviously exemplify 'educational technology' in one or other meaning, but a surprising number of teachers would indignantly deny that they had been practising it; in some cases, this implies disagreement or scepticism with the claims made by some self-styled 'educational technologists' (meaning 5) and in other cases derives simply from a misunderstanding. It makes better sense in any event to look for more specific and precise terms. As far as personnel are concerned, every attempt will be made to refer to them according to skills, professions or areas of activity (e.g. audio-visual technicians, media producers, design consultants), and normally the expression 'educational technologist' will imply someone consciously identifying himself with the theory and methodology of the movement. We shall perhaps all in due course become 'educational technologists', in which case the term will be ready, like the state, to wither away. I feel it should do so now and not keep us waiting.

Two professions and a need for help

The perceptive teacher has already, as we saw, moved very decisively from the traditional view of his role as a primary information source. He is persistently encouraged to see himself rather as the person responsible for seeing that learning happens. Curriculum developers aim not so much to 'cover a given area of knowledge' as to convey basic concepts, teach relevant skills, and create an appetite for, and the ability to pursue, further research and enquiry at later stages. Increasingly the major aim of teachers and schools is to produce competent and interested autonomous individual learners, participating in their own development.

Thus to the expository lesson, the period of exercise and drill, the set readings from the class textbook, the tests of memory and comprehension, and all the other useful ploys of the good teacher, have now been added sessions when the student is placed in direct confrontation with a variety of information sources, print-form, audiovisual and three-dimensional, in small groups or on his own, in a situation which requires his active involvement and which can to a greater or lesser extent be tailored to meet his individual needs. Much of the activity (and one says this with both elation and exasperation) is the kind which good teacher–librarians, not tied to purely literary objectives, have long advocated, but extended to include not only the 'newer' media but also the resources of the world outside. But in each case individual differences, and differences of the class as a whole, will have been taken into account as factors in planning for participation.

For this purpose the existence of the multiple varieties of communication media, and the emergence of professionals skilled in the application of these media to particular problems and occasions, are major advantages and despite persistent grass-roots suspicion there is plenty of evidence that teachers at some stage or other in their careers are ready to experiment and take advice. Yet despite fine work going on in many schools, classrooms and library resource centres, it is all too common to find teachers reverting to type, schools with equipment stowed away unused, library resource centres which have become simply print shops for the production of worksheets and diagrams, supplementing teacher-exposition and drill.

If this was the result of a series of carefully planned experiments leading to the conclusion that resource-based learning was ineffective, there would be no problem. We could all move along and apply our skills and intelligences to other approaches. Some teachers will, of course, say when asked, 'it didn't work', but in a surprising number of cases this turns out to mean, not that the students' learning or involvement was less than had been predicted or hoped for, but that the exercise for one reason or another was too difficult to set up. 'It didn't work' meant 'We didn't get it properly going'. It is very easy to have all the right motives, intentions and objectives; it is often very difficult to put these intentions effectively into practice. Without doubt, one of the most cogent reasons for disaster and dissatisfaction has been that the planning of effective resource-based activities took an inordinate or unacceptable amount of teacher-time in preparation.

One of the outstanding American innovators in the university teaching sector is Dr Samuel Postlethwait, head of the Department of Botany at Purdue University, Indiana. Dr Postlethwait pioneered the influential 'audio-tutorial' method of teaching freshman botany, stimulated by finding himself faced with the task of teaching freshman botany to some 500 and more new students every semester and with a timetable allocation of three weekly hours of lecture or lab time. In the resultant Postlethwait audio-tutorial laboratory, open from around 7.00 a.m. to 11.30 p.m., the student could come at a time of his own choosing; at the entrance he would receive a descriptive hand-out explaining what books, notes, equipment would be necessary to bring along; once inside he would be given a botanical specimen and would enter a pleasant area equipped with a multiplicity of booths or carrels. Each carrel contained a tape recorder and headphones, probably a microscope, and whatever audio-visual equipment and software was required for the week's exercise: perhaps a slide viewer, or a loop-film viewer, or a filmstrip projector. Guided by the tape, the student would examine his specimen, consult his workbook, compare with a slide, perform a task, consider implications and respond to questions; he could stop the tape and replay it whenever he wished, and if he was really stuck he could seek guidance from a teaching assistant, or Dr Postlethwait, or a fellow student, or the library. When he had completed the tape, he had absorbed a required unit of work, and subsequent testing generally demonstrated that students were rapidly improving in their grasp of essential material, as well as responding positively to this method of instruction.

The method has fascinated botany teachers, and others, from all over the world. Undoubtedly the method works in Purdue, and reports are that its adoption elsewhere has been generally successful. Yet when asked how long it takes each week to prepare and construct the next sequence, Dr Postlethwait is accustomed to laugh heartily (as he did when I asked him) and reply, 'Oh, about fifty hours.' (For further information, see Postlethwait et al, 1969.)

Those who have laboured long at programmed learning sequences, even if less wholeheartedly multi-media in scope, will agree that such units take time to prepare. The problem is no less with open-ended exercises and unstructured enquiry projects in humanities work, where the teachers need to anticipate and prepare for a wide variety of student response and reaction. Structured or non-structured, such activities demand time and thought and imagination and knowledge and research to get ready: at any age or ability level. Planners need a thorough understanding of the subject field to be explored, and its structure in enquiry; they need to know what materials, print-form or audio-visual, are available, and suitable, and what special problems they may reveal; they need to have available at the right time suitable equipment, and places where the equipment may be used, and they need to be sure that the student is able to find and make use of all the resources he may need in the periods of the timetable allotted to the activity. Moreover, as far as possible these units have to be planned with the knowledge of the personalities involved and their likely responses to the exercise.

Inexperienced teachers embarking on such experiments are likely to land in the same sort of confusion and chaos that resulted in those primary schools that went headlong into the 'integrated day' without a preliminary survey of their available resources and their knowledge of children's interests and reactions. All such activities demand thorough pre-planning and a type of organization not customary in many schools. Innovative and creative teachers are not necessarily those most accustomed to such disciplines or amenable to them; perhaps the opposite is also true. Yet the programmers and the educational technologists are undoubtedly right when they insist that current trends and changes in education require more systematic thinking, whether or not we always adopt on every occasion their particular model for it.

The injection of considerable sums of federal money into many American schools in the 1960s, together with the programmes and methodologies that resulted, arose from and sometimes led to the conclusion that change in education was primarily a matter of provision. We could solve our problems only if education received a higher and higher budget, either from the proceeds of an expanding economy or from receiving a higher proportion of an economy in steady-state. The economic conditions of the 1970s do not lead to optimism if one continues to hold this view. They make nonsense of the aspirations of developing countries, who not only lack the funds available to some American schools in the 1960s but who lack the meagre finances spared to education in Britain in her declining 1970s. At a Unesco conference in Geneva in 1974, an administrator from central Africa told me: 'We shall have great difficulties in establishing media centres in our rural schools.' 'They are short of money?' I asked innocently. He laughed joyously and replied: 'They have no electricity!' Yet he was proposing to begin, because he held, was indeed forced to hold, the alternative view, that although additional finance was welcome and desirable, the primary requirement would always be systematic planning, sensible co-operation, and the full utilization of what one already had. And this, more than anything else, requires organization.

Organization cannot, of itself, free the teacher from the hours of planning and thought that lie behind the achievement of successful learning in his students. It can, none the less, cut out many of the worst frustrations: material that takes hours to trace, is never found, or is unavailable at the right time; teacher-made material that takes too long, is botched in process or inexpertly designed; equipment that doesn't work, or works badly, or is pre-empted by someone else at the crucial moment; timetables that don't, when it comes to the point, allow sufficient flexibility; help that one feels ought to be available but somehow never is. Organization can help to overcome the isolation, the loneliness, all too often felt by the would-be-innovatory teacher, the need for someone else to talk things over with, plan with, compare notes with. Organization can pool abilities, share loads, bring in local talents and interest, identify sources. It can ensure compatibility, avoid unnecessary duplication of effort, enable economies to be made by co-operative use and the full employment of existing facilities. It can free energies and abilities for creative change.

Now equally of course organization can stultify progress, enmesh teachers and students alike in a nightmare of regulations and restrictions, tie up materials and equipment that could otherwise be productively used, and generally contribute more to the personal empires of individuals than to liberation of either teachers or students. Organization must be appropriate, and must make a positive contribution to the problems whose identification called it into being. As Keith Evans rightly reminded us, some attempts to stimulate and support resource-based learning resulted in 'magnificently equipped Resource Centres with highly trained staff, from which teachers retreat, their confidence undermined!' (Evans 1971: 5.) In particular, organization must avoid a common error, which Evans again picks on with much justification, the attempt 'to provide a superstructure of provision without securing the foundations of demand.' (p. 4)

As we insisted during the period of the Schools Council Resource Centre Project, there are many possible patterns of organization within and without a school, and what is experimented with or decided upon must relate to the local situation and to the needs of the school as its staff see them. The impressive thing about the British experience in this respect is the variety of patterns which have resulted and the good sense of each of them in their own contexts. Organization need not involve the importation of para-professionals, the compulsory centralization of materials and equipment, or an authority-wide standardization of all procedures (although in particular instances a good case can be argued for each of these examples). Support for experimentation, innovation, resource-based learning activities and other desirable or interesting ventures can involve anything from a reorganization of a school timetable to a series of local education authority decisions on staffing and materials provision.

Hugh Cunningham has listed four simple but major difficulties he faced as a teacher when trying to break away from 'too great a reliance upon the textbook':

> The first was simply obtaining suitable material ... The second was having the material produced ... The third was ensuring that whatever equipment was required was at the right place – and would work. The fourth, perhaps the most important, was in establishing some way of evaluating the material ... (1971: 25.)

The solution in Cunningham's own school (Madeley Court, Telford) was a sophisticated library resource centre, on two levels, with a multi-media collection of materials, reprographic and audio-visual production facilities, and trunking to the library and other areas of the school through which audio-programmes could be distributed on command. Naturally, the facility required ancillary staffing in all areas, as well as a teacher as Head of Resources with a curriculum development brief. At the time this was perhaps the most lavishly equipped school of its kind in the UK (though there were many more lavish examples still in the richer areas of the USA) but its strength was to be the participation of its library resource centre personnel and the head of resources in the in-service education of the teachers. A new school beginning from scratch can plan in this way without arousing the instant suspicion and hostility of old stagers in the staff room.

At an already existing school with much less lavish provision, Ron Mitson of Codsall Comprehensive established a thorough change of the total organizational pattern of the school in order to provoke, stimulate and support the kind of thinking and innovation he sought from his staff. His analysis of objectives reinforces Cunningham's:

> In concerning ourselves with the needs of pupils, we may too long have ignored the need to give our teachers services and support and help them to feel adequate to cope with the demands that education in the modern world is making upon them. At Codsall I was hoping to link this to the achievement of a balance of teaching methods ... The ultimate aim would be complete, self-contained courses in particular subjects in the upper part of the school. (Mitson 1972: 46.)

The school is described in detail in *Organizing Resources*, and was very influential in the early 1970s because of its thorough-going use of *existing* resources: staff, equipment, space, finances and enthusiasm. Working from a basis not impossibly different from a very great many comprehensive schools in the UK, it achieved by this single-minded disposition of resources and energy an organization of support for teacher and pupil alike. For the teacher its aim was specific; not only was it an organization of materials and equipment, but: 'Our Centre is an agency for curriculum innovation and teacher development. One of its main functions is that of giving in-service training on the shop floor.' (Mitson 1972: 48)

Keith Evans' charge that some American school media centres actually undermined the morale of teachers (a charge he did not, incidentally, document) was not one which could be levelled at centres on the Madeley and Codsall model, and their influence was such that many examples existed, at least for periods of time. Evans' caution, however, is understandable, and until the effectiveness or otherwise of more elaborate organizations could be tested in a variety of settings it made sense to list more modest requirements for supportive bases to innovative and resource-based work. In an interesting wrestle with, on the one hand, his mistrust of centralized empires and, on the other hand, his recognition of the necessities of the situation, he concluded that:

> There must, however, be some central point, some 'nerve centre', which will contain:
> (a) Some form of index to all the resources distributed at strategic points throughout the school.
> (b) a central collection of works of reference of all kinds, e.g. encyclopaedias, film catalogues.
> (c) master equipment for recording and reproducing, e.g. recording a programme off air on to $\frac{1}{4}$" tape and then transferring to cassettes for use at the satellites.
> (d) a pool of equipment too expensive to duplicate, e.g. 16mm film projectors. (Evans 1971: 5.)

In addition, there would be 'a number of satellite, decentralized resource collections, each one under the control of the Head of Department or Head of faculty,' (*ibid.*) and a Resources Adviser, who it was important should be:

> ... an experienced teacher, someone aware of the educational possibilities and problems offered by the use of multi-media materials ... a person enthusiastic to extend the range of learning methods employed in schools and keenly interested in educational technology. (*ibid.*)

Spelt out in such terms one had a fairly elaborate model system, whose strength was its intended contiguity to the teacher and the place of use, which was obviously the classroom. This type of decentralized model had already been advocated in the USA by, among others, the influential J. L. Trump (see, for instance, Trump 1966, and for a later appraisal from a librarian's viewpoint, Ahlers and Sypert 1969). For many schools it was a necessary reality, shorn of its resources adviser and of any space for the departmental resource areas.

Both models approach the question of organizational support

from within the school, and in terms of what the school itself is able to do by shuffling its priorities and arranging its disposition of resources and staff. The decentralized Evans model underestimates the amount of material which lies unused in departments for long periods of the year and which might be of value to another discipline, or to a pupil in the enquiry mode; it certainly contains no element which would stress interdisciplinary thinking, inter-departmental co-operation or the sharing of acquisitions and experience. The Codsall model, which included substantial departmental collections closely co-ordinated by a central collection and organization, avoided this danger but, by its heavy concentration on production of new materials, provided no incentive for the teacher to consult or seek material already available from published sources; this can often provide an educational input which is both high in quality and economical in teacher effort, in the time spent in laborious production.

It was the special contribution of the ILEA, and in particular of the advisory team headed by Mr Leslie Ryder, that it considered what types of ancillary personnel were called for by the new methods, and their training and inter-relationships. Elsewhere, significant explorations were made of the types of co-operative support that could be developed, between schools and teachers from different schools, and between a variety of other educational institutions such as colleges, polytechnics, universities and that peculiarly British innovation, the teachers' centre.

The ILEA pattern is superficially similar to that often found in American schools: that is to say, the two aspects of resources production and resources acquisition and management are related to types of para-professional staffing. Discussions with the authority's principal library organizer and his colleagues, together with discussions at local area and school level, showed that the professional librarians already on the strength of most of the ILEA secondary schools would be quite competent and also sufficiently willing to organize and administer school collections of audio-visual and other resources, as well as the print-form items with which they were already associated.

Where schools patently did need greater assistance, Leslie Ryder reasoned, was in the production of materials, in the planning of course units making use of resources, and in the use and operation of audio-visual and reprographic equipment. For this need, another type of para-professional was envisaged, with sound training in all these areas, able to work with teachers and give support to teachers, and with a thorough understanding of educational principles and methods. Such a person would not himself act as a teacher (though there was no reason why a person with teaching experience might not make, as it were, a sideways step into this area of work); he would not be a 'leader of teachers', and he would certainly not be anything approaching the Head of Resources envisaged in both the Codsall and Evans models mentioned above, with a curriculum development brief. In no sense was the new para-professional a threat to teachers, therefore, nor did he detract from or erode the professional autonomy which British teachers enjoy. After much deliberation, and with the susceptibilities of Audio-Visual Technicians (a very different breed) in mind, the new man was termed a Media Resource Officer, and a special training was devised for him in association with Wandsworth Technical College.

Schools were not compelled to employ an MRO; in fact, to have an MRO a school had to prove to the media advisory team that it both needed and valued the skills offered. By offering skilled help of a kind that teachers recognized and respected, it was hoped the MRO would prove to be an agent of change, and would work in co-operation with the librarian to develop imaginative resources use and high quality practices. This was in line with the general authority policy, not of compelling change or forcing patterns, programmes and methods upon schools, but on the contrary providing the means whereby the kinds of action it wanted could be supported and rewarded and developed: the carrot and not the stick.

The MRO was greeted with some initial suspicion, understandably. None the less the sheer ability and enthusiasm of the first generation established the value of the MRO and the important contribution he or she could bring to teachers and schools, both primary and secondary. Use of resources improved quite strikingly, and the extra dimension added to curriculum planning and the discussion of methodology was unmistakable. MROs worked in close association with librarians to develop library resource centres of an active kind where pupils could make use of whatever format most suited them and their enquiry problems, and where teachers could find materials, equipment, catalogues, guidance and practical assistance.

The ILEA has supported such work in other useful ways. Very noteworthy was the imaginative decision to give help and advice to those schools which had shown by their own efforts that their thinking and planning had reached a stage where they were ready to make more effective use of innovative methods and resource materials. The resources support team organized by Mr Ryder's advisory section brought together experienced MROs and school librarians; the team as a whole planned a range of activities, including exhibitions, in-service training, and the compilation of catalogues and lists, and in addition supplied pairs of specialists who would '"immerse themselves" in schools for up to several weeks at a time building up a resources centre and advising on the use of resources generally.' (Albert 1975: 27)

Finance of any resulting centre was on a one-for-one basis, the ILEA matching expenditure of school funds by a grant of its own if the advice and guidance of its support team was carried out in practice. In practice the team has not only explored what can be provided within individual schools, but developed and encouraged co-operative schemes between schools and colleges within particular neighbourhoods; and all this work was further supported by the existence of the authority's education library, media resources centre, film library, television service and related activities.

No other education authorities in Great Britain have the advantages and facilities of Inner London, though ILEA can also claim to have more than its fair share of inner city problems to cope with. Its response sets it well in advance of other major cities in the country. Some authorities, on the other hand, have been able to develop another type of supportive service, utilizing the education advisory staff in co-operation with burgeoning teachers' centres. This latter institution developed rapidly in the 1960s, with the particular blessing of the Schools Council, which recognized its value as an agency of teacher involvement in curriculum development. Teachers' centres vary enormously from place to place, but typically provide facilities for teachers to meet, formally or informally, to attend short courses, to hold exhibitions and displays, and consult materials. Teachers' centre wardens (usually themselves experienced teachers anxious to develop active supportive programmes) keep in close touch with teachers and schools as well as with local advisers and 'the office', and centre management is frequently run on quasi-democratic lines with a significant element of teacher-participation (the local authority none the less is responsible for finance). Centres have been used for co-operative curriculum development planning (what in America would be called 'curriculum workshops'), teachers in similar subject fields from a number of neighbouring schools meeting together to share inspiration, experience and effort. LEA advisers develop meetings and courses aimed at stimulating new thought and experiment in their subject areas and the investigation of common problems and current thinking. As a result of such activities, teachers' centres have found themselves closely involved in a variety of support activities relevant to the development of resource-based learning.

One typical activity has been the production and dissemination of locally planned materials. Electronic stencil cutters, offset litho machines and many audio-visual reproduction facilities are, in today's circumstances, beyond the budget of small and medium-sized schools, but can be provided at a teachers' centre for co-operative use. Planning teams developing materials in a local area can have them produced on high quality equipment, and the materials can be available to others who may find them useful at minimal cost. Often what begin as experimental course-work exercises of only medium-to-poor standard become high-quality on-going productions as teachers not only get accustomed to the requirements of curriculum materials planning but recognize through experience the stimulating value of these materials in their work with students. The steady rise in quality of the materials produced and developed at Dudley Teachers' Centre, for instance, is an excellent example; the centre has an enthusiastic warden and much of the work has developed under the stimulus of an outstanding educational adviser, but the content of the materials has been developed by local teachers with admirable results (mostly limited at present to print-form).

In other counties (Oxfordshire was an early example) the linking together of teachers' centres into a county network means that high quality work produced anywhere in the county can be disseminated on requirement to other schools. The Regional Resource Centre at Exeter University Institute of Education hopes to build further upon the network possibilities in this respect, making the teachers' centres the teacher-entry points to an informal organization of schools, colleges, polytechnics, the university and other agencies, including individuals in the community (Walton and Ruck 1975), and we shall be examining such possibilities in closer detail in a later chapter. The importance of such developments will be clear: planning for resource-based learning is a taxing and time-consuming activity for teachers, but if the work can be shared, if the expertise and creativity of colleagues can be made easily available, and if the teacher can have ready access to advice, guidance and encouragement, an important contribution has been made and some of the burden shifted.

Teachers' centres also make themselves responsible in some areas for the servicing of school equipment, the provision of an exhibition collection of equipment and materials, and in some cases even for equipment loans.

Such ventures in teacher-support contrast (at first glance perhaps quite sharply) with the type of provision advocated in *Media programs, district and school*, the latest media center standards issued jointly by the American Association of School Librarians and the Association for Educational Communications and Technology in 1975. This document envisages several levels of support and provision. It lays down standards for the media programme within the school, in terms of the provision of skilled personnel and plentiful materials in appropriate surrounds; it specifies in some detail the media programme for the 'school district' (the American equivalent of the local education authority) in similar terms of personnel, materials and distribution. It goes on to discuss, in rather general terms, regional, state and network possibilities. The lavishness of specification is appropriate to a country which still, in spite of economic recession, is by most standards a very wealthy one, though it should be noted that the document is far from describing typical or *current* practice: this is what the two associations concerned regard as logical developments to be pursued during the next decade in line with the best available practice.

A British parallel would be the discussion in Fothergill (1973: 123), where the respective roles of local, area, regional and national services are analysed. Yet even if such provision were available in every area, this would not in the least preclude the kinds of support and networking discussed in the preceding pages. Provision of materials and expert personnel is only part of the requirement; teachers need opportunities to pool ideas and programmes, share one another's resources on a personal advice basis, find compatible people to whom to turn for educational and emotional support, meet together in courses and workshops at a variety of levels, often very informally, and find the unusual people or collections in the community that the Exeter project is noting and which have played such a useful part in the work of Devon schools. In other words, the British have been compelled by financial limitations to concentrate much of their attention on co-operation, on neighbourhood resources, and on the person-to-person aspects of support work, but this is a valuable area to develop.

Resource-based learning therefore turns out to involve much more than simply a method of revitalizing and individualizing learning. It involves a multiplicity of provision, the necessity of co-operation, the discipline of organization and the welcoming of para-professional skills. We need a variety of materials in a wide range of formats utilizing therefore a number of different types of equipment; because it will never make sense to have maximum collections in every classroom, we are likely to value a central pool from which everyone can draw, and the ability to inspect, copy and borrow materials from other schools and central LEA collections. We need to produce materials to match the individual needs of students and curricula; because this is very time-consuming and difficult, we co-operate at school level by team teaching, by keeping a central indexed pool of locally produced materials, and by intelligent planning, and at out of school level by co-ordinating our efforts through teachers' centres and curriculum development schemes. Because few of us possess universal skills, we learn to value one another's and to look for the unexpected amongst our colleagues (the music teacher who is a professional photographer, the lab technician skilled in electronics); and because teachers must necessarily concentrate mostly on what is pre-eminently their task, the design and communication of learning experiences, we value those para-professionals able to concentrate on related areas, such as the production of resources from our basic design, and the collection and organization of recorded information and communication in all formats.

Later chapters will analyse particular aspects of this situation in closer detail. At this point it is useful to extract from the account a number of basic questions which teacher or student essentially ask and for which it is the task of a resources organization to provide answers.

1. The teacher in preparing a unit or sequence of resource-based or enquiry learning asks: *What have we already?* and the answer to his question requires the systematic selection and acquisition of book and non-book materials in all formats, their arrangement and storage for retrieval, the preparation of a suitable index or retrieval tool allowing the identification of suitable items however sought, and some system of controlling or monitoring the use of the materials so that wanted items can be located and reserved even when in use.

2. The same teacher then asks: *What can we borrow from elsewhere?* requiring a system for identifying the existence of other collections and their major contents, for arranging loan services from them, and supervising the use and return of borrowed items.

3. The same teacher also asks: *What can we buy to add to our collection?* requiring not only the systematic acquisition of catalogues, bibliographies, reviewing services and lists, but also wherever possible knowledgeable people who can advise on the process and on the items themselves.

4. Moreover the teacher asks, *What can we make?* requiring competent guidance and help with the variety of productive and reprographic equipment and facilities available, from the standpoints both of technical excellence and educational design.

5. The younger teacher, or the older teacher inexperienced in modern methods, also asks: *What should I be bearing in mind?* and perhaps also: *What alternatives of educational methodology are in fact open to me?* requiring experienced guidance from a well-qualified senior teacher, including those trained in the full meaning of the term 'educational technology'.

Moreover, the pupil or student equally has questions, especially if his assignment is of an open-ended kind, or if his teacher has included (as one hopes he increasingly will) the objectives of developing autonomy and self-confidence in research in his instructional design.

6. *What materials are available to me here, relevant to my quest?* and the student will require the same indexes and organization as the teacher.

7. *What other libraries, museums and centres may help me?* reminding us that the maturer student will wish to venture further and work in his own time.

8. *What study area is available to me to work in, where a range of materials is readily to hand?* a question obviously involving the provision of a multi-media library.

9. *What facilities are available to me to respond to my assignment in multi-media terms?* a question which should importantly remind us all of the ready way in which many young people today think in visual or audio-visual terms. (There are young people, functionally illiterate, whose involvement in educational pursuits has been greatly stimulated by allowing them to make slide-sequences or videotapes; the acquisition of reading skills sometimes comes after the motivation has been established by other communication experiences.)

Many of these questions fit very comfortably within that group of activities we call 'librarianship': the building up of collections of information materials, their organization for retrieval and use, the provision of suitable areas and facilities for prolonged study, the development of lending and reservation systems, of co-operative interlending procedures and networks, and the provision of full bibliographic and reference guidance. In both Britain and America, the educational preparation of librarians includes all these aspects and more, although individual librarians naturally tend to specialize in depth in only a selection. In all these areas, librarianship has developed a considerable body of constantly re-examined knowledge, a fact duly recognized by (for example) the Council for Educational Technology, which turned to it naturally and appropriately as issues developed within its purview.

Recent years have seen a great expansion in the number of librarians working in educational institutions and specializing in educational librarianship; in Britain this was a later development than in the USA, but none the less the libraries of almost all colleges of education, further education and technology are now run by chartered librarians, and some five hundred or more librarians are also found in secondary schools. The development of the 'resources revolution' has if anything increased the trend, as librarians offered services now actually valued by overburdened teachers. Because this is so it is unnecessary to make extravagant claims; the provision of a multimedia library, with the fullest integration of catalogues and shelves, and the finest collection of viewing and listening equipment, still meets only questions 1, 2, 3, 6, 7 and 8. Work with teachers and students producing materials of their own is a very important part of resource provision, and librarianship training is less sufficient here (but see 'Production: one mode of acquisition; in Chapter 6). Equally, question 5 is properly best answered, neither by a librarian nor by an ILEA media resource officer, but by an experienced teacher with a leadership role in curriculum development and methodology.

Moreover, to say that a set of activities and skills partakes of the general discipline of librarianship is not the same thing as saying that all people who have ever been trained as librarians can perform them, or that they must be performed by people whose training is *only* that of the professional librarian. The educational background and training of chartered librarians in Britain has not been well understood by teachers, and in particular it has been noticeable how

reluctant spokesmen of the School Library Association have been to
acknowledge that *some* librarians have received a special training in
work with children of school age, with materials for children of
school age, and involving more than an acquaintance with the study
of educational systems and methods and of child development. On
the other hand, there is no law saying that librarianship, or teaching, or media production, cannot be learned at professional level by
people who already have a professional accreditation in another
field. This is an assumption or misunderstanding that can only have
arisen from the curious vagaries of the student grants system in
Britain. In the USA, with its flexible and adaptable system of
higher education and its tradition of easy access to university summer
courses, it is common to meet teachers who have, over a period of
time, gained professional competence in each field and become
fully professional in every sense, able to talk on terms of complete
parity with professional colleagues in each group. This situation
would (as we shall see) be very desirable in the UK; some librarians,
some teachers and some media specialists have painstakingly and at
much personal cost gained dual or multiple status, and the extension
of this practice would go far towards resolving unnecessary anta-
gonisms between professional interest groups.

The contribution of librarianship as a whole, including the public
library sector with its schools services, as well as other groups within
the profession, to supporting the needs of teachers and students, is
increasing and important, and not only in the resource-based
learning field. We shall have occasion later to examine the evidence
submitted to and conclusions of the Bullock Committee, and it is
sufficient here to note not only the submissions from educational and
public librarians but also the committee's support for the work of
librarians in schools, and its welcome for the now-emerging courses
leading to people dually qualified as both teachers and librarians.
But the relationship of librarians to the developments we have so far
examined, including the knowledge and publications explosions, the
development of new teaching methods, and the rapid expansion of
audio-visual communication media, is something we must now
examine in closer detail, so that the later arguments and conclusions
of this book can be made clear.

3 New Disciplines for Library Science

New formats come for custody

Some years ago an advertisement aroused great wrath among the touchier members of the library profession: 'I used to be the mainstay of the public library until I tried . . .' (out of deference to the protesters, the brand name of the vodka in question is here suppressed). The advertisement was particularly ironic, inasmuch as in the nineteenth century the public library movement was undoubtedly supported by many reformers in the expectation that libraries would provide a healthy alternative to drunkenness among the working class. Libraries in general have an image of unparticularized worthiness and sobriety, and many young librarians have an admirable messianic zeal about them, a firm belief that what their library has is good for people and that membership lists and issue figures must be pushed up for their own sake. The zeal does not always survive the pedestrian management structures of local government, and perhaps it takes a more than ordinary enthusiasm to persist after the efforts of economizing councillors under pressure to do something about the rates. Moreover when I once tried a word-association test with a class of college of education students, the word 'library' for quite a large minority of them meant 'fines' (although there was no fines system in the college library). Libraries have a slightly tattered, establishment image, hoary with antiquarian overtones and bureaucratic regulations, symbolizing a society from which the whole advertisement series referred to was enticingly suggesting we should drop out.

There have been, and are, scholar–librarians of the old school, wedded to the codex format and to classical culture, but for most librarians their profession is a management exercise and a service among people: on the one hand, the wealth of recorded information and its producers (authors, editors, directors, photographers, researchers) and on the other hand, the readership and audience, the people needing access not only to the items stored but to their subject contents. The task is to devise an organization that gives the greatest and most flexible access to the items and their contents, in a manner that takes note of the needs and the habits of the clientele and of such precautions as may be necessary for the protection of the library's purposes. Individual 'reader guidance' has high priority.

There is a sense in which this task has remained the same since libraries began (clay tablets were gathered into organized collections in Mesopotamia at least as early as 2700 BC) but modern librarianship properly dates from the nineteenth century, from Panizzi's reign at the British Museum, from the spread of the public library movement in Britain, the USA and Scandinavia, and from the new techniques initiated by such creative geniuses (in their day) as Melvil Dewey and Charles Amni Cutter. The foundation material in that formative period was undoubtedly and properly print-form: the book, the pamphlet, the journal; yet libraries before that time had not necessarily always been uni-media. Ashton's ordinance for setting up Shrewsbury School is often quoted today for its specification that the building should include 'a library and a gallery for the said school, furnished with all manner of books, mappes, spheres, instruments of astronomy and all things apperteyning to learning.' The ordinance was dated 1578. Three hundred and forty years later, in 1918, the National Education Association and the North Central Association of Colleges and Secondary Schools, in the United States, approved the so-called Certain Standards (named after the chairman of its working party, Carl Caspar Certain) which laid down the first standard specifications for a secondary school library. It included the memorable paragraph:

> The library should serve as the center and co-ordinating agency for all materials used in the school for visual instruction, such as stereopticons, portable motion picture machines, stereopticon slides, moving picture films, pictures, maps, globes, bulletin board material, museum loans, etc. Such material should be regularly accessioned and cataloged, and its movements recorded, and directed from the library. (NEA and NCACSS 1920: 21.)

The American Library Association also endorsed the document and published it in 1920, and for twenty-five years the Certain Standards were acclaimed as the basis of all school library accreditation in the United States. The library resource centre was born, and re-born, and I have traced its development in the USA through successive decades of perpetual re-discovery, in two papers published elsewhere (Beswick 1970; 1971).

The noteworthy thing, considering this half-century of official recognition, is the regularity with which the multi-media library concept was hailed as a new idea and canvassed with a sense of surprised discovery, as if no library or librarian had ever considered it before. Classification creator Melvil Dewey made an unmistakable point as an influential member of the American profession:

> Libraries are rapidly accepting the doctrine for which we have contended for many years. The name 'library' has lost its etymologic meaning and means not a collection of books, but the central agency for disseminating information, innocent recreation, or, best of all, inspiration among people. Whenever this can be done better, more quickly, or cheaply by a picture than a book, the picture is entitled to a place on the shelves and in the catalog. (1906: 10.)

New York State Library had, in fact, 60,000 prints in stock that year. By 1923, the public library in Springfield (Mass.) was circulating gramophone records (this had been proposed in Britain by H. A. Sharp in 1922) and in 1929 the public library in Kalamazoo (Mich.) began a first experiment with film distribution. Meanwhile, in the UK, W. C. Berwick Sayers in his famous *Manual of Classification* (1926) included instructions on the classification of maps and charts, and in a later edition 'prints, illustrations, lantern slides and negatives'.

Official American Library Association publications in the 1930s paid regular tribute to the multi-media idea (there is some evidence that British librarians maintained illustrations collections and by 1935 record collections without so much publicity). Edith Lathrop's study of American rural schools in 1934 revealed many supportive agencies lending slides, stereographs and movies, often to libraries. Yet when Professor Lester Williams as an educationist addressed the American Library Association conference on 'What the school expects of the school librarian' there was something of a ring of novelty in his style when (after the usual platitudes about 'the library as a workshop') he went on: 'Teachers expect librarians to act as a service agency in providing and dispensing all manner of instructional aids, such as phonograph records, clippings of fleeting materials, films, slides, pictures . . .' (Williams 1939: 679) Librarians were also expected to 'participate actively in the curriculum revision program' and 'suggest sources for instructional materials not traditionally considered within the province of library materials'. (Williams 1939)

This long flirtation between the teaching and library professions in the United States in the matter of audio-visual media became something rather warmer in the 1940s. Educators made specific proposals. The Forty-Second Yearbook of the National Society for the Study of Education, published in 1943, devoted a whole volume (Part Two) to 'The library in general education', once again assuming that the whole idea was totally novel.

> The newer types of school programs . . . make wide use of nonreading as well as reading materials in promoting learning . . . The library

service provided in many schools is being expanded to include a generous supply of nonreading materials ... and by conference and work rooms where materials appropriate for the study of specific problems may be assembled and used by individuals or groups. (NSSE 1943: 24.)

As in the Certain Standards, among the many audio-visual items to be included were stereographic materials, apparently in plentiful supply at the time. None the less it was not until the 1960s that American school libraries really came into their own as multi-media centres. The decade began with the American Library Association's *Standards for school library programs*, which gave a very thorough rationale for the new type of services the school libraries were now to support:

> Services, not words, portray the image of the school library. The *school library* is a *materials center, an instructional materials center*, or any of the equivalent terms now springing into existence. In like manner, the *school librarian* is a *materials specialist*, or an *instructional resources consultant* ... For the school library, through books, films, recordings, and other materials, goes beyond the requirements of the instructional program, and unfolds for the many private quests of children and young people the imagination of mankind. (ALA 1960: 13.)

By any other name, it smelled as sweet to the eager school librarian, and this paragraph will remind many British readers of the arguments a decade later as to whether 'library', 'resource centre' or 'library resource centre' (among many other terms) best described the new organization called into being by the demands of resource-based learning and new curriculum projects. And even though many schools and school authorities in the United States were slow to be convinced, the 1960s was the decade of the famous Knapp School Libraries Project, of federal grants for multi-media developments under the Elementary and Secondary Education Acts, and of the development of the electronic study carrel and dial-access. Senior High Schools put microfilm reader-printers into their libraries and were thought conservative (the microfilm, after all, was only another version of the printed page).

The decade ended with *Standards for school media programs*, published jointly by the American Library Association and the National Education Association in 1969, embodying what was undoubtedly the most advanced and breathtaking model of the role of the school library media centre that had ever received official imprimatur. (It has now been superseded by the 1975 *Media programs, district and school*.) The ALA pushed on, with its School Library Manpower Project, funded by the Knapp Foundation, investigating the personnel needs of the new multi-media services they were advocating. Even the budget cutbacks of the 1970s, which put a brake on the heady optimism of the mid-1960s, were modest by anything but American standards, and an impressive number of schools in the States today receives a multi-media library service far removed from the early print-dominated public image. Yet when one talks to leading figures in American school librarianship one detects an uneasy dissatisfaction. So much has been achieved, and yet in many ways so little has changed. There are splendid examples of schools whose whole educational strategy has dramatically altered as a result of the revolution of which the school library media centre was a part; and yet in so many others, the facilities remain underused, the teaching in the classrooms remains traditional, and the librarians in the media centre complain of being peripheral, neglected and undervalued.

Change in itself is not enough; it must happen with the acceptance and understanding of those who are most affected. There is much evidence to suggest that the American transformation was in many cases too sudden, too linked with immediately available federal grants, too concerned in fact with the importance of material provision rather than with steady and persistent thought and experimentation. However it is also fair to say that the professional leaders sometimes expected too much from the change; it is no slur on an honourable movement within the American profession that its initial success did not immediately bring the golden age. Many British teachers would cheerfully give their eye-teeth for facilities and activities which the visionaries write off as unsuccessful.

In one sense the comparison with Britain is humiliating. Not only has British school librarianship no very long tradition of multi-media interest (Shrewsbury School in 1578 notwithstanding), there is not even a very secure tradition of school librarianship at all until the post-1945 era, despite the admirable work of many grammar school teachers in the 1930s. (The Library Association School Libraries Section was not founded till 1936, and the School Library Association till 1937; when the two came together in 1945 under the latter name, the sad separation of school librarianship from other branches of one profession was reinforced.) Even today it is possible to come across a secondary school without any library, in the sense of a collection housed in a room set aside entirely for that purpose; some of these libraryless schools are in the private sector, and eager parents pay heavily for the 'privilege'. Moreover, whereas America has a substantial history of the employment of professionals trained for their role (most states lay down a minimum requirement of so many credit hours in education and library science at undergraduate and postgraduate levels), by far the majority of secondary school libraries in Britain are run in a few supposedly 'free' periods during a week, by classroom teachers with little or no librarianship training. That the work of many of them is first class is without question, but it is an achievement against great odds. Until a few years ago, only what was the London County Council, and is now the Inner London Education Authority, employed chartered librarians in schools, though counties such as Nottinghamshire, Somerset, and Cheshire have now followed suit. Opportunities for dual qualification, in both education and librarianship, barely existed until the pioneer establishment of a Teacher–Librarianship Diploma at University College London in the late 1960s, and although a variety of different courses are now emerging there has been precious little encouragement or inducement for ambitious people to take advantage of them. (Perhaps the Bullock Report 1975 will help.)

This situation was not, until very recently, deplored very widely by anyone but some librarians. Curriculum development made a difference; resource-based learning brought about a total change of attitude and need. The old school library, print-based or not, was essentially peripheral, cultural, recreational, linked largely with reading for pleasure and the work of the English teacher. There is nothing wrong with any of these aspects; practice in reading and the development of the habit of reading is a vitally important part of all education, and the Library Association very properly made representations on this score to the Bullock Committee. The usefulness of the library to the English teacher must also not be under-emphasized, although very often 'work in English' calls for only the simplest of library skills from the pupil. But the old false syllogism, 'English Literature is printed in books: books are in libraries: therefore the English teacher should be the school librarian', overlooks those sections of the stock that are scientific or concern number, those sections of the stock that are not in English at all, and those sections of the stock largely in pictorial form – quite apart from the service of the library to history, geography, sociology, crafts, and other subject departments, and the usefulness of non-book formats to all comers. The ability to enjoy, create and teach literature does not at all imply an equal ability to organize recorded knowledge for retrieval, though it is not necessarily its opposite. It took radical change in teaching method, requiring greater use of an organized collection of resource materials, to point up the need for a greater degree of professionalism and for larger and more ambitious organizations.

This need began to become apparent in the later 1960s. The astonishing (and sometimes astonished) response to my own journal articles in 1967, describing American practice, was one small pointer. When Dyer, Brown and Goldstein (1970) were writing their book in the later 1960s, there was very little practice to guide their comments on non-book media, which were therefore very general, but the importance was recognized and the book made a brave, if insufficient, attempt at a new educational basis for a library programme. Leicestershire County, in the meantime, was planning new school buildings for the resource-based learning concept, placing the library resource centre of Manor High School, Oadby, at the heart of the school in a very real sense (Edwards 1969). In 1970, the Library Association produced the first set of specific standards for school libraries that Great Britain had ever had, embodying the library's new name, and including an analysis of implications for finance, planning, staffing and service which was immediately recognized as being incomplete. The *Supplement on nonbook materials 1972* sought to redress the balance, and announced a level of provision to test the nerves and ambitions of school librarians and library advisers for years to come

For many people, the major change was the simple addition of new formats to the library collection. In the same year that the Library Association produced its *Supplement* and the Schools Council published my own Working Paper 43, the School Library Association published its *Libraries in secondary schools* (Morris *et al.* 1972). Yet the SLA document, excellent though it was, was little more than a description, sensitively written, of what school librarianship had aspired towards since the SLA was first formed; audio-visual resources received a polite page and a quarter, and there were two references to curriculum change. The ferment of the 1960s and early 1970s could hardly be guessed from its otherwise admirable pages, and the document remains the culmination of the lifetime devotion of eminent, elderly and retired authors. Very properly, they regarded the changes around them with interested caution, and the book leaves the reader with the impression that the recent changes have been primarily the modest addition of audio-visual materials to those items already included for enquiry and project research. The Association issued in 1975 a compendium, *Not by books alone* (Waite and Colebourne 1975) but few of the reprinted articles were initiated within the SLA, which has unfortunately tended to resemble a pressure-group of teachers of English i/c Libraries rather than an innovatory body. Indeed, although the SLA is composed overwhelmingly of qualified teachers, it seems to some to have shown itself less aware of the pressures of educational change than the Library Association, with its royal charter to oversee the interests of libraries of all kinds. It would be delightful if this pessimistic and disappointed paragraph were to be proved false by subsequent activities.

However, the misunderstandings were not only on one side or in one organization. The uncomprehending response of some professional librarians to the question of retrieval systems in the library resource centre has shown the underlying belief that what was at issue was simply the addition of new *formats*. If audio-visual items could be included in the very simple card catalogue systems previously devised for school libraries, they felt that the retrieval argument was over: a very comfortable conclusion for those who did not in any case understand indexing principles very thoroughly, were not very interested in the activity and valued most of all their own face-to-face contact with the clientele, making up in personal (and psychologically boosting) service for the shortcomings of their own indexes. The 'OCCI boom' (Optical Coincidence Co-ordinate Indexing) spreading through school resources centres in the early 1970s was not, however, based only upon a misunderstanding about media formats, although there was evidence of a considerable confusion about general principles of information retrieval; what teachers in particular were signalling (as I explained in *Organizing resources*) was great dissatisfaction with the effectiveness of conventional catalogues in practice. They did not, in the experience of these teachers work. This was partly because the traditional school library catalogue, devised by teachers untrained in library methods, aimed to meet only the very simple demands which, alas, were made of it in the long decades of neglect. When, under the influence of the newer curriculum methods, the approach to the library by teacher and student became more sophisticated, the catalogues no longer served. But this is not all.

If any one activity is thought, in the public mind, to represent the essence of librarianship it is undoubtedly classification and cataloguing: the organization of library materials into a system for their displayed storage and the easy retrieval of the subject content of the collection. This, teachers and educational technologists will always happily agree, is the librarian's professional job, and what surprises people is not that librarians classify and catalogue but that they sometimes believe they know something about the contents of their books and AV items, offer advice on quality and relevance, and have pronounced views on how they would like their libraries to be used. Yet in their courses of professional training, it is normally the information retrieval classes that most students describe as boring, difficult and irrelevant. Many librarians argue that all classification and cataloguing should wherever possible be done nationally, or even internationally, allowing librarians to get on with their 'real work'. To most school librarians (chartered librarians or otherwise) it is the individual work with teachers and particularly pupils which is most satisfying and rewarding, and their knowledge of the books and other items available for children is what they most importantly claim as their special expertise. When teachers ask what librarians can offer in pupil-guidance, chartered librarians often retort that their own knowledge of children's literature greatly exceeds that of the average teacher (usually strikingly untutored in such matters), and when self-styled educational technologists wonder what a librarian can tell a student about a filmstrip, the retort in recent years has been prompt, and along the same lines.

Yet the new interdisciplinary approaches, the new stress on enquiry and research, and the increased stress on the teacher in the devising of resource-based approaches, require more flexible, efficient and detailed methods of information retrieval than has been typically the case in schools, or in most academic and public libraries hitherto.

It is not that librarians had no practice in the classification and cataloguing of non-book materials. Although the British profession has not adopted a multi-media outlook with the celerity that many would wish, there are plenty of examples of public libraries with visual and aural collections, and the counties of Wiltshire, Somerset and Leicestershire have in recent years been offering significant audio-visual services to teachers and schools. Moreover, there is a wealth of experience among the specialized libraries represented in the Aslib Audio-Visual Group, including such distinguished collections as the Slade Film History Register, the BBC Film Library, the British Film Institute, the Imperial War Museum, the British Institute of Recorded Sound, the BBC Record Library, and many others. In the United States, the Library of Congress has been classifying and cataloguing audio-visual materials for many years, so long as they were deposited at the Library for copyright purposes. The *Anglo-American Cataloguing Rules*, prepared jointly by the Library Association, the American Library Association, the Canadian Library Association and the Library of Congress, were published in 1967 with some sixty-six pages devoted to rules for non-book materials, and dissatisfaction with these rules produced further publications from the Canadian Library Association (Riddle 1970; Weihs, Lewis and Macdonald 1973), the Department of Audio-Visual Instruction of the National Education Association (1968), and the very impressive LA/NCET rules issued by the Library Association and the (then) National Council for Educational Technology (1973).

It is not that librarians did not know, nor that they did not care. It is partly that the teachers were asking for a depth of cataloguing, a level of retrieval, that is very expensive. But it also happens that in the organization of recorded knowledge for retrieval the profession of librarianship finds itself at an interesting point of crisis. Just as teachers found the knowledge explosion and the publications explosion causes of considerable difficulty, so certainly did librarians, and a brief examination of some of the problems may at this point be instructive.

The organization of exploding knowledge

It is no accident that the nineteenth century saw a tremendous acceleration of interest among librarians in classification and indexing procedures. In the medieval monastic library, knowledge fell into such simple categories that broad grouping on shelves could be accompanied by only the simplest of catalogue descriptions. The publishing explosion following the development of printing made it necessary for catalogues to give rather more detail: for instance, the edition and date of a book might now be more crucial to the reader, because there were so many variants. But by the nineteenth century knowledge itself had expanded so rapidly, and interest in locating published accounts of very specific knowledge units had developed so greatly, that all previous expedients had to some extent broken down, and the new public libraries proliferating in the UK, the USA, and elsewhere gave an added impetus to invention.

There are still libraries where books and materials themselves are kept on 'closed access', in other words available only on request to the library staff; the catalogue carries the whole burden of revealing to the clientele the contents of the stock, by subject or author or whatever 'retrieval handle' is thought to be worth displaying. This is exactly the system which many teacher–librarians and resource centre directors in Great Britain adopted for reprographic and audio-visual materials when they began consciously organizing resource collections (rather than 'libraries') in the late 1960s and early 1970s. Yet most libraries, whether public, academic or specialized, these days operate on the 'open access' principle, whereby as many items as possible are displayed on shelves or in other units immediately available for browsing and consultation. Such systems depend on a classified array; most libraries adopt schemes that enable the reader not only to find 'where the science books are kept' but a particular sub-section 'where the books on sub-atomic particles are kept'. The shelf display is supplemented by an indexing system flexibly organized to allow for a variety of approaches, to lead the enquirer to the right 'shelf address' and to remedy any deficiencies in the system for particular types of user.

A library is an organization of recorded knowledge for the autonomous individual learner. Its system of display and retrieval must therefore be such that this kind of learning can proceed: that the individual user can, to a very great extent, progress himself through the various pathways to knowledge provided by the library, with the minimum of unnecessary difficulty and the maximum reinforcement. For teachers and other educators therefore the effectiveness of the library's retrieval system is a matter of concern, and for some of them the way in which the retrieval system forces the enquirer to conceptualize his need is in itself a matter for educational as well as bibliothecal decision. A system where the user presses a series of buttons without thought and gets exactly what he *needs* (rather than what he at that stage *thinks he wants*) is efficient but not entirely educational, any more than one so difficult that the user could only throw himself at the mercy of the person sitting at the reader's adviser desk. It is this concept that lies at the back of R. P. A. Edwards' attack on dial-access retrieval systems:

> If it is considered that the information content is of paramount importance then it is valid to so construct a resource centre that every student may spend most of his time wired up to a dial-access system so that all he need do is dial a number, press a button and then sit passively absorbing what he sees on a screen and hears in his headphones . . . If this latter is to be the ultimate model, with the student's role being somewhere between that of a battery hen and a laboratory rat, then surely most teachers would wish to have no part in its evolution. Surely it is the learning process that is important! (Edwards 1973: 2.)

Mr Edwards mistakes his target, in fact; in his anxiety that the student should have the experience of search and enquiry, he is attacking the unimaginative, closely programmed learning package or the teacher-dominated reading list, rather than dial-access systems. For if the student can retrieve an item by dialling a number, he still has to discover *what* number, and to conceptualize how he might arrive at the correct answer that would give it to him. The problem for librarian and teacher alike is to devise a system which will enable him to achieve reasonable success in spite of all the colossal problems that the size and growth of human knowledge present.

Monastic libraries were small enough, and their rate of growth low enough, for the 'shelf-mark' system of organization to work tolerably well. Shelf 4 of bay E could be designated to hold all the histories of England likely to be added to stock during the next hundred years or more. The distinctive breakthrough of the great classification makers of the later nineteenth century was in response to a new need: books on all subjects proliferated, and unpredictably, so in Dewey's scheme, for instance, the classification number did not represent a fixed shelf but a subject's position within a sequence. As library users have found to their cost, the shelf that held the books marked 636.7 last week might hold books quite differently numbered today, as the stock grows and books move along, and yet the position of a subject's bookstock can rapidly be found once the all-important subject number is identified from the index.

The 'new' classification schemes offered the possibility of flexible display in a one-dimensional sequence (i.e. along shelves), and the differences between the Library of Congress Classification, Cutter's Expansive Classification, Melvil Dewey's Decimal Classification, Brown's Subject Classification and Bliss's Bibliographic Classification (to name the prominent enumerative schemes that arose) were mainly of notation (the symbols used to express and mechanize the position of each subject within the sequence) and of general order. Like subjects were grouped together; thus Dewey's scheme grouped together material on the electron and located it with material on other sub-atomic particles, which was grouped together with material on molecular and atomic physics in general, which was grouped together with other aspects of physics; physics itself was in the science section of the scheme, together with other sciences. Yet in reading this, the alert reader will immediately demand a correction; the whole of atomic and sub-atomic physics developed well after the year 1876, when the first edition of Dewey's scheme appeared. In fact Dewey had left unassigned the section 539, in the physics schedules, allowing, very fortunately, for future developments, and it was only later that the new subjects received their allotted positions in subsequent editions of the scheme.

It is the characteristic of a good classification scheme that it will allow for later addition, showing the prescience of the compiler and the hospitality of the notation. If 500 was Sciences, 530 Physics, and 539 Atomic Physics, revisers at DDC headquarters could subdivide decimally to produce 539.7311, the number for the Electron; and should the electron itself reveal hidden depths in future, presumably they can continue to subdivide by adding numbers to the right hand end. But knowledge develops unevenly; Dewey's luck was not so conspicuous when it came to, say, radio engineering, where relatively simple new subjects end up with a classification symbol of twelve digits or more. Moreover, the whole shape of knowledge changes; the intermingling of psychology, philosophy and occultism in early editions of Dewey became a classifier's nightmare, until a recent edition caused havoc in innumerable libraries by radically uprooting whole sections and re-assigning them. The same muddle is evident in Mathematics, 510, whose arrangement is practically meaningless to modern mathematicians, and in the artificial separation of closely related topics in physics, mathematics, chemistry and biology, which these days are regarded as interdisciplinary whole subject areas of their own, relating tangentially rather than unidimensionally to the general scheme. Nor is it only in science where problems arise; Dewey's assumptions in politics, philosophy, economics, and religion, are typically western/racist/capitalist/Christian; and his division of the arts into 'Fine' and 'Applied' has caused many a pottery teacher to gnash his teeth.

The problem is no easier with other schemes of the same kind; accusations of chauvinism, racism, and inability to transcend the limited nineteenth-century world view can be successfully applied to them all. A classification of knowledge is as good as its times, and begins to crumble to pieces when times dramatically change. Economics, good marketing methods, an easy notation and the difficulty of building an acceptable alternative are, one suspects, the only factors that have kept Dewey Decimal alive. It is an appalling muddle: but so are they all. The general order of a library classification scheme was often claimed (notably by Henry Evelyn Bliss) to be best based upon 'an educational and scientific consensus of opinion', but even if such a consensus is at any one time conceivable, in present circumstances it is increasingly unlikely to persist in any recognizable sense. As we become open to the thought and influences of other societies, and as our own society develops unexpected and unpredictable sub-groups and alternative cultures, the question, 'Whose consensus?' may well be very pointed.

A way forward seemed to have emerged some decades ago with the school of 'facet analysis' developed from the work of Dr S. R. Ranganathan, whose revolutionary Colon Classification is widely in use throughout India. Whereas previous schemes, such as that of Dewey, presented an enumerated list of subjects in hierarchical layout with appended notation (e.g. decimal numbers) to express the system in practice, the Colon Classification distinguishes a range of 'facets' in each major subject area, which the classifier combines (like a set of parts) to form an extended symbol which both expresses the specific subject and its relationships and also allows for its easy insertion in and retrieval from a store sequence (e.g. a shelf). The symbol for the 5th edition of Ranganathan's own scheme (1957) for instance, is $2:51N3 \ qN57.1$, and each digit represents one part of the concept which the scheme itself exemplifies. It is claimed that new subjects can frequently be accommodated without addition to the scheme, by a judicious deployment of existing facets. Ranganathan's work was enormously influential. Specialist libraries employed facet analysis with great success in the creation of classification schemes for the depth classification of specialist subjects, e.g. Education. A Classification Research Group of the Library Association formed itself with great hopes of constructing the ultimate universal scheme which could be adopted by all libraries. The day of Dewey Decimal, it was believed, was nearly over.

Like some other examples of futurology, this prediction did not come true. The knowledge explosion means what it implies; the task of producing a scheme that would really satisfy all needs, and avoid the criticisms which had very rightly been levied at all the previous schemes, was enormous. Dr Ranganathan was one of the most brilliant and imaginative figures the profession has seen; his Colon Classification went through many revisions and new editions, and is widely in use in his own country, yet elsewhere it is admired but, for good reasons, not employed. It is doubtful whether ever again the one-man universal classification schemes will make any sense; it is too big a task. A new classification would need to have unusual authority, to gain immediate and widespread acceptance, and to be assured of a steady and unshakeable future. There are a lot of libraries, and the cost of reclassification of their entire stock would be enormous. No sensible librarian would agree to such a change (or be able to get the necessary financial backing from his authority) without very persuasive evidence indeed.

One of the trickiest problems with a faceted classification scheme has been notation, that is to say, the symbols (e.g. decimal numbers) which represent the subject and mechanize its place in a shelf or catalogue array. It is fairly easy for a library user to learn that a subject whose symbol is 623.4 will be found 'in the 600s', and somewhere in between 623 and 624; and untrained assistants can after a little guidance cope with the shelving and filing problems. But the complexity of Ranganathan's own scheme required a variety of symbols: not only capital letters and decimal numbers (without the decimal point), but also inverted commas, commas, colons, semicolons, lower-case letters and even Greek letters as the subject matter expanded wider than the available symbols. C. D. Needham (1971) gives examples of the filing difficulties that result; he points out that a decision must be made at every stage – does L 7 file before or after L:7? Does L'N file before or after L.2? A user may after a while remember that 'Surgery' is represented by L:4:7 and he may remember that 'The stomach' is represented by the symbol L24. One can represent the subject 'Surgery of the stomach' by combining these symbols, and Ranganathan's scheme provides, a 'preferred order' by which such combinations are to be made (its explanation would take up many pages and the reader is therefore referred to basic textbooks on library classification, including Needham's already cited, if he is intrigued to know); the result is L24:4:7. One can go on to specify Surgery of the stomach in the nineteenth century (L24:4:7'M) and Surgery of the stomach in nineteenth-century Britain (L24:4:7.2'M) but the problems for the shelver on a busy afternoon in the medical library are obvious.

The notation of a classification scheme is important, and in the context of the knowledge explosion one requirement is that this notation should be 'hospitable', that is, that it should allow for addition at any point in the scheme in the light of new knowledge and new concepts. But any notation (representing order as well as description) will run into problems here. One can, for instance, employ letters of the alphabet, but if the list of major subjects goes past 26 one is in trouble. Dewey, as is well known, divided knowledge into tens so that he could employ decimal notation; when a particular subject turned out to have more than nine facets he had to group them together, often at the expense of logic, and if a new facet arrived inconveniently there was no way of including it at an appropriate place in the hierarchy. Similarly, a special-subject faceted classification, the London Education Classification, devised for the Institute of Education Library, University of London, by its librarian, Douglas Foskett, experimented with a notation that used pronounceable symbols – Bab Bin Bux Fab Lib Liv Rix Rog Ruf Rur Tab and so on. (Experience had shown, as the introduction pointed out, that whenever a letter notation was used, people tended to pronounce it if at all possible.) Alas for the purity of the LEC, however; by the time of the second edition (1974) the number of facets had increased so considerably that such unpronounceable symbols as Lmn, Jbb, Dvv, had crept in. Meanwhile, Ranganathan had yet again made a creative, if difficult, contribution, with his invention of the so-called 'octave device'. This in essence meant that one digit in a sequence (usually 9 or Z) was used solely for the purpose of continuing that sequence further if new editions needed to be made. As an example, the section 530 could have been developed as follows for a sequence: 530, 531, 532 ... 537, 538, 5391, 5392, 5393 ... etc. By not assigning 9, but using it as 'an octave device', one could establish as a convention a way of producing a hierarchy of numbers allowing for almost infinite addition in array. The difficulty came when one imagined these numbers written on the spine of a book, or on the can of a filmstrip or an audio-cassette, and given to an un-trained person to shelve or file in a sequence.

Of course, whereas human beings would be expected to find difficulties with such notation, computers would not; it would be a simple matter to programme the computer to recognize such symbols in any sense that was necessary. Just as most large organizations and systems have found important uses for the computer in accounting and housekeeping operations, so also large libraries, whether public, academic or special, have tended to put their acquisitions and other operations on to computer, and considerable experiment has been going on with the applications of computerization to information retrieval. It is perfectly simple, relatively speaking, to store on magnetic tape within a computer a full catalogue entry, including a classification symbol or symbols, and to label each segment of the information in such a way that the computer can be programmed to find it on demand. Thus a computer catalogue could print out on demand all the items of which Dr Rhodes Boyson was the author; or those which had his name in the title; or all the items having to do with a specific topic, even something so very specific as 'The effect of solvents on the killing of bacteria by phenol'; or all the items in tape-slide format; or all the items published in Bletchley in 1975. For that matter, a computer catalogue could relate different demands together, so that one could find out what was in the collection in tape-slide format on the emigration of Cornish tin-miners to southern Wisconsin in the nineteenth century, suitable for advanced students in the sixth form (ages 17–18). One could then find out what else was available on emigration, or on Cornish tin-miners, or on southern Wisconsin, or the nineteenth century, or any permutation of two or more in relation to other topics, such as the design of houses or the techniques of mining, or at another level of student understanding, or another format entirely.

The computer could reveal this information, *if* it had been previously fed into the data store. Once the material is there, it can be retrieved again at an astonishing speed, so long as the method of input is sufficiently well devised. For instance, a computer can search the words of titles and print out all items containing the relevant key terms, but if an astronomer asks for anything to do with black holes, he may find himself presented with material on the Black Hole of Calcutta, or titles in which the two words appear separately and accidentally, unless the search procedure is more tightly controlled. Moreover, in the humanities and much professional and social science literature, titles are by no means the precise description of the subject matter that one usually expects in *Nature*; in a notorious example, an article on information retrieval appeared in the *Library Association Record* entitled 'How golden is your retriever?' – an article which would greatly puzzle dog fanciers who had turned to the computer for search along these simple lines. The computer is very fast; it can be set to scan the text of journal articles and print out the titles of all which use significant key words more than a stated number of times, and it can be set to tell us how many times Shakespeare used a particular expression, and in each case it can give the results quite astonishingly quickly. On the other hand, by itself it is entirely stupid, able to take no decisions other than those included in its programme and entirely dependent on the skill and foresight of programmers and questioners.

The abilities of the computer will remind some readers of the experiments in many school resource centres using, instead of the Dewey Classification and a simple card catalogue, one or other variety of post co-ordinate indexing, frequently with optical coincidence punched cards. As I have explained in *Working Paper 43*, and developed in *Organizing Resources*, this indexing system depends upon the initial production of 'features lists', or lists of subject headings, the subject facets which it is desired to be able to retrieve from the system. The subject content of an item is then analysed into these facets, and the item is indexed under each one, usually by punching a hole in a topic card representing each facet. Two examples might be a book on the education of women in India in the first half of the twentieth century, and a film on the extension of the suffrage in Britain from 1830 to 1930. The first might be indexed: EDUCATION – WOMEN – INDIA – 1900/1950; the second perhaps SUFFRAGE – BRITAIN – 1830/1930 (perhaps also POLITICS). It will be noticed that these two items have common elements; their time periods overlap, so that anyone doing a comprehensive study on the first half of the twentieth century would want both items if he was really very thorough, and the interest of Women's Liberation students would be caught by the first item and by part of the second item. But this women's suffrage element is only a part of the second item's subject field and not explicit in the title; it would require competent and perceptive indexing to bring it out, if it was desired that this should be attempted in the index.

Control of the terms chosen for the headings list (what is technically called the 'thesaurus') is of crucial importance if the co-ordinate index is to attempt to provide a service over the whole field of knowledge, and if it is to provide the depth of service that is technically feasible. Whether computerized or on punched-cards or any other system, an index is only as good as its initial design and its indexers. In particular, unless very rigidly controlled it is subject to what is technically called 'a false drop', that is to say, the combination of facet headings that produce false or unsought information. For instance, a book on the influence of religious tradition on the education of women in Britain and India might include substantial chapters or whole sections on Hinduism, Buddhism and Christianity; if the indexer therefore indexed HINDUISM, BUD-DHISM, CHRISTIANITY, RELIGION, EDUCATION, WOMEN, INDIA, BRITAIN, the later combination of individual facets such as HINDUISM and BRITAIN might suggest, falsely, that the book was about Hinduism in Britain when in fact it was nothing of the kind.

Thus co-ordinate indexing was not recommended for use in schools without very skilled staff being present to operate and co-ordinate its use. In the wider field of information processing in general, the development of computers and other sophisticated instruments has opened up a great many possibilities for really elaborate information retrieval techniques, but there remain very substantial difficulties of thesaurus control which librarians and information scientists in, particularly, the United Kingdom are at present exhaustively examining. With the phenomenal expansion of knowledge, and the development of new concepts and the re-appraisal of old ones, computerized retrieval facilities are becoming both increasingly necessary and increasingly difficult to organize and control.

For the simpler tasks of cataloguing, none the less, the computer has a major contribution to make and is already making it. National and international bibliographic data can be fed into computers in machine-readable form. Already, Anglo-American co-operation between the Library of Congress and the British National Bibliography section of the British Library, using the MARC II format, enables a basic data storage of catalogue entries to be made, from which classified, author, title and other lists can as required be produced. The Library of Congress Catalog and printed card service, and the weekly, monthly, quarterly, annual and subsequent cumulations of *British National Bibliography*, plus its own printed card service, derive from this data base, and it is hoped to begin experiments towards the provision of a similar computer store of catalogue data on audio-visual materials in due course from which all manner of useful selected print-outs can be derived. Catalogue data on international publication would be available to all.

Futurologists, of course, see enormous possibilities ahead for the computer. *Automated Education Letter* in December 1972 reported a talk by R. P. Henderson to the Royal Canadian Institute in Toronto:

In the not too distant future we will see the world's knowledge recorded electronically rather than on the printed page. We will see enormous archival computerised knowledge banks replacing books and libraries. (Henderson 1972: 6.)

Well, perhaps. The discipline of information science, which attempts to study all the ways in which human beings communicate information with each other and the many facilities which make it easier to perform, is in its earliest formative years, and it will be a long time before we can be sure either that the science of information is a true discipline or that it can deliver its present optimistic promises. Like educational technologists, they have a number of prophets ready to announce the millenium a little before its arrival. There is still a big task ahead and we cannot be sure how well it can be accomplished. Certainly schools will not be handling such retrieval techniques in the present economic circumstances for a long time yet; though a service to teachers and educational researchers is offered in the United States (and is available here in some libraries) by the ERIC system, which provides micro-copies of research papers together with a tolerably thorough indexing system which can be computerized for quick search. British librarians have strongly criticized the thesaurus of the ERIC scheme, with good reason, but this is an indication of what is immediately possible, at a price. Meanwhile we should await further developments with a suitably optimistic scepticism.

The organization of knowledge by classification and indexing is a valuable activity in which much more work must still be done. Yet as we explained, most librarians would reject it as a definition of what librarians actually do. Librarians working in the various educational institutions see their work and their libraries in an active light, and tend to dismiss classification and indexing as necessary but tedious backroom tasks of a housekeeping kind. Whatever one thinks about this, it is certainly important that teachers and media producers should understand the various movements which have swept the library profession over recent decades and which see the librarian as educator rather than curator. We turn to this aspect in the next section.

From storehouse to learning centre

In almost every decade of this century, and before, librarians have been congratulating one another at having shaken off the custodial image and become active disseminators and publicists. Many of the earliest public libraries were busily involved in adult education, providing lectures and discussion meetings, arranging exhibitions and displays, and going out with some of their stock to societies and schools and clubs in the most admirably proselytizing manner;

many actually had art galleries and museums under their care as well, providing an early example of multi-media provision. Children's librarians have notoriously never sat still in their back rooms (or anywhere) but provide regular story-hours, give introductory talks to classes brought in from local schools, and get to know their young clientele very thoroughly indeed. In our rural areas, libraries have taken their stock out to the people in bookmobiles and (to the astonishment of visiting Americans) made available from these peripatetic points full access to the national interlending system of which Britain is justifiably rather proud. Across the Atlantic, American city librarians have developed remarkable programmes of 'outreach' to the disadvantaged in slum and ghetto, and many have recently developed active information services somewhat on the lines of our Citizens Advice Bureaux but with a more active involvement and identification with the needs and problems of those who approach them.

So librarians are surprised, and a little hurt, when it is still suggested (as I have heard educational technologists and others suggest at conferences) that they are shy, retiring administrators, concerned more with order than with use. Of course librarians are far from being a heterogeneous group, and there need be no doubt that all types of personality and approach are represented within the profession. What is here stressed is that there is, and for many decades has consistently been, an active and relatively vociferous body of thought among librarians concerned with the active exploitation of the collection and the development of busy programmes of dissemination.

This must not, of course, get out of hand. A librarian must be able to merge unnoticeably into the background, develop when necessary Keats' 'negative personality', or as Douglas Foskett puts it:

... during reference service the librarian ought virtually to vanish as an individual person, except insofar as his personality sheds light on the working of the library. He must be the reader's alter ego, immersed in his politics, his religion, his morals. (Foskett, D. J. 1962: 10.)

(In a different way, the teacher must also know when to hold himself back and allow the student's personality to flower.) But equally, a librarian must be able to show firm, out-going interest and competence, encouraging the trust of his clientele. The good librarian is sensitive to individual difference, omnivorously interested in all areas of knowledge and in all problems of access to it, politely at ease with people, able to assert authority when it is required, and to employ systematic thinking in relation to all aspects of his work. It is no job for a shy mouse, and some of us have been sad to come across schools which have preferred to appoint inexperienced and nervous introverts rather than business-like mature librarians with a clear idea of their role. (One suspects that some head teachers

regard such librarians as potential trouble-makers, but is it wise to
buy a quiet life at the expense of quality of service?)

When librarians and others consider the educational functions of
libraries there is a variety of aspects and contributions which it will
be useful here to distinguish.

1. The library can serve an educational role by the simple provision
of books and learning resources, providing both immediate access to
knowledge and practice in the use of knowledge sources, for instance
practice in reading.

2. The library can serve as a laboratory for practice in the skills of
using an organized collection, through the use of bibliographies and
catalogues, the understanding of the classification scheme, and the
proper consultation of works of reference such as encyclopaedias
and atlases.

3. The library staff can serve an educational role in their explana-
tions of the processes of library research, both by displayed expositions and by individual or group instruction.

4. They can also educate in the way they handle reference requests
(whether they supply the answer, for instance, or the way of *finding*
the answer); and they can be valuable stimulators of book use and
enquiry by giving readings, quality advisory services and reading
lists, and knowledgeable enthusiasm.

5. Finally, librarians can collaborate with teachers in the planning
of more formal periods of organized research as part of a wider
programme of study; it is here that the librarian can often explain
to the teacher the problems which readers have been observed to
encounter in such activities, so that the resolution of these can be
built into the overall plan.

Libraries and librarians have for a long time sought to play a role
in the educational development of young children in the formative
and primary years, particularly in the simple stimulation of the
reading habit. As the Bullock Report put it:

> Potentially, the most important source of help is the Children's Libra-
> rian. One from whom we heard lends collections of books to the
> borough's hundred or so pre-school organizations, which include day
> nurseries, playgroups and private nurseries. She and her colleagues
> visit as many of them as possible at fortnightly intervals to tell the
> children stories from picture books, and to get to know the supervisors
> and staff and the children's mothers. A travelling exhibition has been
> assembled, containing books for children up to the age of seven, and
> this visits health centres, teachers' centres, colleges of education and
> community associations. Another proposal is to take a double-decker
> bus to areas of greatest need, determined by consultation with local
> community visitors, health visitors and social workers. The lower deck
> will be equipped with books for young people and their mothers, and
> the upper deck fitted out for story-telling and audio-visual programmes
> ... We recommend that all Authorities should make possible and

encourage enterprises of this kind. (Great Britain, D.E.S. 1975: 98, para. 7.3.)

Peggy Heeks described the function of a children's librarian in this way:

> Children's reading tastes are unformed, their use of book reviews slight, and their requests are likely to be limited ... The librarian must gather together, lovingly and with care, the best imaginative literature and factual material that is available and then proceed to get it used. This is creative work and exciting work, but it is not a sentimental journey ... The essence of personal guidance is tact and sensitivity; it implies a knowledge of people and a knowledge of books, and a skilful marrying of the two. The dogmatic approach spells death to the delicate business of transferring enthusiasm from the librarian to the reader; the slantwise, almost casual introduction is more likely to meet with success. (1967: 11.)

There are arguments about what is 'the best', and how far one goes in meeting present taste before developing it; there are arguments about paternalism and mandarin or upper-class standards; but no children's librarian would accept a purely passive supply function; all would agree that one hopes to provide opportunities for wider exploration and the growth of informed taste, whatever it turns out to be. The wealth of literature available for young people today is enormous, the poverty of provision in the average commercial bookshop quite appalling, and the children's librarian's assumption of a broadening and educational role is not only understandable but very necessary.

How does the children's librarian in a public library service differ from the good primary teacher or the teacher–librarian in a school? Both are hoping to develop the reading habit, to encourage the child to explore the many pleasures of reading (and of the growing number of items in audio-visual format), and to gain practice in this essential skill as well as in discrimination. The librarian is not, however, tied to a developmental programme or syllabus, and need not consider any other aspects of educational growth, such as the teacher in school must take into account. In a sense the children's librarian is freer, but also is forced to work in a more oblique and informal way; the teacher may work directly, can initiate activities and be more directive, for instance in requiring the child to respond with his own written or pictorial work or linking the reading to another activity in the classroom. Yet both teachers and children's librarians have much in common, and it is always desirable that there should be continual personal dialogue between them. Each should respect the other's strengths: that the teacher can intervene in a positive way to prevent the acquisition of bad learning and reading habits and to ensure that broad aims and objectives are, as far as it is possible to ensure, reached; and that the librarian, working in a permissive non-authority setting, can by indirection and suggestion, using the child's natural behaviour and personally chosen interests, foster the development of activities and skills from which learning and motivation arise.

This difference in approach and method was noted at a very different level at a seminar on the availability, management and application of learning resources in teacher education (CET 1975: 17):

> It had been suggested during the conference that a librarian tends to be 'liberal': to offer his whole stock and invite the student to select; whereas the educational technologist tends to be directive: he guides tutors and students to particular ends.

As a broad generalization there is much truth in this, and both groups can usefully remember from their own education how sometimes learning is 'taught' and at other times 'caught'. Patricia Knapp, in the United States, once commented that one could get a perfectly good liberal education from a paperback bookshop: the sense in which this is true must not however blind us to the fact that self-learning of this kind has its weaknesses, is unreliable, and depends very much on the way in which the student undertakes his task. Sartre's character the Auto-Didact was working his way through an alphabetical subject catalogue, with the result that he knew nothing of subjects beginning with the later letters; to learn mathematics by the route Algebra, Arithmetic, Calculus, Geometry . . . and on to Trigonometry would be bizarre by any conventional standard. Equally, however, if the only learning experience one encountered was in closely programmed format there would be no scope for those intuitive leaps and imaginative forays most of us remember, or for those times in which one pursues a sudden enthusiasm almost to saturation.

The achievement of a good 'liberal education' was much in the minds of those concerned with technical college education in Britain in the 1950s. The government's advice in the famous circular 323, *Liberal education in technical colleges* urged teachers and others to foster habits of reflection, independent study and free enquiry into the broader implications of their technical occupations (Great Britain Ministry of Education 1957). Hertfordshire in consequence of this feeling initiated an influential and controversial scheme, whereby as part of the work of increasing the research and learning competence of the student, as well as stimulating his general reading, courses and tutorial supervision were provided in the use of libraries and library materials. These courses were *taught* by the college librarian, who for the first time in Britain was included on the teaching staff of the college on a teaching scale, and styled 'Tutor–Librarian'.

His teaching programme was far more ambitious than the Cook's tour round the library shelves plus a hand-out, which was probably the best typical kind of library induction up to then provided in further and higher education. Moreover, in acting as a teacher the librarian was offering structured and directed courses with declared objectives, and frequently with examined results. Gordon H. Wright, very much the driving force of the movement so far as librarians were concerned, declared in a letter to the *Library Association Record* in September 1961:

> ... many professional librarians believe that running a College Library is no different from administering a public library and therefore the former can be staffed by public library assistants. This policy has undoubtedly lowered the standards of library provision ... Providing a library for a College which has never had one before is a simple professional task but ensuring that the library becomes an integral part of the College educational structure is another matter ... This is the significance of the term 'Tutor' as distinct from administrator – a librarian who is *actively* engaged in seeking to encourage others to use books for pleasure and profit. (Wright 1961: 314.)

As an example of what such courses required, we can consider an example from Hatfield College of Technology (Carey 1964), serving at the time some 200 full-time and 1,800 block and day-release students for external degrees, diplomas, and other qualifications. The educational background of the students was generally quite high. Carey summarized their needs under six headings:

> (i) ... an appreciation of the need for information and of the practical value of records of other people's work and ideas.
> (ii) Awareness of the availability of information and of the complex nature of communication ...
> (iii) Help ... to break down the complexity of documentation so that broad categories and patterns can be observed.
> (iv) ... basic ability to use bibliographical aids such as abstracts, indexes and review publications.
> (v) A systematic approach towards literature searching ...
> (vi) The opportunity ... to read a wide range of documents and to communicate information in writing and orally. (Carey 1964: 14.)

The resulting courses were spread over eighteen three-quarter-hour or twelve one-hour periods; they began with an introductory review of the college library, its purpose, stock, arrangement and services, including standard reference books, and then proceeded through the detailed study of a specialist literature, in a field closely integrated with the students' own subject courses. At the completion of the course the student presented information in the form of a technical report or literature survey. There were sometimes optional questions in an exam paper. Much experimentation went on at Hatfield and other colleges into courses of this kind, and the above example is only one out of very many which might have been cited.

The tutor-librarian model, and title, was for some years highly contentious in the library profession as well as among many teachers.

For librarians the title smacked of the days when running a library was undertaken by a lecturer 'in his spare time' (compare the teacher–librarian in most British secondary schools) and they resented the possible implications that running a library was not a full-time job. Many tutor–librarians were also required, as a condition of appointment to teacher-scales, to teach a minimum number of hours in the Liberal Studies programme, and this often included the teaching of subjects not essentially part of the librarian's speciality. Although Hertfordshire distinguished between tutor–librarians (whose job was primarily educational) and 'college librarians', whose job was supposed to be entirely administrative, many felt that such distinctions were meaningless or misleading; it was all a matter of proportion, and nobody (it was argued) working in a college library could avoid at some stage taking part in the educational process. Teachers, on the other hand, objected; teaching work should be carried out by people with teaching qualifications (although here they were indeed on shaky ground as the majority of technical college lecturers at that time did not themselves possess qualifications in education). Many librarians, especially in Hertfordshire, remedied their lack by attending Garnett College for a one-year course preparing them as teachers in further education.

Much of the heat has by now gone out of these arguments, and it is fairly generally accepted, first that college librarians should be appointed on teaching scales and given academic status by nature of their work and secondly that the work of a college librarian implies the librarian's own active participation *as a librarian* in the college's educational programme. R. O. Linden summarized the legitimate teaching commitments of the Tutor–Librarian as follows:

1. Short induction courses on library use for all students.
2. Supervision of, and bibliographic guidance in, private study and project work.
3. Co-operation with teaching staff or subject departments in the use of the library as part of a specific teaching programme.
4. Tutorials or seminars for teaching staff on the library's resources.
5. Special courses for student Tutor–Librarians, Teacher–Librarians and other trainee librarians.
6. Extra-mural lectures, etc. to outside bodies on college libraries, etc. (Linden 1967: 354.)

By 1971, the Library Association's recommended standards of library provision in Colleges of Technology and other establishments of further education stated:

No college leaves the use of a laboratory, workshop or studio to the choice of individual students but incorporates such activity within the curriculum. Similarly, education in library use, often involving planned programmes should be given by the professional library staff. (Library Association 1971: 7.)

Meanwhile in Colleges of Education, the gradual replacement of lecturers i/c library by professional librarians, on academic salary scales and conditions of service, showed a parallel development. Librarians in colleges of education, as befitted people closely in touch with the professional education of teachers, made considerable advances in the integration of the teaching and administrative roles of their collections and their staffs, and increasingly regarded a wide range of teaching commitments as being suitable to them. Librarians provided library induction courses, further courses in the bibliography of education and other subject fields, in school librarianship, children's literature and even, on occasions, participated in the supervision of students on teaching practice. The Library Association standards for college of education libraries (1967) specified (p. 10):

> The Librarian should be paid on the Pelham scale or its exact equivalent ... irrespective of the number of hours of formal teaching he is called upon to do. His work will include much personal advisory work with students, which is similar to a lecturer's tutorial responsibilities.

A substantial chapter on 'The tutorial function of the college library' is included in an authoritative collection on all aspects of college education library work, published by the Library Association (Platt 1972).

Such aspirations, and such a view of the inter-relationship of librarians and educators, are not confined to this side of the Atlantic. In April 1960, Wayne State University entered into a contract with the US Office of Education to conduct at Monteith College a research project concerned with exploring methods of developing a more vital relationship between the library and college teaching.

> The ultimate purposes of the Montieth Library Program is to stimulate and guide students in developing sophisticated understanding of the library and increasing competence in its use. To achieve this end, it proposes to provide students with experiences which are functionally related to their course work. Planning such experiences will involve library instructional coordination on an unprecedented scale. The specific objectives of the first phase of the Program, the pilot project, therefore, are (1) an appraisal of a structure established for the purpose of attaining this coordination, (2) an exploration of new methods of relating the library to the instructional program, and (3) a preliminary assessment of the effectiveness of these methods. (Knapp 1966: 11.)

The initial proposal cited evidence in research literature to support its contention:

> Traditional college instruction fails to exploit fully the library's resources available for it and ... the average college student's experiences with the library constitute a limited and fairly insignificant part of his education. (*op. cit.*: 11.)

Such conclusions had been growing in force in American higher education for many years, and especially since the investigation carried out by Harvie Branscomb, librarian of Duke University, in the later 1930s at the request of the Association of American Colleges. Branscomb studied the typical college library 'from the standpoint of its educational effectiveness rather than its administrative efficiency.' (Branscomb 1940: ix) His conclusions were published in *Teaching with books* (1940) and were widely influential among librarians and their academic allies. His conclusion that: 'The necessity for a reconsideration of the library arises . . . from the adoption by many institutions of methods of teaching which emphasize student responsibility and self-direction,' (*op. cit.*: 8) led directly to the kind of experimentation which took place at Monteith, and which is vividly recorded in Dr Knapp's seminal account. The Monteith experiment (summarized very baldly) concluded that its experience had been broadly encouraging, that there appeared to be some evidence of correlation of a student's personal library effectiveness and other measures of educational development, and that (of course) more research was necessary. Since that time, no other organization has, to our knowledge, undertaken so comprehensive an enquiry. This is a pity because, as Hazel Mews has indicated, there is some reason to be cautiously disappointed about the effectiveness of library instruction programmes at present:

> . . . reader instruction as at present interpreted remains largely instructional rather than educational, and emphasizes the value of the library as a storehouse of knowledge rather than a storehouse of wisdom and understanding. (Mews 1972: 84.)

The typical tutor–librarian premise, that the library matters and that an understanding use of it is crucial to a fully rounded and successful education, received its most dramatic promotion in the United States in the 1960s with the growth of the Library–College movement. This group, characterized by enthusiastic missionary zeal, comprises librarians, educators and administrators, partly from the two-year community colleges, liberal arts colleges and similar burgeoning establishments; they are in rebellion against the typical American college's stress on the importance of class attendance and the lecture–textbook–assignment–grade process, as well as much else that smacks of authoritarianism and rigidity. Library–Collegians reverse the usual conceptual model, as their name implies. For them the library essentially *is* the college and *contains* it; it is not a question of libraries being placed in departments, but of departments being regarded as essential facets of, and often included within, the library. In a Library–College (if one existed) the library contains rooms which may be used by teachers for small or large group sessions, and there are laboratories, gymnasia, music rooms and so forth leading off, but essentially the library is the dominant body. This view of teaching method and learning strategy places an unusually heavy concentration on the use of instructional materials; as Louis Shores, the movement's father-figure, wrote thirty years earlier, his model of a college:

> ... reverses the conventional college's practice of compulsory, regular class attendance supplemented by voluntary and irregular library reading. The library arts college student is definitely scheduled for supervised reading periods and permitted to ask for a class meeting whenever he feels his readings have failed to answer questions. (Shores *et al.* 1966: 8.)

Expanded later into a more humane and flexible pattern the system presupposed a heavy concentration on individual study using a wide variety of self-instructional materials: and developments in audio-visual education and in the theoretical base of educational technology make this somewhat more feasible than in the heavily print-based Shores model mark I. The object was not to abolish the teacher, but to re-examine what his proper role might now be. How much of what teachers currently feel they have to do could be accomplished as well or better by the use of a library of varied instructional materials supervised by well-trained staff with both bibliographical and subject-teaching competence? The movement spawned conferences and books (Shores *et al.* 1966; Shores 1970) and founded a journal at first entitled *Library–College Journal* and later re-named *Learning Today*. It is still very active in terms of publications and conferences, and claims many successes in the design of new institutions and the planning of new educational programmes.

At first sight, the objectives of the Library–College movement seem very similar to those of mainstream educational technologists, particularly those with a predominant interest in self-instructional packages. However, whereas educational technologists are, in theory, uncommitted design consultants, looking at each educational unit and set of objectives and then (and only then) prescribing suitable methodologies and media, Library–Collegians give the immediate appearance of preferring 'their' answers. They see themselves as belonging to a radical and anti-establishment tradition.

Louis Shores foresees the student shaping his own course and his own curriculum, with the library providing the main means of achievement of his objectives as he sees them; the teacher is to be available 'when needed'. This places the Library–College movement somewhere along the road that leads to the free-schoolers and de-schoolers, which will strike the reader as odd considering the sophistication and media-centredness of the facilities they envisage. A prominent figure at conferences has been Dr Stafford North, who as Dean of Instruction master-minded the elaborate Library Learning Center at Oklahoma Christian College, where every student had his own electronic study-carrel (with random dial-access to a large

collection of audio-tapes and other materials) in which a large part
of his education took place. Another has been Dr Samuel Postlethwait
of Purdue, already mentioned in Chapter 2, and who exemplifies a
carefully pre-planned and programmed teaching approach, devised
by a subject-specialist academic, and taking place (as it happens) in
a laboratory not a library. In neither instance could it reasonably be
said that student choice was as wide open as the Shores model would
require, and the main area of decision was at what time to go to one's
carrel and enter the process. While this is not insignificant (a weakness of the lecture or the teacher-directed lesson is that it must take
place at a pre-set time irrespective of student readiness) it is hardly
Liberty Hall.

Generally speaking, Library–Collegians are better at exhortation
and generalization than on detailed analysis of how to achieve their
objectives or even what all their objectives should be. As Wayne
Gossage has said: 'Patricia Knapp was one of the few people in the
inner circle of the library–college vanguard who was in any way
critical' (Gossage 1975: 8) and this has been a sad weakness in a
movement which, with its enthusiasm and provocative reversal of
traditional priorities, has aroused much interest and thought amongst
educators, librarians and administrators. The early death of Dr
Knapp was a serious blow to those who respected her careful and
meticulous studies and research, as well as her analyses of library
objectives within the educational system.

Mr Gossage's critical examination of some of the major concepts
of the Library–College movement usefully dwells on some of the
present flaws in the movement's thinking: the woolliness of their
approach to curriculum, their silence on student motivation, their
too-easy dismissal of the usefulness of the lecture. At the same time,
he makes useful points which can lead us to other conclusions:

> Certainly the good reference librarian is the most Socratic of teachers
> in academic groves. He teaches by asking questions to help the student
> clarify his question. The good reference librarian doesn't give the student
> the answers, except in matters of simple fact. Rather he guides the
> student to likely sources and tries to teach him how to find paths to
> other sources. The student is then left to discover answers for himself.
> (Gossage 1975: 17.)

This is surely the kernel of the argument, that there is an unrecognized potential in the library situation which is capable of
much greater development. Library materials, as they include a
wider range of formats and a greater proportion of locally produced
items planned for the known needs of known students, can make a
more varied contribution to student learning than hitherto; individual study has an increasingly important role in contemporary
education, and the new potential of library materials is therefore
timely. The contribution librarians could make to student develop-

ment has been underestimated, and includes not only the librarian's contribution to taught courses on library research methodology, leading to greater confidence and autonomy, but also the day-to-day interaction with students and librarians at reader's advisory and reference desks. I concluded in 1967:

> ... perhaps the main value of the Library–College movement is that it provides a speculative model for use in our thinking. It will help us to re-examine two questions which are central to any educational institution: (i) what contributions to the learning process can be made by libraries, independent study, the new media and the computer? and (ii) what are tutorial staff *for*? It is the present role and perhaps dominance of the tutor which is most usefully challenged. (Beswick 1967: 201.)

And the purpose of challenging that role is not to downgrade the tutorial staff and thus advance the hegemony of the empire-building librarian, but to place the perceptiveness, energies and special training of teachers to work in their areas of greatest concern and competence, with the appropriate encouragement and support of other concerned professionals wherever present.

Teachers in today's schools and colleges have to concern themselves with a bewildering multiplicity of factors; some of them were hinted at in preceding chapters and there are more that were ignored because they were not directly relevant to our theme. It makes sense to see what the crucial contribution of the teacher is, and to test other models of the learning process which may from time to time be proposed to see what help they can give. This section has paused long on the views held by some librarians on the nature of their role, and that of their collections, in the educational process because it was felt that such views were not as widely known among educators as perhaps they should be. The development of resource-based learning brings the question of a revision of professional roles sharply into focus. In the heady 1960s it was possible to suggest that:

> ... the old distinctions between teaching-staff and librarians will become hopelessly blurred ... both tutors and advisers will need to have a thorough understanding of subject fields and the various generic-book materials available within them, and their uses and applications. Moreover, regular consultation will be essential between those who are 'mainly' tutors and those who are 'mainly' librarians ... (Beswick 1967: 200.)

In the mid-1970s, in Great Britain, the polytechnics of Liverpool and Newcastle-upon-Tyne are offering a three-year degree course in librarianship which can be transformed into an honours degree by a fourth-year course in education, leading to dual qualification; Leeds Polytechnic plans to follow suit, and already offers three-year-trained teachers the chance to turn their qualification into a bachelor's degree by intensive part-time study of librarianship.

Loughborough University offers a four-year joint degree in Education and Library Studies, taught concurrently, and leading again
to full dual qualification. The Froebel Institute College of Education,
in London, offers a one-year course to experienced chartered librarians, leading to a teaching qualification. University College London
has for some years been offering a one-year postgraduate diploma
course in librarianship to experienced graduate teachers.[1] And
Garnett College, already mentioned, has offered a one-year course in
further education to qualified librarians. This recognition of the
'blurred roles' of teachers and librarians, and of the importance of
providing opportunities for those who wish to gain an understanding
of and professional accreditation in both professions, has long been
the case at school level in the USA, where school librarians are
generally required to have a proportion of undergraduate and
graduate credits in both disciplines (the regulations vary from state
to state), and the education system has long been flexible enough to
meet the need without the provision of special courses (though this
has its disadvantage in that some students may therefore miss the
opportunity to make direct cross-disciplinary comparisons under
academic supervision).

Thus in discussing the role of 'the teacher', 'the media producer'
and 'the librarian', we must not forget that individuals acting in
these roles may well have other qualifications and experience in
addition. In the changing world of the late twentieth century, not
even professional groups remain static and unitary. Succeeding
chapters of this book hope to examine professional roles and inter-
relationships further in the light of the specific requirements of
resource-based learning and its related educational trends. Among
other things, we shall have to examine how far the hopes and claims
of librarians match up to present realities. As Ronald Linden
admonished:

> ... in the present era of super-professionalism, whether of the blended
> variety or not ... we must not overlook the need for a measure of
> professional *restraint*. Books are books; education is education. A 'good'
> book (or any other form of record) is arguably superior to a poor teacher.
> Ultimately we cannot safely substitute the one for the other. (Linden
> 1967: 355.)

---

[1] This course is now taught at London University Institute of Education.

PART TWO

Three Professions and Resource-Based Learning

4 Curriculum Renewal

The movement to re-examine curriculum and methodology, which has been shown to be characteristic of teachers and educationists since the end of the Second World War, may take a variety of different forms, and become associated with a number of different fashions and bandwagons, but it is unlikely to come to a halt. The world will not stop still, and economic depression and even national economic collapse (so regularly forecast by the doom-mongers) will not alter the nature of the educational challenge, though it may drastically affect the means we have to employ to face up to our challenges. Some learning resources are cheaper than others, and British primary schools have improvised for a long time with the very simplest materials including the discarded packaging of the consumer society. Where ancillaries cannot be afforded, their skills can often be found less conveniently amongst teaching staffs themselves, or else acquired; and it was noted by many schools visited during the Resource Centre Project that a surprising potential sometimes existed in voluntary form in the community.

But of course it is one thing to argue for change, and to explain (as preceding pages have tried to do) the readiness and degree of involvement of para-professional colleagues and groups; it is quite another to analyse in helpful detail the types of learning systems and units that might be relevant, and their implications in terms of planning and organized provision. Succeeding chapters will therefore address themselves to at least a beginning attempt at this task. It is all too clear from many published accounts of ventures in educational innovation that they have frequently been less successful than was hoped simply because the necessary consequences in terms of processes and support had not (or could not have) been foreseen.

Organizing resources: six case studies was a research report into specific aspects of resource centre organization and so concentrated on matters such as indexing and the allocation of funds. That this was a part only of a very much broader problem was cheerfully conceded from the beginning; it happened to be the project's brief and that was that. It cannot be claimed that even as much testing as was possible of the information retrieval systems during the Resource Centre Project has been applied to the discussion in these subsequent pages. What is offered is not the results of detailed observation and validation, but an attempt to argue out from a comparison of, on the one hand, declared principles and objectives, and on the other hand, personal experience and published accounts, the fuller implications of resource-based learning in practice.

We shall be drawing our examples from the professional knowledge, not only of teachers, but of media specialists and librarians, because they have much to suggest to us, and because their contributions within schools and without are important to what can be attempted and achieved. This may lead both author and reader into difficulties unless one point is emphasized and remembered: the terms 'teacher', 'media specialist', 'educational technologist', and 'librarian', are not necessarily mutually exclusive. A media specialist, for instance, may well be a teacher who has through additional training and experience gained an extra competency; a person with full professional qualifications and experience as a librarian may also (as we saw) be a recognized teacher, or have a diploma in educational technology. When in subsequent pages therefore we speak of 'the teacher' or 'the librarian' or 'the media specialist' or any other professional, we mean a person acting with that background and in that capacity at any one moment. A graduate chartered librarian with a full teaching qualification and working in schools is a teacher when he is engaged with a class, and mostly a librarian when he is devising an alphabetical subject index, and so on. As *Working Paper 43* stressed, the work of the library resource centre requires different skills, but these skills may be present in different ways in different individuals; many people can learn and practice at least two.

We must begin with the initial decision-making within educational institutions themselves, and with the choice of what learning sequence or task will be presented to the students and for what reasons and with what expectations. This focuses attention squarely and inescapably upon a person acting in the capacity and with the necessary professional background of a qualified teacher.

Teachers articulate purpose

Such developments as we have outlined have caused a distinct uneasiness among some British teachers. They fear that responsibilities and attitudes once a prominent part of a teacher's life may no longer be regarded as essential; they fear an erosion of the teacher's role

and status, and see changes as signalling moves to squeeze him out
of concerns that were and are rightly his. In particular, they note
that resource-based learning has sometimes been presented as if it
'replaced' the teacher. In universities, educational technologists
have sometimes seemed to be suggesting that a mixture of cinema,
television and self-instructional systems could make possible economies in the teacher–student ratio. In schools the increasing number of para-professionals creeping in under the resources umbrella
have understandably aroused suspicions in teachers' union branches.
Sir Brynmor Jones said jocularly: 'The teacher who can be replaced
by a teaching machine or any audio-visual aid deserves to be!'
(1968: 281) and this might be thought also to be true of replacement by ancillaries. Teachers have long called for more opportunity
to get on with what they regard as quintessentially 'their' work;
they should normally welcome the opportunity to off-load tasks
which can just as effectively be performed by other people. But this
is only half the story. The resources movement is an instance of an
educational trend that calls, not for less from teachers, but for very
much more. It is not simply a matter of reassuring teachers that their
jobs and prerequisites are secure; they must be drawn into discussions and decision-making which many have been able and happy
to avoid. Resource-based learning places the pupil in the active
mode, but equally its demand on the teacher is for his full creative
involvement. In such circumstances he needs all the help that it
makes economic sense to provide.

This is predicated in the very reasons for embarking upon
resource-based learning in the first instance. If the individual pupil
is to be presented with opportunities for learning that will arouse
his active response, the circumstances and the materials have to be
judged with considerable care. What do we need to know if we are
to teach Humanities to Johnny? Answer: among other things, Johnny
himself, as no textbook can. Fortunately, although Johnny and Susan
and Harbajahn and Khadijah are individual personalities with a
myriad variety of individual differences, they are all recognizably
part of the genus homo sapiens, whatever the embattled teacher
may sometimes wonder. L. C. Taylor rightly reminds us:

> True, no set of children or of circumstances is entirely like any other,
> but then nor are they entirely different; nor do we need to postulate,
> as the only alternative to a whole set of materials being produced
> centrally, that every item should be made locally. (L. C. Taylor 1972:
> 239.)

Thus the desperate position which tended to be the teacher's in
the days of the Dalton Plan, with no help available, almost no bibliographic service for the location of likely materials, and the consequent necessity of having to produce a daily flood of work-sheets
and data sheets, is no longer the case in schools sensibly organized.

But the teacher cannot sit in splendid and comfortable isolation in staff room or on classroom dais while his pupils are busily engrossed in resource-based exercises; he is involved at every point in the process, from the preliminary planning and assembly of available materials, the creation of additional resources and linking items, the initial presentation and motivation sessions, the follow-up work as the pupils proceed, and the eventual summing up and validation at the end. Moreover, few types of resource-based learning are as clear-cut as perhaps they sound to the newcomer; there is always the possibility, indeed the likelihood, that at any one point the teacher may find it necessary to intervene, to establish a point, to correct a set of errors, to reinforce an insight, or to bring in an additional set of experiences, including the experience of argument and group debate while the interest is hot. As Holly puts it: 'One of the skillls required by the resources approach, in fact, lies in achieving a nice balance between independent working, group discussion and direct exposition by the teacher.' (Holly 1971: 9) Nobody but the teacher can make such decisions or deploy such skills

Thus the title of this section is 'Teachers articulate purpose'. What aims, objectives, hopes, wishes and intentions are gathered together under the broad heading of resource-based learning? Some of the points that follow are re-phrased from L. C. Taylor's summary (Taylor 1972, pp. 156–7), while others will be recognized as emerging from the arguments of Chapters 1 and 2.

1. *Resource-based learning hopes to replace the essential passivity of the student in class teaching with an active learning mode stimulating interest and involvement.* For this to be so, the activity must be varied, continuous and within the student's capability; it must be meaningful and not just 'busy work', and it must be progressive. Equally, the involvement is more likely to be won if the student's choices and decisions are genuine and not bogus, allowing him or her to feel personally responsible for at least part of it.

2. *RBL hopes to increase student motivation by presenting varied possibilities, of subject matter, method of working, and medium of communication, in contrast to the class lesson where all must learn one thing in one way.* Again the motivation is more likely to arise if the choices are real and begin from propositions or activities acceptable to the student. (An example may make this clearer: how does one dramatically improve the spoken English, reading and writing ability, and the IQ, of backward rural children? Knudson [1971] reports impressive results by getting them to prepare their own videotaped dramas – during which varied language activities were practised absorbedly.) The concentration is less on the covering of a specific range of subject matter than on the acquisition of essential skills and increased insight into 'modes of understanding', of which History, Sociology, Biology and other subject fields are examples.

3. *It hopes to allow, and induce, students to work at the pace best suited to them as individuals, rather than having to proceed at the standard class rate.* It is important to stress that this means some students working much faster, and probing much deeper, as well as others plodding at a much slower and more generalized rate. For either student, going at the wrong pace can well mean not learning as much as the average, or not learning at all, and this is true for the highly intelligent student as well as the one with learning difficulties. The boredom of the gifted has been well documented (see, for instance, Gallagher 1965 *passim*); so, of course, has the alienation of the slow learner.

4. *It hopes to allow for more flexible use of time and available spaces, both within subjects and between subjects.* When the major source of information is the teacher, it is essential that students gather at fixed times, 'to catch the teacher's words during their moments of fleeting life' as Taylor puts it. This places particular limitations on the time-tabling. Once these limitations are reduced, a wider variety of possibilities becomes open. This does not mean that the timetable disappears, although in the smaller primary schools operating the integrated day it does so to a very great extent, leaving only such activities as physical education and music needing some organized attention. In larger schools, and at the secondary stage, the organization of spaces and necessary reservation of particular areas remains a complex job, but can be approached from a different viewpoint. Teamwork, flexible use of spaces and rooms, and day-to-day adjustment of time allocations within block periods, become more possible.

5. *RBL aims to make fullest use of all available sources for information and stimulus, as 'learning resources' as well as simply 'teaching aids', and provides the opportunity to plan learning activities fully with this in mind.* This does not mean the abolition of expository teaching, whether in person or by sequenced AV materials; it means that the whole range of possible methods is thrown open, for the selection of the appropriate mode and appropriate input at any one point. Working around a resource-based pattern, especially when what Holly has called 'structured heurism' is expected to play an important role, the teacher-team can plan more readily for multiple methodologies than if the basic pattern is what might in contrast be termed 'developed exposition'.

6. *RBL hopes to be able to respond more imaginatively to changes in attitudes towards authority.* Adolescents are less acquiescent than (it is said) they used to be. It is foolish and unnatural to employ teaching methods that enforce and seem to advocate their quiet passivity. A well-devised range of resource-based opportunities seeks to channel their energies and restlessness into interesting and positive activity leading to an educationally useful result. It is no panacea for the teacher with discipline problems, but has its contribution to make to one of them.

7. *RBL seeks to contribute towards the development of self-confidence and ability in continuing education: the student who is able to pursue further studies in later life and with at least a latent readiness to do so.* This necessity of the pace of social and industrial change has its implications for teaching method: the student must increasingly develop and practise the skills of enquiry and discovery, in order to experience the confidence and pleasure of it and to be able to make fullest use of 'recurrent education' possibilities and requirements in later life. Closely structured work must lead, through 'structured heurism', to a succession of increasingly open-ended exercises, projects and other activities. This again throws the emphasis on to skills rather than coverage of facts, although a comprehension of the structures of subject disciplines (even the idea that subjects *have* structures) is an important element. The Bruner material in *Man: a Course of Study* is an interesting example in the middle part of the process, paving the way for freer, more student-originated activity.

8. *RBL seeks to give the student insight into the wide range of information sources, and practise in their creative deployment.* Thus community resources (such as people, buildings and associations), printed materials and libraries, audio-visual materials and equipment, all form part of a guided series of activities which 'round out' the student as a learning individual. The techniques of field work in local history and geography, the techniques of using books, reference guides and libraries, the ability to 'read' pictures and to assess critically film and television material, as well as to use creatively the various facilities and pieces of equipment that now exist, are valuable facets of the educated individual, and each type of activity offers a possible key to individual confidence and interest in learning. (This process, incidentally, may begin much earlier than many secondary teachers suppose. Stephanie Connell (in 1973) described the use of cameras and tape recorders by infants of 5 and 6 years old. Moreover, the oft-repeated statement by teachers that 'children don't understand Dewey Decimal Classification' has been consistently denied by librarians able to work with primary and middle-school pupils, let alone those at the secondary stage. And the age at which children begin studies leading to an understanding of the computer and its interrogation gets younger and younger.)

No doubt many readers will wish to expand or amend this list, and many more will want to argue with the points made and perhaps contradict some of them. However, enough will have emerged, I believe, to show that:

1. There is no question, in RBL, of the student sitting like a battery hen being forcibly fed with passively received 'facts'.
2. Equally, there can be no question, in RBL, of the teacher sitting back with his feet up, or worse still, joining the dole queue, while his students gain their education from impersonal sources.

But if the teacher remains the chief articulator of purpose and the planner and executor of method, this leaves him in a fairly exposed position even if he is surrounded by technical, production and librarianship support. The university teacher in Britain, thinking of producing a tape-slide sequence to explain a particular concept or process to his students, may well need only to consider, with a production assistant, the learning objectives, the structure of the process to be considered, the best ways to exemplify this in the photographs to be taken, the graphics to design, and the commentary to write, and then turn it all over to the producer to put into effect, with his guidelines and help. He can usually take for granted initial student motivation, educational level and intelligence; he is part of a system which already expects the student to spend a considerable proportion of his time in private study, and which usually provides at least minimal facilities for this to take place. He can add consultation of the tape-slide sequence to the student's required work-load without altering his own pattern of lectures and seminars in the least, if he so wishes.

For the teacher in secondary school (and even more for teachers in primary and middle schools) this situation simply does not obtain. In the first place, he can make no common assumptions about motivation, previous knowledge and IQ: his students will be very various, even in a selective school. Secondly, most schools at present do not expect the student to spend very much of his school time in individual study except at the whim or discretion of the teacher, and the only facilities for such study are the school library (when available) and, for the older students in the sixth form, sometimes a sixth-form study room. When the library is a multi-media centre, it may be possible for the tape-slide sequence to be studied there, but in the typical school there would be severe limitations if more than a small proportion of students were set to do such study; the library is usually too small for more than a tenth of the school population at best to use it at any one time. Moreover, few British schools at present include private study periods on the timetable, except for the sixth form, so the teacher knows that his students can only see the sequence in breaks and before and after school, unless he allows time in his own assigned periods with them. This he will normally be planning to do, but it involves him in a more considerable recasting of his planned activities than the university teacher, and brings him into contact with many more parts of the school life. He cannot plan in isolation.

For instance, in good planning the teacher would take into account, not only what the students would be doing and receiving in his subject and his periods, but with other teachers in other subjects at other times of the day. Students who come to him after an hour or more of reception learning may be more ready to take an active part than students who have already spent most of the morning burrowing in the library or measuring the school buildings. Skills that he wishes to rehearse with them may be part of the programme of another department also, and it makes good sense to have some consultation and perhaps co-ordination. (Teachers used to living in subject blinkers are sometimes startled to find that films chosen as 'starters' for topic work in their subject may already have been shown by another teacher in a different context. This need not be a problem, especially as each will have a different approach to the same material, but it makes obvious sense on many counts if the teachers are each prepared for this by consultation.)

The situation is much easier if the teacher is not working in isolation, but is part of a planned and co-ordinated programme. The advantages of team teaching, for instance, include the fact that the teacher is no longer dependent on his own wit and abilities, nor on his own lobbying power; the team can plan with more flexibility and more confidence, drawing on the insights and specialist skills of its members and with a broader knowledge of what the pupils are receiving and needing. It is evident from accounts such as those in John Freeman's book (1969) that much experimentation in team teaching was the forerunner of the resource centre boom of the early 1970s in the UK, just as its early proclamation in J. Lloyd Trump's *Images of the future* (1959) presupposed and helped to develop departmental and centralized resource collections in the USA. If, as is commonly asserted, 'the teacher is a resource', then so are other teachers, and it makes sense in the resource-based mode to make available by timetabling and co-operation those varied 'personal reference sources', the staff.

A disadvantage of team teaching, of course, has been that it required the teacher, normally an individualistic person accustomed to complete authority within the four walls of his classroom, to sink his authority and his subject speciality within a group. M. F. D. Young has pointed out that, while scientists of different persuasions can be said to form a professional group sharing assumptions and methodologies, the same is not by any means true of the humanities or the social sciences, with the result that there is not the same readiness to combine forces nor the same understanding of what such combination might produce (Young 1971: 35). It may be that in attempting to start team teaching without the experience of preliminary resource-based and other approaches and without a great deal of shared discussion and curriculum planning some schools have plunged their staffs into an experience for which they were by no means ready. As David Warwick says:

> ... teachers *decide* to take action. Team teaching is not imposed on them from above, nor is it likely to succeed if this happens. A headmaster may suggest the possibilities of team-work within his school ... But unless the staff concerned are enthusiastic about the project, fully

understand it, and are thus prepared to give the time and energy to make it work team teaching will be doomed to failure. (Warwick 1971: 18.)

It is probably better to think of team teaching as one eventual culmination of resource-based learning rather than the other way about, and some schools will usefully move towards it by stages rather than in one giant leap. On the other hand, a school with a high rate of staff turnover cannot usually afford to wait for a consensus and readiness that may never come; and a staff hand-picked in a new school, or for a new school situation such as amalgamation or unstreaming, is usually in a mood for bigger adventures.

What is well documented is that any attempt to prepare enquiry and discovery activities based on the pupil's own interests and starting points will most frequently and helpfully lead to thematic work, breaking out of the narrow specialisms of the traditional timetable. 'Famine in India' includes history, geography, agriculture and (importantly) religion, as well as contemporary politics and international relations. 'The medieval village', based on a useful example in the neighbourhood, spreads through history, geography and rural studies into art, literature, architecture, crafts, domestic science and music. 'Space travel' immediately involves, not only astronomy and engineering, but mathematics and physics to hold the wilder speculators in check, and religion and literature to stimulate the creative imagination. The hazards for the individual teacher in such exercises are considerable in that he is unlikely to be equally knowledgeable, or equally enthusiastic, in all these fields. Certainly he can turn to the school library resource centre for relevant books and audio-visual resources, but how is he to judge their quality and relevance, how can he know what other materials to order, and how can he confidently set about resource production? The existence of other colleagues is an obvious source of satisfaction and help: he needs their advice; he may be glad to have their personal help with the students, perhaps supervising or guiding a group, or talking to the entire class; and he needs their selections and productions. Where work can be planned in co-operation, in any modification or adaptation of team teaching, not only are there obvious gains for the students but the teacher himself receives much needed support.

'Resources' is about co-operation, and the maximization of use of existing facilities. We shall be examining in due course how organization can make fullest use of books, materials, equipment and ancillaries; we have reminded ourselves that it can also make fullest use of the many abilities in the staff room. As Warwick rather archly puts it:

... in the course of team teaching, interests and experiences are revealed which hitherto have been unsuspected ... Who would have thought that Mr Jones, the R.E. teacher, was an expert in modelling ships? This skill can be put to use in the 'Voyages of Discovery' programme next term. Miss Smith, who is in the Domestic Science Department, actually visited the Lascaux Caves two years ago and has a complete set of slides. The 'Origins of Religion' is coming up with Year One in two weeks time . . . Did you know the French master was fluent in Anglo-Saxon – part of his degree was in Old English – how about bringing him in on 'The Coming of Christianity' with 'The Lord's Prayer' as it was spoken by Alfred the Great? (Warwick *op. cit.*: 30.)

The traditional school's isolation of the teacher typically allows such useful knowledge to lie unused, or at least under-used, the people concerned being unaware of the circumstances in which their skills could be deployed, their colleagues unmindful of the possibilities or unable because of lack of timetable time or other simple machinery to bring them in.

The usefulness of some system of co-operation and team work is not only that the particular subject knowledge or skills of teachers can be pooled and shared, The teacher also needs support and advice in a more personal and practical sense. All of us who teach know well the moments of self-doubt, the anxieties and the hesitations, as work is planned and executed and evaluated, the apparent failures and inadequacies bulking large in the mind's eye. Much of it is a matter of planning and approach, and most of us from time to time talk with colleagues and seek advice from older and perhaps wiser hands. If teachers are, as we saw, to 'articulate purpose', they must know what purposes are possible and what is involved in putting them into effect. It is one thing to speak of involving the student, 'teaching concepts rather than facts', 'practising skills' and all the other catch phrases of educational discourse; it is quite another thing to put them into practice, to find out *how* to involve the student, to elucidate which concepts are of most importance and which facts are necessary to their understanding, and particularly to distinguish which are the key skills and how they are to be most usefully practised with these students in this situation. It is here that team work gives extra support and guidance, providing a discussion framework in which such matters can be aired. Team teaching, or something very like it, is an important element in the continuing professional development of the teacher.

We saw in an earlier chapter how innovatory schools such as Madeley Court and Codsall Comprehensive regarded 'in-service training' as an important factor in their planning, and how such training was provided, not only from courses outside the school, but also from within, by judicious deployment of available personnel. Good schools have always regarded advice and guidance as part of the responsibilities of senior teachers, and department heads are chosen not only for their administrative abilities but also for their qualities of leadership in developing sound methodologies amongst their staff. (This presupposes the British system, where seniority and higher salary depend upon promotion to such leadership positions; in some schools in the USA, on the contrary, the system of rewards is such that there is less incentive to a fine teacher to seek, or, accept what we would call 'promotion'.) It is common in British schools for a deputy head, or someone with similar experience and seniority, to have general oversight of curriculum matters, and often, as we have seen, such a person bears the title 'Head of Resources' with a particular brief to develop the organization of and for resource-based learning. Where the school maintains regular curriculum discussions, departmentally, in faculties, or throughout the entire staff, there will normally be plenty of opportunity to share experiences and raise questions. These occasions can be the beginnings of more determined initiatives in continuing teacher education.

There is nothing derogatory to the teacher intended in such a suggestion. Indeed, if 'éducation permanente' is a necessary feature for anyone, it is surely the educator himself, as methods develop, available materials burgeon, and technical equipment improves. For many of us, one of the fascinations of teaching is that it is not a static affair, a series of learned techniques regularly applied, but a continuing exploration of possibilities. The teacher claims his professional status, and demonstrates it by his readiness to adapt and change. We recognize this by our willingness to go on courses, keep up with professional reading, and sometimes update our qualifications; education authorities recognize this when they encourage us to do so by paying expenses, granting leave of absence, and sometimes secondment on full pay. What is often overlooked, none the less, is the in-service training potential within the school itself, both among teachers and ancillary and para-professional staff.

A feature of the in-service programme at Codsall Comprehensive School, for instance, was a guided tour of the school, the Director of Resources showing teachers what was actually going on in other departments. Even in a school where plenty of interdisciplinary discussion took place, this was often a revelation; 'new methods' were no longer something one heard of elsewhere, but something going on in familiar surroundings. In the context of a directed consideration of methodology in general, the explanation by a colleague of how he planned a particular exercise or sequence can be a greater source of stimulation than a high-level lecture by an educational pundit whose circumstances and limitations are not immediately clear. A description by an ancillary of the abilities of the school's stencil cutter or Caramate slide-tape presenter can be the key to innovation, because the teacher suddenly recognizes what is possible, as distinct from a lot of theory whose implementation he has previously understood imperfectly if at all. Moreover (and this point has already been appreciated by alert education advisers) in-service training within the school does not require extra staff, extra

equipment or extra classroom space; it makes use of what is immediately and necessarily available.

The limitations will also be obvious: the dangers of inward-
looking, of a restricted range of materials and equipment, of partial
understanding and incomplete experience, and all the hazards of
parochial insularity. The good adviser will value schools' own programmes, and be willing to participate in them and provide additional help, but he will also try to stimulate other opportunities of
co-operation between schools, wide-ranging discussion in courses
and occasional meetings, and curriculum development planning
meetings at teachers' centres and colleges and departments of
education. The enthusiasm sometimes generated by a teachers' centre
whose advisory courses are backed up by a practical service can be
considerable, and most valuable. It is surprising how often courses
and exhortations aimed at teachers ignore the affective and practical
domains. For that matter it is disconcerting how often the response
to a call for advice and help on resource-based and discovery learning is a series of formal lectures, and how the Library–College
movement in the USA has typically propounded its ideas by
'lectures against the lecture'! If teachers are to be encouraged to
develop learning programmes and sequences for their pupils in
styles which go counter to the traditional (and easily prepared)
pattern, we must pay attention to their development of prerequisite
skills and prerequisite understanding.

We shall be able to understand these more clearly if we look more
closely at what teachers will be planning for their students

Units, sequences and themes

Resource-based learning is a mode with many aspects and facets.
When applied in practice it may be short or long, structured or open-
ended, teacher-directed or pupil-operated, subject-specific or inter-
disciplinary, individualized or class-based. It may consist of a tape-
slide sequence which can be shown to classes and groups or viewed
singly by individuals, and conveying a particular unit of information
or stimulus; it may, on the other hand, be half a term's work programme for a class, meeting twice weekly for an hour and three
quarters each time. It may appear as a number of elements in a
schedule of work which also includes directed teaching, use of text
book, and practical formal exercises, as well as enquiry work, the
consultation of sources, and a problem-solving exercise involving the
study of a filmstrip in relation to a work-sheet or a passage in a
novel. It may well resemble, or actually be called, enquiry work,
project work, thematic work, individualized learning, activity learning, integrated studies or inter-disciplinary enquiry.

The wrong thing to do is to think, 'I hear a lot about resource-based learning: it is obviously the thing to do: therefore I will experiment with it next term.' A teaching mode should be selected because it best fits one's intentions and the needs of one's students in a particular instance. As always, what you try depends on what you want to do. We saw earlier that there is disagreement about the helpfulness or universality of the 'objectives' model, and certainly many teaching situations involve so many objectives that one wonders where to stop enunciating them. Moreover it is often difficult to specify every objective in precise enough terms, and sometimes hopeless to devise ways of ensuring that the objectives have been achieved. Some teachers and writers, perhaps carried away by behaviourist doctrine in the narrower sense, or thinking only in terms of sequential and very logically organized subject-matter, have over-emphasized what is involved and over-simplified the usefulness and effectiveness of 'specifying objectives'. None the less the opposite argument is equally shaky; it would be frightening to imagine teachers embarking on the planning of a term's work or even one single-period unit without asking themselves the simplest questions: 'Why am I doing this? What do I hope will happen?' and 'Why am I doing it this way?' We have a duty to be as clear as we can, and to articulate at all times what we are trying to do, in at least a general sense, and it will help us to ask (even if we cannot always easily answer) what the result might be in terms of student ability or behaviour.

The stated aim of the Nuffield Science units, for instance, was to place the student as far as possible in the experimental mode, to give experience of 'thinking like a scientist'. This had obvious implications for methodology which went beyond the simpler objectives of transferring information from teacher to student. Gestalt psychologists insist that we not only learn by the steady accretion of tiny units of knowledge but also by the recognition of broad patterns. Most of us have experienced the moments of intuition when we 'grasp' a broad and sometimes even global concept from a minimum of hints or indications, and know the excitement of such occasions. Science teaching, like any other, hopes to make provision for this to happen, as well as to provide the necessary detailed cross-checking and testing to see whether our intuitions have been correct. 'Thinking like a scientist' includes both. It has been questioned whether there is much resemblance between a student working in the Nuffield mode and an experimental scientist working in his laboratory, and probably many a teacher of science has wondered whether it logically follows that this objective *requires* the use of discovery learning. Certainly scientists and fifth-formers are not working in identical circumstances or in identical ways, and it may seem that the objective has been over-simplified or exaggerated. (Do we need to practice 'thinking like a scientist' *every time* we learn something in a science course?) The answer must lie to some degree in effectiveness and involvement, in other words whether the discovery method as well as giving some general introduction to scientific method satisfies the educator's broader aims of working through the affective domain, of stimulating active thought rather than passive reception, of positively influencing motivation. Whatever else a scientist 'does', he certainly *cares*.

Thus many schools concerned to teach scientific subjects in a more active fashion, Nuffield-based or not, have sought to employ a judicious mixture of 'lead lessons', directed laboratory practice, and increasingly open-ended problem-solving activity. This brings into view a number of sub-sequences and minor objectives, as well as forcing the teacher to state to himself what the pupil will need, not only to do, but be able to do, in order to take part in the work. He may need to be able to use apparatus, and generally speaking science teachers are accustomed to explaining necessary points about its use and keeping a close watch on safety. On the other hand, the student's difficulties may be of another kind: that his reading ability is poor and he has trouble in comprehending the work-card, for instance. Sometimes such problems are tackled by putting the students to work in twos and threes, so that good readers can help the slower ones; in the case of fairly lengthy work-cards, where more explanation is given, it is also helpful to record the text on a cassette, which the slower reader can listen to with the words before him, increasing his familiarity with the written word at the same time as giving him the information that he needs. The student who finds difficulty in writing out his results may equally use audio-recording as a tool, perhaps later transcribing his account into written form after he has formulated it. These are two, rather simple examples of the type of flexibility in approach which is now possible, and which can sometimes remove the intermediate barriers between students and better achievement.

'Lead lessons' provide an excellent opportunity for the use of projected and three-dimensional items, including slides, overhead transparencies, models and television. Closed circuit TV or video-tape can present to a large class visual stimuli in close-up that would otherwise be impossible to show except to individuals, as well as include out-of-school experience from schools broadcasts and specially recorded field work. It is interesting to note that some, if not all, of this initial stimulus work can be recorded and made available individually for refreshing the memory, checking particular phenomena or making up for absence. Pupils have sometimes asked to see again particular slides, or overhead transparencies, while checking a hunch or clarifying their recollections, and this was one reason why in *Organizing resources* it was recommended that they be kept in the library resource centre or some other suitable place after use, properly indexed. The Postlethwait method brings to everyday work some of the vividness of the lead lesson, but presents it individually in a carrel, and offers what is really a sort of heavily guided 'discovery'. However, quite often the valuable function of a lead lesson is not only the stimulus and information conveyed by the materials but the way these are deployed by the live teacher at the moment of performance, responding to little hints and reactions from his class.

Because of the nature of scientific work, much of the earlier 'practical' work has to be carefully structured and supervised, especially when it involves the possibility of dangerous accident. There is plenty of experience now of varied class patterns, students working individually or in pairs from work-cards or other guidance material, proceeding through a series of experiments calculated to introduce and reinforce processes, concepts and information, and doing so at their own pace. It is no longer essential for everyone to do the same experiment at the same time, and be held up when a few find unexpected difficulties. A term's work can be planned with a variety of experiences in different modes, enabling the slower students at least to master basic points and others to fill out this minimum with what the jargon calls 'horizontal enrichment', in other words different facets of the topic in wider contexts and re-lationships. But 'thinking like a scientist' sooner or later involves greater autonomy, a bigger share of the decision-making: not simply discussing with the teacher and learning to guess from his facial expressions or other clues what the 'right' answer might be, but actually wrestling unprompted with the methodology and materials in order to find it out for oneself.

This leads to the general observation, that if the aim of resource-based learning or any other teaching–learning mode is to produce the independent autonomous learner, then the tendency of closely structured sequences or units of work must be towards eventual loosening of structure, the emergence of open-ended situations where the student can exercise his choice and decision-making in a meaningful way, and 'learn how to learn by learning'. One does not learn to 'think like a scientist' by perpetually following instructions on work-cards, just as one does not learn how to 'think like an artist' by perpetually joining up dotted lines or painting in colours according to numbers. Moreover, how *does* a scientist think? Some-times, perhaps, instead of setting up a series of difficult and time-consuming experiments, he checks to see whether the answer is already known. He may be dissatisfied with what he then learns, but that is a later stage. And to test whether this is in fact true of how scientists think, the only way to work is to observe, not oneself as a student doing discovery learning, but scientists themselves. This is the relevance of the history of science, past and present, and the value of supplementing investigation of the process of experimental discovery with reading. Many science courses involve elements of library research as well as its laboratory equivalent.

The history of science is of course an important part of our contemporary culture, to be considered not only in the context of the
Science department's work but also in History, Humanities, Religious Education and other fields of study, and in the process of
inter-disciplinary thematic work in general. When integrated work
is being developed, through team teaching or departmental co-
operation, a great many areas of cross-fertilization can be identified
and prepared for, and their relevance not only to the student's
mastery of concepts but also to the more narrowly specific requirements of examining boards brought out. In simple co-operative
work, the Art Department can plan to examine particular patterns
and structures at much the same time as the Science Department
looks at crystals and lattices; the Geography Department can look
at climatology and weather charting at the same time as the Mathematics Department studies or revises graphs. The hope here is that
each will reinforce the other, and make the school experience less of
a bewildering succession of totally disparate experiences. In Inter-
disciplinary education (IDE) and other broad team work, the
possibilities of bringing in both specific basic scientific units and
topics for all on the one hand, and opportunities for further scientific activity at a later stage for those choosing to develop their
assignment in that direction, will also be remembered in the initial
planning.

Scientific interests have been chosen for these few pages of examples
because of the tendency in some quarters to assume that resource-
based learning is a Humanities or Social Studies prerogative. In fact
any subject matter can be examined and taught with a significant
resource-based component, although as in our examples above there
is likely always to be an important place for the directed expository
lesson, whether 'lead' or otherwise. What basically emerges from the
planning point of view is the number of objectives that need to be
considered in terms of pupil performance – not only what he will be
able to do at completion (on which educational technologists have
understandably concentrated) but also what he will have to be able
to do in the process. Let us try to summarize some of the things that
will need to be kept in mind.

1. *Previous knowledge.* This comes in two parts: the teacher's previous
knowledge of the students, and their own previous knowledge of the
subject-matter to be considered. The teacher will want to note down
any relevant information he may have about the interests, previous
skills and behaviour of the students, including their home backgrounds, so that where possible he can build items or experiences or
practices of special importance or usefulness into his planning. This
may also indicate preparatory drill in reading skills and the handling
of information sources.

2. *Overall aims and objectives.* This will include not only the subject

matter it is essential to master, but the skills it is essential to practise, as well as social and motivational aims, and subsidiary objectives. This will have its immediate relevance for choice of methodology in both the broad sense and in the development of sub-units within the whole. If the subject-matter is sequential, the teacher must ask himself whether it is essential that step A is known to have been mastered before the beginning of step B, and what is the essential minimum; he will then go on to decide how the achievement of that minimum can be tested, what can be done for those who do not reach it, and whether the material is such that comprehension or insight might be expected to dawn at later stages after more exposure to the subject field. In any case, it will do no harm for the teacher to ask himself how he will know whether the expected learning is taking place; it is all too easy for a teacher to assume that 'they must be learning – after all, I'm teaching'. Even though the subject-matter may be such that it is difficult to come to rapid conclusions by, say, an objective test, the question should still be asked so that the teacher can explain to himself in all honesty what he is about.

3. *Choice of methodologies.* These will be dictated by the objectives, as well as (other things being equal) by the style preferences of the teacher or teaching team. In a broad programme of work, a variety of methods or types of activity can be reasonably expected; planning will begin to lay out the sequence in increasing detail, even when allowing for a number of variant paths or for the switching of the course according to observed student response: improvisation or student decision-making works best when possibilities have been foreseen and prepared for. The identification of particular units and requirements can proceed, and will probably include the following elements (not necessarily in this order):

— presentation and exposition
— discussion and debate
— activity with tools (lab-work, use of mathematical instruments, etc.)
— activity in the environment (visits, field-work, exploration, examination)
— activity with learning resources (books, a-v materials, work-cards, project booklets, etc.)
— creative activity (drama, artwork, music, crafts, etc.)

Throughout much of these types of activity, the practice of careful observation, note-taking and written accounts will play an important part; several of the schools reporting in Freeman's (1969) book on team teaching stated that their students had gained a valuable facility in note-taking which was required not only for science but in other subject fields. There may also be practice with audio-visual equipment itself, not only in the receiving mode but also in creative and other production, such as photography, interviewing with a tape recorder, and use of a tape recorder to make oral notes during practical work and visits.

4. *Collection and preparation of materials.* Some of these materials will be used for periods of presentation and exposition, not only at the beginning but at helpful points during the programme. All types of a-v, museum, artefact and other stimulus material may be involved, and if it is not immediately available it may have to be purchased, borrowed or created. The materials may be part of a formal presentation by a teacher, or series of teachers; but may also be made into individualized or self-instructional form, for instance a project booklet with all relevant 'starter' material including basic data, examples for further study, assignments or suggested activities, and a booklist. Equally it may be a tape-slide sequence or an 8mm movie or film-loop. Discussion and debate may need (as with the Humanities Curriculum Project) packs of supporting data, and if paper is short some of it may well be put on overhead transparencies and projected when relevant. Activity with tools may be undertaken by the whole class as a supervised group, or may be later activities undertaken by small groups of their own volition, and the circumstances under which this latter is to take place must be carefully organized in advance.

Materials for environmental or other field-work may include cameras and tape recorders, or simply measuring tapes and surveying equipment, but in many cases there will also be a work-card or outline to guide the activity. This may again be necessary for work with learning resources, but librarians and experienced teachers will in any case want to stress the absolute necessity of previous detailed checking to see that the resources likely to be helpful and required are actually available. This calls for an act of the imagination, in foreseeing the ways in which the enquiry is likely to develop, the types of information necessary, the reading ages and levels of attainment of the students in relation to what is currently available, and the weaknesses of the collection as it stands in relation to this analysis. Numbers are vital: if thirty students are each likely to want a biography of a scientist, or a map of the Lake District, or the text of the Race Relations Act, and at roughly the same time, then copies must be available. It is sometimes noticeable that teachers who would blush to begin a lesson without the requisite number of sharp pencils and sheets of properly stencilled paper, make unrealistic assumptions about the hospitality and usefulness of the stock of the school library, or worse, the local public library branch. Where the material to be used in enquiry work is audio-visual (as for instance a filmstrip, perhaps with the accompanying booklet transcribed on to audio-cassette so that the eye can concentrate on the pictures and the slower readers have quick access to the text) then of course suitable equipment must be available in sufficient quantity for the expected numbers of students at any one time. The same is true for materials for creative activity.

5. *Provision of necessary space(s).* All these planned activities must happen somewhere, and the spaces must relate sensibly to convenient use. As with all the items listed so far, there will normally be compromises necessary in most schools as few of us work in ideal premises; this calls for advance consideration of the possibilities and contingency planning. If some students are to use laboratory, workshop, craftroom or drama department facilities, we have to know that these spaces are available at the required times and with suitable staff, and what numbers can be accommodated in each. Some students may be creating a videotaped drama, in which case numbers and technicians must be calculated and provided. If the library resource centre is to receive a possible influx of busy researchers, it is wise to find out whether any other classes or years will also be present, and what the maximum capacity is. If many students are likely to be moving from room to room, and even leaving the school altogether, some system of control and supervision will certainly be necessary so that no one gets lost, or is tempted to fritter away time or abscond.

Space is often one of the most limiting factors in any attempt to create a genuinely open-ended learning situation, and planning for its most effective use puts heavy demands on the imagination and organizing ability of teachers and administrators. On the other hand, because the perfect answer is not always immediately available does not mean that the whole exercise can or should be abandoned as a foolish pipe-dream. The answer may mean harsher timetabling, or it may mean reconsidering the school's traditional use of its premises and their parts, but neither of these answers is impossible. One school, deciding that extra space for resource-based learning was a priority, took over a classroom for use in unstructured individualized work, with the result that other classrooms including some specialist rooms were more heavily used than before; teachers complained that they could not get in to put up work on the blackboard beforehand, and were introduced to the more thorough use of the overhead projector; the timetabler had to bear in mind the needs of some practical subjects where the previous laying-out of equipment was vital, but the exercise was valuable in focusing attention on such priorities and making them clear to everyone. At other schools, the amount of space given to exhibitions and displays, to secretarial work, and to counselling activities, has been analysed carefully and sympathetically, and some compromises of multiple use achieved without sacrifice of principle or utility. For instance, careers information is a very important part of a secondary school, and the work of the careers teacher or team requires publicity, time and space; but where is the material most effectively displayed for regular consultation by students themselves, where is the careers interviewing most advantageously sited, and what proportion of the school term or year is spent on it? There is no one answer applicable to all schools, but systematic analysis in each institution may sometimes yield answers helpful to overall planning of accommodation allocation.

With these five factors examined and the results of preliminary thinking kept in mind, the teacher or the planning team will be able to settle down to detailed planning of the specific learning sequence in question, whether it is a short piece of structured work with a work-sheet, tape-slide sequence or programmed unit, or whether it occupies several weeks of varied work. The basic theme, topic, or specific subject-matter will be selected, and examined for its facets, concepts and possible sub-units as well as for the skills that are necessary for its full comprehension and others that can be usefully practised within its general ambit. The knowledge the teacher has, or the team has, of the students themselves and their particular aptitudes, interests and needs, can at this stage be related to and integrated with the chosen theme. The planning must then design the introductory and motivating unit (the 'lead lesson', the 'starter pack', an introductory film, or whatever is the best agent for the particular purpose), a schedule of subsequent activity anticipating varieties of use and as many of the consequent hazards as can be foreseen, and the expected conclusion; and at every stage it is important to be clear about intentions and objectives, learning points, and how it is proposed to monitor the continuing success of the work in achieving these objectives.

What this might mean in practice

At this point it will be useful to look more closely at particular examples. Let us begin with an inter-disciplinary theme in Humanities, devised in Leicestershire under the stimulus of the Curriculum Resources Development Project in 1970, with Emmeline Garnett as Project Director. The theme chosen was 'Creation', and it was planned for use with 11-year-olds in a team-teaching situation. The Handbook produced by the Project for use in co-operating schools is still useful for its analysis of the contributing factors, available resources and major themes and concepts, as well as including for discussion purposes an examination of what one particular school had used as a basis for its own planning. In addition, the Project produced a box of materials, including the texts of nine myths on tape and in duplicated script form, and a record of one song (by Rolf Harris) which was also relevant. In the first trial year the Project material was used by ten schools, and in its improved form was used the following year by eleven schools; and in most cases this involved some 120 children at a time. It was assumed that schools would be using the materials and theme for about twelve periods a week for six weeks, as Miss Garnett noted: 'This is probably as long as the steam stays in a theme for this age, and nobody should feel embarrassed about pulling out of it quicker if it seems right to do so' (Leicester/Leicestershire Curriculum Development Project 1970: 1). 'Creation' is in many ways typical of the kind of theme chosen for inter-disciplinary studies in thematic work. As Miss Garnett pointed out:

> . . . the theme is the exploration of answers, actual and possible, to the question 'how has man conceived of the beginning of things?' This is part mythological, part anthropological, part historical, geographical, literary and creative. It does not include the scientific, which it ought to do – it is hoped that schools will build in this element for themselves . . . the original teams of teachers who came together to build the project did not include a scientist . . . (*ibid.*).

The planning notes from one of the participating schools assumed a basic team of four teachers (styled A, B, C & D) with a basic humanities teaching background in English, Religious Education, History and Social Studies, involved in all twelve periods a week. Two teachers (E & F) were art and music-drama specialists, and were able to give four periods a week. A young probationary teacher and a student-teacher were also available for some periods of 'fringe help, mostly supervisory' (*op. cit.*: 5), but played little part in the planning discussions. Occasionally other teachers who wanted to take 'a cautious look' were brought in for specific purposes.

The 120 pupils met normally in groups of thirty, but for these occasions were divided into eight groups of fifteen, and the twelve periods a week in fact came out as two double periods, one whole morning and one whole afternoon. The work mostly took place in the first year base, which was described as: 'a large hall and four small rooms each capable of taking a group of twenty. It might equally well be a hall, four classrooms along a corridor and the corridor itself.' (*op. cit.*: 6) Art sessions took place in the Art Room itself at the far end of the school, and Drama work happened in the hall. Learning resources were divided into eight sections kept separate so that individual groups could concentrate on them. 'Movable "libraries" are ideal, for instance, old tea trolleys which hold books, slides, pictures, a hand viewer, box of assignment cards etc. These can be wheeled out of the way when not needed.' (*ibid*) Paper stocks and model-making materials, together with other practical resources, were also available.

At different times in the week, the teachers found themselves taking different roles. A teacher could be called upon to be a lecturer to 120 children, fairly infrequently, on 'lead lesson' lines: 'a full-scale highly polished performance, carefully prepared, and using any necessary ancillary aids.' (*ibid*) He could be a seminar leader to a subsequent discussion or work group. He could be a group teacher to fifteen pupils, dealing with the general theme but making full use of his own specialism. When the children worked individually or in smaller groups he acted as adviser/supervisor to 'wander round, look over shoulders, give encouragement, ask pertinent questions, look at folders of work, help on slow groups, etc.' (*ibid.*) Finally he served regularly as pastoral tutor, responsible for the general progress of thirty children, monitoring their work and progress, and in charge of assessment. The learning mode was a judicious mixture of lecture, class lessons, practical sessions and (on Friday afternoons) individual/ small group work, using work-cards or booklets; these latter varied, being strictly or loosely structured according to need, allowing for different kinds of work, not all of it written.

Creation stories from eight cultures had been distinguished – Egyptian, Norse, African, Oceanic, Greek, Mexican, Indian and the Genesis account – and these could be divided amongst the eight groups very happily, with the addition of timetabled periods of art and music-drama for double groups, in which basic techniques were linked to suitable themes (for instance, shrine-building, rain-making ceremonies). The lecture periods could be used for outside visitors, or for specific and relevant accounts by teachers who did not normally participate in the work; examples were the playing of records of part of Haydn's *Creation* with explanation and commentary, by a teacher made specially available, and a talk on Red Indian tribes by a visitor from a local museum, together with overhead transparencies, slides and objects from the museum collection.

The Friday individual/small group work spread the children throughout all the available accommodation. It involved reading, the consultation of several books and resources, the study of visual or aural material, and the production of work or the answering of questions from all these sources; it could also involve creative writing or drama, and small group work following productive discussion. It was possible with work-card and booklets to give scope and variety to this work as well as necessary structure, and 'the members of the team in their original discussions, will have built into the courses the skills and techniques they think should be learnt and practised by eleven-year-olds.' (*op. cit.*: 8)

Miss Garnett's Project team supported this work, in all the schools, with considerable detail on available resources, and suggestions of useful sub-topics to explore with the children; it also listed works which the teachers themselves should read for their own preparation, as distinct from other works and materials suitable for the children. It distinguished five categories of creation story (taken from Philip Freund's useful book *Myths of creation*), and picked out eight characteristics or linked elements that were worth pursuing. General sources of further help were listed, especially the services of various museums, with their addresses and specialities. There can be no doubt that this sort of help is most valuable for teachers, and where it cannot be provided from a curriculum development project itself might in less ambitious form be offered from a teachers' centre or from a schools library service, although in the latter case the advice on sub-themes and topics would necessarily be tentative rather than prescriptive.

When one looks more closely at the individual creation myths one recognizes that the work will involve more than simple description of the myths themselves; it will be necessary to go into the societies from which they sprang in at least sufficient detail for the myths to be appreciated in context. This is where anthropological studies prove helpful as well as archaeology. The Mexican creation story, for instance, requires an explanation of the Mayan, Aztec and Incan societies and cultures, so very different from the Mediterranean civilizations from which our own society emerged. As the booklet explains:

> The incredible ruined cities, many more of which still remain to be discovered in the jungle areas, are one fascination, if only to speculate as to how they were built in a civilisation which had no beast of burden bigger than a llama, no wheels, and no cutting edge except stone. (*op. cit.*: 35.)

Suggestions for the children's own work, as well as the simple ones of drawing, model-making, painting, writing and drama, included:

> Problems that involve working out what a culture may owe to certain technological discoveries – e.g. the wheel, the use of iron, the domestication of the horse, the discovery of writing.
> Working out the rules and trying to play the Aztec ball-game.
> Inventing rituals, music, chants and poems.
> Studying connections between geography and culture. Many features of the early American cultures were based on maize. Trying to build a culture on the basis of some other food (the potato?) or some other animal than the llama (the cow?).
> Making up calendars on a different time-scheme from the solar.
> Making up a mathematic with different bases and signs. (*op. cit.*: 35–6.)

This may seem to have moved a long way away from the Creation, but not if the full significances of the Mayan story are to be enjoyed. The interesting feature is the variety of sub-topics and activities arising out of this one unit, offering to pupils a considerable element of choice as well as of imaginative 'playing-out'.

To underpin this work requires a sizeable resources collection, and we shall be examining more closely in Chapter 5 the ways in which resources provision can be planned. Block loans through the public library service will have an important part to play, and it will be advantageous to both sides if the teachers have provided a detailed breakdown of likely sub-themes and activities for the library staff to use (although their own examination of stock may throw up additional possibilities which could be suggested). The C. R. D. Project was able to produce and duplicate considerable packs of material, in several formats, and to reveal the existence of suitable 16mm films available for hire. There is no mention in the Project booklet of the use of the school library resource centre itself, and it may be that for this age group in their first extended piece of work in the school it was felt that moving out of the year base into another area involved more planning, supervision or simple hazard than the staff were ready to face. At other schools, however, in other counties (and especially when a full-time librarian is available to receive the youngsters and add his or her strength to the teaching team) the library resource centre is a useful additional area for work, and the use of its indexes and bibliographical reference tools an important part of the skill-learning aspect of the project. Use of the library resource centre means that the children would have immediate access to a much larger collection than can normally be gathered in a series of project or topic boxes, of the kind that were to be gathered for the use of the eight groups in this example. 'Starter packs' should have the admirable function of motivating the children to seek elsewhere, including in encyclopedias, atlases, art books and (for instance) the poetry section, as well as the world outside.

Items in the world outside can be a valuable resource. In local studies, for instance, there is a local church, particularly if it is a fairly old village church with a few hundred years of history behind it. When Miss Garnett's Project team set about producing a curriculum guide to the study of local churches, they were greatly assisted by a schematic study or flow-chart of possible work that might arise, devised for them by Mrs Mary Ball of the Leicester Museum. This valuable example of a local non-teacher specialist's advice will show the many different ways in which work can arise from one study focus. The offering of such guidelines or suggestions does not in any way detract from the professional integrity of the teacher, who must then select what suits him best for his own purposes, but there will be few teachers who will have had the time or the imagination to think of all of them. Different types of pupil will gravitate towards different sub-topics, but all will have the common link of starting from the same stimulus; it will be possible for all children to contribute to whatever may be the concluding feature, such as an exhibition, poster or class booklet.

In the school on whose work the Curriculum Development Project's notebook was based, not all the sub-topics picked out by Mrs Ball were taken up, and of course it is the joy of a topic of this kind that this does not matter; one is not concerned with 'covering the syllabus' and 'getting everything in', but providing the stimulus for valuable enquiry, the development of interest and of concepts, and the practice of a variety of skills. One of these skills must certainly be analytical thinking. The children visit the church and learn to look at it and describe what they see, and this is in itself a valuable exercise; but it becomes more valuable still if as well as noting that the fabric is stone, they are provoked to go on to enquire what type of stone, is it all the same stone, why were these types of stone preferred, where do they come from, and how do they come to be what they are? Thus two of the individual contributions which the children were asked to make or able to make were put in this way:

2. Write notes, in sentences, about the appearance of the stones you have chosen, e.g. their colour; size; shape; markings and position in the church should be included.
3. Write some short notes about where the stones have come from and how they have got their particular markings and colour. (Curric. Resources Development Project. Curriculum Notebooks No. 1. 1970: 8.)

Other questions asked about the tools that would have been used to shape them and the reasons for these shapes. Information on varieties of stone was given in the duplicated project booklet which the children received at the start of their work, but with some children this would not have been necessary had the school library resource centre contained suitable information in an easily discovered form.

The sources from which the children could find information enabling them to make fullest use of the church study were not confined to what they saw in the booklet nor what they could see and think out for themselves; a number of people, both inside and outside the school, were enthusiastic and available for consultation. But the notebook gives a dismaying picture:

Material resources were few; cameras were privately owned, though the school bought the film. A few reference books were collected from the library, from people's own shelves; somebody found a couple of Leicester guide books in a Yorkshire second-hand shop. The resulting list was about seven titles long. The pamphlets were produced on the school duplicating machine. (*op. cit.*: 6)

Despite this, quite a lot of good work was done by the eighty fourth-year 'leavers' (aged 14-plus) who were the trial group for the project. Many had considerable reading and writing skills, but about 20 per cent were recent immigrants, often with language difficulties. Much of their work was individual (though carefully timetabled and monitored) over eight periods a week: it included a survey of the church, tombstone rubbings, individual written work and folders, and something approaching a survey of the parish, including street plans, dates and arrangements of buildings. It will be easy to pick out from these products the types of learning objective that might have been achieved; one hopes that in general these correlated with those the teachers had in mind from the beginning, and that they learnt from their examination of the results.

Not all our units and sequences will be as long or as detailed as the foregoing examples. Resource-based learning can last as little as ten minutes: a child's scrutiny of a repeating film-loop which teaches him a concept or skill he will need for the next part of his programme; a short programmed exercise that enables him to test his grasp of an idea or piece of knowledge before embarking on a larger exercise; a work-card unit giving practise in loading a projector or using a subject catalogue. The basic rules of procedure for any such exercise, short or prolonged, remain very much the same: a six-week programme may well include a series of short ten-minute sequences as well as other episodes and exercises and in devising materials for either one would take into account the basic procedures of materials production which we shall have occasion to examine in a later chapter. Moreover, it should not be forgotten that if the teacher is 'a resource' as well as books, audio-visual materials and three-dimensional items, then a similar claim can very properly be made for items of resource equipment. Using a camera to record the progress of plant growth or of an experiment not only gives useful experience of photographic work but gives a particular slant to, or stimulus point for, subject study. Knudson's work cited earlier, using the challenge of producing video playlets as a stimulus to bringing about general improvement in the language work of under-achieving pupils, is a case in point. The equipment need not be videotaped, which admittedly is expensive and less common in many schools; audiotape provides another catalytic agency at a much more modest price. In the creation of an audiotaped sequence, the pupil or group can make use not only of verbal messages and a variety of voices, but also of natural and artificial sounds, and of course music. Other pupils can take the matter further, and with a quite simple automatic camera create perfectly acceptable photographs, perhaps in colour slide form to lead to a tape-slide sequence. The hazards, difficulties and expense of this have been greatly exaggerated; the usefulness in creating interest and provoking genuine subject study can be considerable.

One of the major reasons, however, for the interest in resource-based learning has been the recognition that children must learn, during the course of their schooling, to be increasingly self-sufficient in learning, to become the 'independent autonomous learners' most fitted to survive in a society undergoing constant change, and in the context of the knowledge explosion. Being able to find out for oneself has a number of contributory sub-skills attached to it, and in planning resource-based programmes for our classes we must take into account such sub-skills so that we can give the chance for them to develop and mature. Some of these skills are essentially verbal: the ability to articulate one's need, to understand expositions of the subject-matter in written or spoken form, to make notes and in due course write reports, essays and synopses, and so on. Some may well be mathematical; to have sufficient grasp of number and of other mathematical concepts to be able to follow the processes required in one's subject study. Mathematical and language skills unite in the understanding of logic and reasoning, an essential component of mature intelligence.

These skills however are only part of the story. To learn for one-self one uses more than the conventional language and number skills, plus one's ability to locate an appropriate evening school class. One needs the basic skills of research, including the ability to use the full resources of a research collection. Much time is spent by teacher–librarians in secondary schools in giving pupils busy intro-ductions to reference books and library catalogues, and we saw in Chapter 3 how tutor–librarians in technical institutions along Hertfordshire lines had built up programmes of instruction in all aspects of information-seeking. There have been differences of opinion as to how such matters should be most advantageously introduced to school children, and some have argued that the 'library period' where children systematically practise 'library skills', in isolation from any other work they may also be doing, is a mistake. This is an understandable reaction to some of the less interesting programmes of what turns out in practice to be a kind of 'library drill': aimless trots through catalogues and reference books by pupils carrying work-cards or slips of typed paper setting them questions to answer which nobody apart from a desperate teacher–librarian would ever think to ask.

There is of course no reason why this should be the way in which library skills are taught, even in library periods; but the use of resource-based learning as an important strategy in a school gives an excellent opportunity to build in the acquisition and practice of library research skills as part of a 'natural situation'.

If we are to do this we must be clear what such skills include, and an advantage in having the librarian working in consultation with the planning team is that such questions can be asked and their proper inclusion sensibly planned. A person who can make good use of a resources library has learnt the following things:

1. The recognition that information can be retrieved from books and other learning materials, and is not beyond reach.
2. The ability to discriminate between types of potential informa-tion source, for instance between consulting an encyclopedia and a dictionary, or either of these and a full-length monograph, as well as recognizing what types of information may best be found in a visual source such as a photograph or chart.
3. The ability to retrieve information from a book or other source, using the various elements in the packaging such as the contents list, chapter headings, index and jacket blurb.
4. The recognition of the limitations of individual sources, includ-ing the existence of bias and error. (As examples of the latter, try

looking up the length of the river Mississippi in as many reference
books as you can find, and compare the answers.)

5. The ability to use an organized *collection* of materials, including
an understanding of the existence of subject arrangement (though
not necessarily the full details of any one such arrangement, such
as the Dewey classification), and the ability to 'browse skilfully'.

6. The ability to use library catalogues, both subject and author, including the important ability to articulate one's subject interest in specific terms and to be aware of possible synonyms and related subjects.

7. The ability to see subjects hierarchically, i.e. to perceive that
specific subjects are often included in more general ones (ROBINS
might be included under BIRDS), as well as vice versa, and that as
well as trying more general subject areas on shelves one might look
for books with more comprehensive titles or filmstrips on more
general themes.

8. The ability to make use of the various services of libraries,
including reservation systems, inter-library loans and copying
services.

9. The ability to use relevant equipment, such as viewers, projectors, players, recorders and headphones.

It will be seen that not all these nine items are of equal weight.
Item 2, for instance, has many facets. A skilled library user knows
when to turn to periodicals for the latest information, how to use
abstracting services, how to find his way through bibliographies, and
how to make best use of atlases and tables and collections of maps.
Item 5 includes remembering that items are of different sizes, and
may sometimes be shelved in different sequences: a simple enough
thing when known, but the cause of much misunderstanding when
its full implications (including the need to consult catalogues) are
not realized. The main point to make, however, is that few teachers
consciously build in such skills when planning resource-based
exercises, and regrettably few teachers could either articulate the
nine simple points above or even demonstrate very convincingly
their own abilities in a library setting. This might, of course, lead
some to the conclusion that the nine skills are unnecessary: after all,
teachers had reached their dizzy heights without them! A moment's
reflection shows how much the confidence of the adolescent in the
learning process depends upon the possibility of success, and enough
of it to give 'reinforcement'. Libraries (and for that matter separate
collections of audio-visual software) have to be organized for retrieval in ways that allow the user fullest access to their subject content;
these methods are not understood by instinct and have to be revealed
through teaching and through use. The student who is confident in
his library skills has a basis of trust upon which to build – and he
will save himself a great deal of humiliation as well as precious time
(a commodity his teachers are themselves equally short of).

Thus the planning of curricula and of resource-based programmes, though basically a teacher-function, takes into consideration many factors on which others may have contributions to make. The librarian knows, not only how his library is organized and what retrieval tools it contains, but also what problems the students (and their teachers) have in its use and what skills need special attention and practice. He also knows the stock and can discuss plans in relation to it (as we shall see more closely in the following chapter). But in recognizing the role of one ancillary, we should not overlook others. The media technician will be able to advise on the suitability of various pieces of equipment to the tasks which teachers may wish them to perform: not only in the presentation of information and stimulus to the students but also in their utilization of hardware in response. Some ideas that sound splendid in theory may, for very good reasons, prove hazardous or impossible in practice. Equally, the media production adviser (under whatever title) may creatively transform the range of what is possible by his suggestions, as we shall see. Thus although it is true that 'teachers articulate purpose', this articulation and its achievement will often be the more effective for professional co-operation. The teacher working on his own, or with the co-operation only of his teaching colleagues, is isolated and detached from useful help. We saw earlier how subject specialists (for instance, working in museums) can provide analytical outlines upon which the teacher can draw; we have seen how the very objectives underlying resource-based learning include an understanding of the skills teacher–librarians have till recently taught alone; we have hinted that other ancillaries will, in their work, help the teacher not only to achieve his objectives but also to modify and even enlarge them. We shall find this co-operative function persisting if we examine in turn the other matters of our concern. The first, very obviously, is the provision of the materials by means of which resource-based learning can proceed.

5 Materials: the Collecting of Resources

The first step in many sensible schools, when contemplating an extension of resource-based learning, has been to gather together all materials available within the school at the time and make an index of them, so that at least the teachers and students could find out what was to hand for them to use. Much of the argument raging at resource centre conferences in the United Kingdom in the early 1970s was about such indexing; the Schools Council Resource Centre Project had to spend much of its time discussing and evaluating indexing methods, and Chapter 7 of this book will look, in more detail than has been possible to date, at the implications of information retrieval for economy and educational effectiveness.

But even the best, most flexible and thorough of indexing systems cannot in the end make up for an inadequate stock. Resource-based learning needs resources: they probably do not have to be elaborate or expensive, there may be a considerable element of local production, we may be able to make wholehearted use of the environment, of materials on loan, and of each other, but we have to start with *something*, and the more varied and extensive our collection the better.

To some teachers, wholly absorbed in their own world, the idea that other people, such as librarians and media producers, may have opinions, training, experience, or even a role in materials selection, has been surprising and even alarming. Some have felt threatened by the suggestion, claiming hotly that *they* were the subject specialists, that they had unique understanding of the students, and of educational purposes and method, and that they were therefore uniquely and properly qualified to decide what items should be included in the school's stock. Professional librarians working in schools and (in the past) colleges have sometimes found themselves debarred from any say in the selection of the books and resources among which they spend their professional lives. Equally, media resource officers and educational technologists have sometimes been regarded as merely 'the men who repair the machines' and their particular insights into the choice of resources have been overlooked.

The exclusions have not only been one-sided. Educational technologists have sometimes made extravagant claims for their abilities, leaving the impression that, in future, subject specialist teachers of long standing will be waiting in a line outside the Educational Technology department for advice on whether to use a particular filmstrip. Librarians, too, have sometimes exaggerated their abilities, in their anxiety to establish the usefulness of their role in education, although they are probably less likely to want to exclude any other group from a part of the selection process.

The truth is that each group has a point to make and a part to play. The educational technologist has often made a careful and advanced study of the points to look for in a sequenced item and the considerations to bear in mind when planning a resource-based exercise; he has frequently made a special study of audio-visual items, and will have views on the characteristics of a good chart or poster, the qualities of a good photograph (whether projected or not) and the potentialities of audiotape for both stimulation and the conveying of information. What he may lack is the knowledge of the subject specialist: he will know if it is a well-made item but not whether it is accurate or whether it gives a genuinely helpful contribution to concept development in that subject. The teacher, especially when he is a specialist teacher, will often have this knowledge, though it would be foolish to pretend that he always has it; moreover he can judge the usefulness of the item for the specific purpose that he is currently considering, that is, whether it will match this particular class or student in this particular context.

Both teachers and educational technologists tend to be at their best when considering a particular and immediate selection problem – what do we want for tomorrow's class? – and this is the area where their training and their day-to-day activities both combine. At this point, the librarian is certainly not at a loss: once the parameters of the problem are explained to him he can bring his training to bear upon his knowledge of the stock and of the bibliographical tools at his disposal. This is the work of a good Reader's Adviser, and it includes the ability by probing and analytical questioning to draw out from the enquirer what he really needs and what factors must be taken into consideration. However, the librarian would not feel himself qualified to lay down in advance what those factors might be; he will, if he is any good, have studied such matters as level of vocabulary and quality of illustration, and apprised himself of the views of leading authorities in these matters, but he will defer to the subject teacher about accuracy and effectiveness, and to the educational technologist about structure and sequencing, if their views differ from his own.

Where the librarian is at his strongest in relation to his other two colleagues, however, is in the long-term planning of a collection, as well as in his training and experience with the wide variety of bibliographical and other selection tools. Working in the multimedia library all day, and dealing regularly with all the many people who make demands upon it, gives him an informed knowledge of its strengths and weaknesses; he knows what actually takes place in the library, as distinct from what teachers and others hope or believe will happen, and he knows how often things are sought and what the failure rate of the collection is. He can build up the gaps in the collection, can help to foresee future needs, and with the co-operation of his teaching colleagues can prepare for subsequent demand. He has the time and the duty, while the teacher is busy with his classes, to probe the various selection tools for materials which will meet the teacher's needs, or which he can suggest to the teacher (and the educational technologist) for their appraisal as subject or methodology specialists.

When teachers, educational technologists and librarians quarrel about whose duty in fact the selection of materials is, they are in fact quarrelling over different meanings of the word and different occasions when it takes place. Each has his speciality; but a unified selection policy, or series of considerations and decisions in relation to the building of a school collection, should employ the insights of all three. This is particularly true when, because of staffing limitations, only one person or type of person is involved in the work. These insights we will try to bring together in the next section.

Selection for now and later

We collect books, pamphlets, periodicals, audio-visual materials, models, educational games, maps and charts, artefacts and museum items for a variety of purposes, and some items will be serviceable for more than one of them. Here are some; there are probably many more.

1. *To convey a concept or simple succession of facts*. Examples would include purchase of a film loop or filmstrip, or an audiotape, or a map or chart, or the preservation of a journal article or set of newspaper cuttings.
2. *To give a broad overview and include a variety of concepts and factual accounts*. This is one of the major usefulnesses of the printed book, and in buying it we may have in mind both its total contents and its parts: its use when read right through and its use as something to consult.
3. *To stimulate interest and activity*. Examples here would be audio-visual presentations used in lead lessons, as well as 'starter packs'

(e.g. those devised by Goldsmith's Curriculum Laboratory, or various Schools Council projects), multi-media kits, books and collections of slides, artefacts, illustrations, etc.

4. *To give pre-determined activities or exercises for the student to follow.* Sets of published work-cards as well as the home-made variety, and of course the exercises at the ends of chapters in textbooks, are commonly found examples, to which one may add in appropriate cases programmed learning sequences if available

5. *To reinforce and supplement what has already been learnt or presented in other ways.* Novels and stories put living flesh on historical periods, moral problems, geographical studies or scientific discoveries. So do biographies, travel books, and popularly written accounts, as well as art-books and similar items. Films also work in this way, although in Britain it is not common for schools to purchase full-length feature films or more than a few items on 16mm.

6. *To give practical examples of things already discussed.* This certainly includes museum items, artefacts, models and specimens; it also includes, for students of languages, audiotapes and records of the spoken word, and for students of music, recorded examples of instruments, composers and individual works and forms.

7. *To present information and stimulus in a variety of different ways.* This means that we seek different media formats wherever possible, to suit the preferences of our varied students. Stories in a book may be recorded on tape, or on a filmstrip with a record. Pictures may be projected or printed. Some material can be explained at length in a duplicated pamphlet, or assembled and worked out by the student in the form of a kit or package. Some items will be closely systematized and structured for one group of students, and presented in open-ended problem-solving form for another.

8. *To give experience in handling different media formats.* Children need plenty of practice in reading, listening, looking, using equipment, making and recording. Some items will be acquired or produced mainly for this purpose.

9. *To give experience in using basic research tools.* This is a similar purpose, and includes use of dictionaries, encyclopedias and atlases, use of indexes and guides, practice in putting together answers using a variety of sources and comparing what they say, and articulating verbally information that is initially presented in visual or non-verbal form.

10. *To provide basic information for teachers and others in the manufacture of their own resources and the planning of lessons.* Such information can be of all kinds and in a variety of formats – including collections of illustrations and maps as well as basic reference books.

11. *To give pleasure and delight.* One of the major revelations of education, one might suppose, would be the sheer enjoyment of good books, pictures, music, poetry, discovery, for their own sakes.

The word 'good' here need not be interpreted in a mandarin or elitist fashion; whatever gives somebody genuine delight is good. We must see that plenty of it is available.

In a school that is primarily teacher-directed, and where most of the learning is carefully pre-structured, it may be possible for the school's collection of learning materials to be largely keyed to immediate curriculum need and purchased or produced as the direct result of the teachers' course preparations. Even here, however, the teachers will have been greatly helped if the collection has tried to forecast their needs or to contain a genuinely balanced and comprehensive stock. Teachers are busy people, and it is easier for them to judge the likely effectiveness of an item if it is available on the spot for them to examine, or if at least something like it (perhaps in the same series) can be consulted.

Where it is hoped that a substantial measure of student participation will be encouraged and developed, it is far less easy for the teacher to predict what will be needed. The work may take an unexpected direction; a group of students may surprise us by the topic they adopt; and there may be a greater variety of topics chosen than the teacher had bargained for. Moreover, if students are to have the chance to choose, they need an introduction to choice: what *can* they choose, what *might* they choose, what are the possibilities? Schools need to provide the resources for them to find out, examples of different topics and treatments. As Holly reminded us, the typical working-class child is *not* freed simply by the removal of supposed restraints, because he has no consciousness of possibilities nor understanding of what freedom entails. One of the prerequisites for participation is an information-rich environment, however provided.

At once our Practical Teacher from the cynical end of the staff room sits up bristling and talks sarcastically about economy cuts and shortage of finances. 'Information-rich environment indeed! What are we going to have, the British Museum?' But it is precisely because there are, and probably will be for a long time, severe economy measures in British and other education systems that selection is so serious a matter. To make the best possible use of the financial resources available to us, we cannot afford the kind of haphazard purchasing that was often typical of schools in the past. We must plan and buy carefully, bearing in mind the many varieties of objectives that may characterize our needs. Eleven possibilities have already been cited, and they certainly will not be the only ones that perceptive teachers can conceive. Moreover, each objective must be seen in relation to a multiplicity of major subjects and subsidiary topics, and to a whole range of mental ages, reading skills, intelligence scores, personality types, media preferences and social and other backgrounds.

This is, at first sight, an intimidating task; many will wonder whether it is possible of achievement. Certainly so far as audio-visual materials are concerned, L. C. Taylor has voiced his own doubts in a note at the end of his seminal book *Resources for learning*:

> In some American schools the library has become a multi-media resource centre . . . an alluring prospect but wasteful . . . Materials in the new media . . . cannot sensibly be bought, like books, on the principle that someone will doubtless find them useful some time. (L. C. Taylor 1972: 283.)

One's response to statements of this kind is to feel that they miss their target by mistaking the nature of what is proposed. Audio-visual materials are bought by schools for a variety of purposes, and it is unthinkable that their purchase should be stopped or slowed down. On the contrary, because of the usefulness of such materials in giving immediate impact, in providing information which is not readily available in other forms, and in catering for the needs and interests of particular types of child or varieties of handicap, among so many other reasons, one hopes that schools will wish to buy rather more. But while they are in the school, it is highly desirable that they should be used as fully as possible, and it makes excellent economic sense to try to maximize their contribution to the school's learning achievement by regarding them as part of a total collection, indexed in the library resource centre and available for individual or group study as well as for occasional use by the teacher in class.

It is very easy to exaggerate the expensiveness of the 'new' media. The cost of simple viewers for individual use of slides and filmstrips is modest by any standards, and the materials themselves are often cheaper than books, though it must be admitted that they carry, generally speaking, much less information. The experience of many British schools has shown that tape recorders, filmstrip projectors and record players can readily and conveniently be shared between classrooms and library resource centre, again maximizing use without greatly increasing the equipment stock. At present the expensive 'new' media formats are videotape and 16mm film (not to mention 35mm), and it is notable that purchase of the latter in American schools tends to occur either in very wealthy areas or in very large schools some distance away from major centres of population, for whom expense of money and time in film hiring would be comparatively high. Neither situation is the case in the United Kingdom.

There is a great deal to be said for the economic provision of a selected number of really well-made learning packages, of the kind Mr Taylor's book proposes, and whose usefulness was investigated in some detail by the Nuffield Resources for Learning Project. No one need quarrel with that, and their selection should properly be in the hands of the teaching staff because of the major role such packages would play in the curriculum. It has been characteristic of the use of some learning packages and kits, none the less, that their components have been listed and sometimes cannibalized for other purposes: and any package containing a variety of individual items, some of them in audio-visual format, might well find its contents being used in ways very different from those which the package designer had in mind.

Meanwhile it is important not to misunderstand the point we are discussing. An information-rich environment is not one that is restricted to the library resource centre, any more than it would be restricted to one classroom in the school. In discussing the selection of materials 'for now and later' we are discussing the total collection of the school, wherever it may at any one time be housed or normally situated. The outlook and skills of a librarian, viewing such a collection as a whole and looking for its necessary growth points, are just as relevant, no more no less, to such a total collection as to a collection housed, maintained and even corralled in the library. American teachers and librarians have an expression for it: 'the library without walls.' Every member of the school's professional team is concerned with its selection. But the usefulness of considering the collection as a whole will be easily evident when one considers the teacher faced with the choice of purchasing a number of similar items for a particular instructional purpose. Each item would meet a number of his ordinary criteria, and he will perhaps hesitate between them; if he is considering the item's usefulness to others as well as to himself, for other purposes than his own, he may well find his hesitation is over.

Teachers and librarians of course will have writhed at Taylor's suggestion that books in a school might be bought 'on the principle that someone will doubtless find them useful some time.' This may sometimes happen when the selector is hurriedly spending the remaining few pounds of the library grant, or snatching what items he can from the public library's travelling van in its fleeting moments of rest in the school playground. It ought not to happen in any school where responsible attitudes to collection-building prevail. Items should be acquired because their use can be reasonably forecast in at least general terms. In the early years of this century, a 10-year-old American girl describing her library wrote: 'In the library there are three kinds of books. Books people like to read. Books people do not like to read and books people never will read.' (Hudson 1963: 40.) No doubt the educational process will hope to reveal unsuspected pleasures in the second and third of these categories but it will be apparent on reflection that any item, book or non-book, which is to be used in enquiry or non-prescriptive work, should have at least some nominal element of attractiveness. In the hallowed phrase, we must 'start from where they are'. But this does not and should not mean that we fill our classrooms and library resource centres indiscriminately with items that are 'just about their level', any more than we would throw in handfuls of slidesets and background books in the simple hope that some teacher or other might find them handy. We need, in other words, selection criteria.

The process of selection has been often enough written about, in books for teachers and equally in books for librarians, and it is worth noting that very similar criteria are laid down for and by both groups. Teachers tend to lay more specific emphasis on the item in relation to specific teaching situations, and more frequently imagine its use in closely supervised and prescribed circumstances; librarians tend to consider the item in relation to their experience of the use of the collection and their examination of weaknesses in its stock. Both however base their purchases on their estimate of needs related to critical examination of available items, and using similar criteria.

We can turn to the criticism of actual items in a moment. First we must consider how we estimate needs. Here the teacher must have the imagination to see the various facets of his subject matter and envisage ways in which, through use of resource materials, the student can be led to their understanding. We saw in the previous chapter how a subject or theme could be analysed into a variety of sub-themes and constituent parts, and how these could be relevant to an understanding of the subject's basic structure, or of its major concepts, or the practice and development of the requisite skills. This analysis must then be related to the particular group of students in question, their abilities, previous knowledge, current skills, and (in any relevant sense) their interests. Both analyses then turn our attention to the relevant resources. What are we looking for? What could we be looking for?

It is useful at this stage to ask ourselves questions about format: the way in which varieties of information source present their contents. In the past, most information not delivered by the teacher himself was conveyed to the pupils through a textbook in the classroom and/or a slightly less rigidly structured book from the library. This had, to put it mildly, serious limitations in the study of music; we can learn 'about' Beethoven by reading, and we can study scores when we are knowledgeable enough, but we gain our fullest understanding of his music through listening (and if possible, playing) and this leads us towards among other things sound recordings on disc or tape. Similarly with foreign language work, there is a valuable reading and writing aspect but our understanding is greatly enhanced by regular and persistent listening. Moreover, illustration in books is now reaching high levels of expressiveness and, where necessary, fidelity, but can normally only be seen by one, two or at most three readers at a time. If small groups are to see the pictures, slide or filmstrip becomes a better medium; and rather than drop our eyes to the foot of the page to read the captions, we often find it easier to have these recorded so that we use our eyes to see what our ears direct us towards.

On the other hand, material which we shall be using for the close study of ideas, figures, and factual data is most conveniently presented in printed or duplicated form, enabling the student to check back, to cross-refer, to scan and to compare. There is no more reason to go overboard for the audio-visual formats than to stick rigidly to the printed book. It may be a matter of the type of information or stimulus conveyed; it may be a question of helping the student to the right response (for instance, if we want him to put something in his own words, it is sometimes a good idea to present the basic information in non-verbal form, through pictures, diagrams or figures); or it may be that we shall be considering the skill to be practised (regular practice in reading is a vital part of the school day for anyone). We might have to consider particular types of student; an immigrant with insecure English may be helped by a visual presentation, or by having a difficult text recorded in slow and clearly enunciated speech, or by having the text presented with visual support on the page. We have all these possibilities and it makes excellent sense to take them into account in our selection planning. We can ask ourselves whether colour is a crucial element, or whether black-and-white will do; we can ask whether movement is involved and how importantly, and consider whether film or videotape are required or whether we can do subtle things with a quick succession of slides.

The weakness of the 'audio-visual' movement of the past was that it tended to concentrate attention on its favourite formats as an accompaniment to the teacher's own exposition (or sometimes, more limitingly still, as an entertaining relief from it), and it is once again stressed here that audio-visual materials can be study materials in their own right, used by the student individually in much the same way as he uses books, and with very little more fuss or expense. But of course this is also true of models, artefacts, specimens and realia, which can be as effective in student use, by groups or individuals, as carefully prepared sequences. The ILEA Media Resources Centre was once asked for a film loop on rabbits, for use in a classroom which had a live rabbit in a cage in the corner; and I remember once, in the United States, seeing a school librarian earnestly preparing to teach a class the parts of a book (titlepage, author, publisher, contents list, index, etc.) by means of a filmstrip, when some 20,000 examples of the actual thing itself were on shelves all around.

A number of formats is of course an effective way to give variety to the work and allow for individual preferences, as well as helping the students to recognize all types of media as possible information providers. (Young children find little difficulty in accepting this latter notion; I have reported elsewhere seeing a junior school pupil turning of his own choice to a filmstrip to help him identify a bird he had just seen, after the book collection was found to be wanting.) There is the further advantage that different students can be engaged in different types of work, perhaps in different areas, as a result. However the printed book has at present the very considerable advantage that it is traditionally well packaged for retrieval and use, with its indexes and contents pages, page numbering and running titles, and its easily portable shape. Producers of filmstrips, slidesets, audiotapes and other formats are hereby begged to take note and pay closer attention to their own packaging.

The materials we collect will be used for most or all of the available learning modes: as aids to the teacher in class presentations, as major information sources in whole-class situations, and as learning sources by the students in their own group and individual work. There are organizational problems involved which we can examine in later chapters; and it may be that among our resources is the index itself, deployed and structured along particular lines to meet educational demands. What should now be clear is the many-sidedness of resource-based learning. Teachers in discussing the method sometimes appear to assume that it acts in only one way: either as a direct provider of instruction which the student is expected to absorb like a battery hen, or as a provoker of frenzied enquiry and endless discussion, the resource centre churning out the over-whelmingly varied evidence for a never-ending debate. But there are some resources which give, interestingly and accessibly, particular units of information – how to spin a cricket ball; how an electric bell works; the journeys of St Paul; the structure of the reproductive system; the varieties of cloud patterns and their significance. There are some resources which stimulate activity of a specified kind – work-cards and the like. There are resources which provoke thought or are objects of study in their own right – poems, models, musical recordings, artworks, specimens. The list is considerable, and some items can be used in many different ways or have aspects which overlap with others. When we select resource items, be they books or whatever, we try to visualize the possible uses and the possible users, and relate them to our overall aims and objectives and to specific circumstances and students.

The practice of selection

Let us now examine the materials that were considered for the 'Creation' project mentioned in the previous chapter. The first format to be used was obviously books, and the Leicestershire County Library Topic Loans Service was able to provide carefully chosen book boxes in consultation with the teachers concerned. The titles were provided in multiple copies, mostly threes or sixes, but sometimes as many as eighteen or twenty-four, according to the nature of the item and its particular usefulness to the work. Titles were collected under seven headings: General (8 titles), Greece (9), Egypt (11), Scandinavia (15), Africa (13), Mexico and Peru (12) and Australasia and Oceania (8). The titles covered a number of different aspects in each area, including myths and legends, art, peoples, history, and travels. The Mexico and Peru section had the following items (numbers of copies in brackets):

Ancient arts of the Americas. Bushnell. (Thames & Hudson)   (3)
Mexican mythology. (Hamlyn)   (9)
South American mythology. (Hamlyn)   (9)
They lived like this in ancient Maya. (Parrish)   (18)
They lived like this in ancient Peru. (Parrish)   (18)
Pizarro and the conquest of Peru. Howard. (Cassell Caravel) (3)
Cortes and the Aztec conquest. (Cassell Caravel)   (3)
Ancient America. (Time-Life)   (6)
Conquest of Mexico (Jackdaw: Cape)   (6)
Everyday life of the Aztecs. Bray. (Batsford)   (3)
The Incas, people of the sun. Von Hagen. (Brockhampton)   (6)
The ancient Maya. Burland. (Weidenfeld & Nicolson:
  Young Historian)   (3)

(This is how the titles were listed in the project booklet, and librarians would normally prefer more detail and consistency of presentation. Note that many other titles may since have appeared.) This gives a grand total of seventy-three titles and 507 copies, to be used over six weeks by about 120 pupils. That quantity of multiple copy provision would be uneconomic for a library or for a total school collection in relation to one, possibly not repeated, theme, and is a clear case for the public library supplementation that was made. The books represented a variety of subjects which would certainly be found in seven or eight very different places in the Dewey Decimal Classification and therefore on widely separated shelves in any library; this brings out the interdisciplinary nature of the theme. It will be noted that although the Genesis account was to be one of the creation stories included, no books about it were included, nor books about the early Jewish people, and one imagines this is based on the assumption that the subject would have been fairly thoroughly treated by the school already and be represented in most school libraries.

Books were not, of course, the only provision made. Twenty-four 16mm films were traced, some of them in local film libraries, the others available on hire from other sources. The films were not included in the project boxes but details of them, including annotation copied from the *British National Film Catalogue*, were given in the project pamphlet. They included historical, travel and geographical films, such as an expedition into an active volcano, an extract from Disney's 'Fantasia', and a dramatization of the Odyssey. In addition, the creation myth from each area was recorded on tape, and the boxes included seven boxes of slides, seven slide packets, a colour supplement and a gramophone record. These items were provided by the Curriculum Development Project, who also added at the end of the project handbook lists of books on other related topics, including the Genesis story earlier mentioned, other mythologies and scientific versions of creation.

To all this material, the schools could add from their own stock, and if they felt it necessary (and had time) could produce further material themselves. A school collection that was at all reasonable would be very likely to have at least some material that was helpful and relevant. If the school had on its staff a person with particular expertise in the field, he or she might well have personal materials to contribute – slides of Greece or Egypt which could be copied and added to the collection, for instance, or a personal account of something seen and visited. Schools in the United Kingdom may well these days have on their staffs teachers from India and Pakistan who could add their own contribution from the culture and religious teaching of their homeland. The scientists missing from the Curriculum Project team probably exist on the staffs of particular schools, and some may have a special interest in cosmology and scientific theories of the origins of the universe. There may also be local people whose interest and knowledge could be a valuable resource and integrated into the work, either in person or through some recorded form.

It is likely that the Curriculum Development Project team, when getting down to the selection of items for inclusion in the project boxes, were presented by the public library service with a variety of items from which to choose. Certainly the process of selection is as much one of rejection as of inclusion. There are many items on the market which are undistinguished, misleading, inappropriate for school needs and sometimes positively bad; publishers and commercial suppliers jump on bandwagons and make grotesque errors of judgement as much as any other aspect of the business world. It cannot always be assumed that every item in a reputable series will be of the usual high quality. Although most teachers, librarians and media specialists will be knowledgeable people with working experience of using and criticizing books and other media, it is useful none the less to consider some of the many factors which will be taken into consideration in the selection process: bearing in mind that selection may be proceeding at two levels, that of the immediate challenge to hand (the course or unit being planned) and that of the overall usefulness of the school's collection in general – as the previous section heading put it, selection 'for now and later'.

Once again it will be helpful to make a list and consider each one:

1. *Accuracy.* The item must give a reasonably true picture of the subject-matter, both in specific factual detail and in overall presentation. This is best judged by subject specialists, and is important whatever the medium under consideration. The idea that librarians will be able to judge books but that audio-visual specialists must judge slides and filmstrips misses the point that a crucial contribution to the selection process comes from neither source but is the prerogative of a person with specialist subject knowledge. None the less it is easy to over-emphasize this, and to forget that subject specialists are found not only on teaching staffs of schools but also in the pages of reviewing journals, not to mention on the editorial panels of some publishers. There are of course simple basic checks that experienced people make when examining an item: one is simply to look up particularly recent or contentious points and see how they are handled or whether they are included at all; another is to compare with a known source whose authority is unimpeachable. Allied to accuracy are up-to-dateness and authority, worth considering further.

2. *Up-to-dateness.* It is unfortunately common for an encyclopedia edition to receive only partial revision, and to contain information which is no longer sufficient. We often forget that this may apply to a filmstrip, some of whose frames may contain (for instance) out of date maps or pictures of ousted political figures. Again we need to check to see whether recent information is included in known instances, and how much revision of previous copy has been made (sometimes the additions are, as it were, stuck on without reference to what has been said in earlier paragraphs); we need to check the bibliographies at the end of sections or chapters, or at the book's conclusion, to see whether recent items are included. Good examples to choose are new names of territories and cities, scientific subjects which have shown dramatic recent change (e.g. quasars, black holes, quarks), technological advances such as space explorations, new aircraft and new processes, and political and social changes. It will be noted in current affairs material how specific key developments, such as the shift of power towards the oil producers, the strength of the trades unions, the spread of economic recession and unemployment, has changed the tone and emphasis of good learning resources. Librarians during their professional education often take part in assessment exercises aimed at developing their detective abilities in identifying inadequately revised items.

3. *Authority.* Another check on accuracy is the item's provenance. There is a filmstrip on writing with an accompanying booklet by David Diringer, and the association of a famous authority of this kind with an item will often be a good clue to its integrity. One looks to see the qualifications of the author, his associations if any with the material at first hand or with universities or other official bodies with research interests in the field. However, although the material may therefore be judged to be reasonably accurate, it does not follow that this is the only criterion that might be used; experts are not always the best people to communicate their subject to young people or to the particular group of young people one has in mind.

4. *Presentation.* We look therefore to see how the material is presented, and this section has many facets worth careful thought. Depending on the subject matter, one looks at the *sequence*, to see whether it is logical or sensible; one looks for *clarity of exposition*, both in overall organization and in actual moment-to-moment narration; one looks for *ease of use*, bearing in mind that one might wish to locate and use a part rather than the whole; and one looks for *unity of parts*, meaning that where verbal, visual, oral or other materials are present in combination (as with an illustrated book, a tape-slide sequence, or a film) they are equally relevant and of equal quality.

5. *Relevance of presentation.* This has two aspects at least: is the presentation relevant to the subject-matter, and is it relevant to the pupils and purpose in mind? I once came across a slide-set on the Impressionist painters which was admirable in choice of examples and in the detail given in the accompanying booklet, but was in black and white! The way in which one would present a subject to well-motivated university students, and the way in which one would attempt the same subject with ill-motivated 15-year-olds whose only desire is to drop out of the whole educational system, will be very different. However, one always takes into account varieties of use; the latter student may sometimes be induced to use an item for specific contents if the class-work itself has been the motivating force, so that even if one can never envisage him reading it through for himself, there may be occasions when it would still be a good purchase with him, among others, in mind. This is true sometimes in relation to number 6.

6. *Vocabulary level.* The main rule here is that a book or item should not normally be below the vocabulary level of those for whom it is intended. It may not matter if it is likely to stretch some of them a little, so long as it is not absolutely beyond them. However, vocabulary level becomes a crucial difficulty for students whose reading age is significantly below their chronological or developmental age. A 15-year-old is insulted if the only material he can decipher is *Janet and John*. Equally, a student for whom English is a second language may lack the broad vocabulary necessary to read stories and non-fiction books at his proper level of interest; there are simplified classics, for instance, for such students, admirable so long as they are used for their stated purpose, and not as short-cuts by other students for whom the original texts are with a little effort perfectly accessible. So far as imaginative literature is concerned, most teachers and children's librarians know that a well-told story can be enjoyed even when some words in its vocabulary are mysterious and advanced; there is nothing simple about the language used by Beatrix Potter, while in contrast the main reason for disquiet about the hugely popular stories by Enid Blyton is that her vocabulary (and her emotional range) is consistently below the level of her readers.

7. *Age level.* This is a matter of emotional and physical development, and with other factors coming into the concept of maturity. It is clearly linked with the problem of vocabulary level already mentioned above. A highly gifted 9-year-old will have the technical facility to read *Lady Chatterley's Lover* but is most unlikely to be ready for such an experience. One feels similarly about certain illustrators of books for children (and some designers of charts and posters), that their concepts are more suitable for sophisticated adults in Hampstead than 11-year-olds in Rochdale or 5-year-olds anywhere.

8. *Technical quality.* This is very important with young people, who are today surrounded with mass-media whose technical standard is usually very high indeed, whatever one may think about its intellectual or imaginative content. One looks at print items and asks whether the print is clear and well placed on the page, whether the illustrations are conveniently placed near the subject-matter they represent, whether the illustrations are well reproduced and whether the colour is faithful and pleasing. One examines the sturdiness of the item – its binding if it is a book, the brittleness of the plastic in the case of a wallet of slides – to see whether it will stand up to the kind of treatment it may be given. One looks at charts to see whether the material presented is readable at a distance (assuming that this is how we want it to be read) and is sensibly organized. One listens to sound recordings to check, not only on the perfection of high fidelity (which may be unnecessary) but on the imaginative use of the facilities of sound recording itself: does a recorded story include sounds, suitable background music, songs and so on, and is the text read in an appropriate accent and with acceptable emphases. (Equally one asks whether sound recording is the most suitable medium in every case: not every recorded discussion between experts is best heard rather than read.) With movie film one looks for appropriate use of the facility of motion as well as for good cutting and high quality of sound and picture; one looks for a sensible use of the ability to add commentary, and to mix images and one asks whether colour is essential or whether black and white will be perfectly acceptable. With any visual material using graphics (including slides and filmstrips) one looks for artistic quality as well as imaginative stimulus, and should be on guard against twee-ness or ambiguity.

All these factors assume, of course, that the item is at least on the face of it worthy of initial consideration: that it is in the appropriate subject area, that it is in a format for which the school has, or will have, equipment, and that it can be used in the circumstances planned or in some circumstances that can easily be predicted. Increasingly we are likely to find that publishers will issue an item in several formats: already we see hardback books simultaneously issued in paperback, and some sound recordings issued simultaneously in disc, cassette and cartridge form, and this development may well increase. Children's stories are now issued as picture-books, or with the pictures reproduced in filmstrip form with an accompanying record carrying the text, and this audio-visual format is very helpful for large-group work or for individual viewing by children for whom reading is a problem or who need a particular stimulus. Clearly if we are thinking of children's own use we shall not buy the AV version if we lack suitable replay equipment, or circumstances in which it can be individually used and supervised; but if we have another use for it this may give us a reason for considering adding to our equipment stock to make fuller use of items we possess only for teacher-dominated display. Selection decisions interlock with decision-making in other fields.

Educational technologists who have read so far will probably be tempted to interject that no mention has been made of the crucial subject of validation. Certainly in connection with the purchase of any programmed-learning unit one should always look to see whether the accompanying literature gives any notion of the size of the test sample and what steps were taken to check that the unit does in fact achieve its objectives. It is one thing to produce a carefully sequenced programme: it is quite another thing to produce a validated one, and this involves an initial co-operative arrangement and the testing of the material with many thousands of students, whose ages, abilities and general characteristics should also be known. To purchase programmed material without such a seal of approval is indeed perilous. This must lead thoughtful selectors to wonder whether we can 'validate' other types of item, and whether there is any way to make the selection process less dependent upon subjective judgement.

In Chapter 1 we had occasion to mention the controversy over the first 'Race pack' produced by the Humanities Curriculum Project, whose efficacy was claimed to have been proved in the classroom by means of the application of an attitudes test. As Christopher Bagley explained:

> The average score of the 60 English boys in the experimental study on the racialism scale was 13.21 before teaching and 11.82 after it. The scores of the 60 control boys actually rose during a similar period, from 13.03 to 13.21 ... What these results show is that the teaching of race relations using the race pack has been followed by moderate unmistakable moves in the direction of the expression of tolerant attitudes. (Bagley 1972: 4.)

This seems to offer the heady possibility that in at least one sphere of teaching activity – the inculcation of mature attitudes – we might be able to measure, not only the effects of our teaching, but the effects of particular sets of materials, so that we were buying guaranteed packages ready to produce socially tolerant and responsible individuals. It is surely not being obscurantist or timidly reactionary to wonder whether this is anything like being the case. Leaving aside the debate on the actual Race pack Mark I itself, on which few of us have the information to make useful comments, we must find ourselves wondering what might be being measured and what other factors might require to be measured for us to make confident statements. How far can the differences between scores of this kind be explained by what some critics will call 'verbal conditioning', that is to say, replacing one set of student articulations by another without much conscious understanding of differences? How much were the students responding to their own perception of their teachers' or their testers' hopes and expectations? What effect does one set of materials and attitude changes have upon other parts of the students' value structures? How many students would need to be tested before we could be sure that teaching charisma, Hawthorne effect, and purely local factors had been screened out, and that the materials would have the desired effect upon a particular class in a particular and peculiar locality?

Let me stress again that I am not taking sides in the Race pack dispute, now in any case very ancient history. But whereas it may be possible to suppose that one can make some sort of measurement of the effects over a period of time of a teaching exercise, it must be quite another thing to be able to measure the specific effects of a particular learning resource. There are too many variables: who used it, knowing what, feeling how, after what experience in what circumstances with what expectations . . .? A carefully programmed item is a different thing; most other resources are loosely structured, may be entirely open-ended, and used for a wide range of purposes and in many different ways. Yet teachers and librarians can and do make judgements on the likely effectiveness of items, and can even be surprised by what happens in practice: 'I never thought that filmstrip would excite the third years as much as it did'; 'Who would have guessed that Gareth would have been stimulated to do all that work just because of that one book?' Would-be censors believe passionately that particular films, books and pictures can have profound effects upon certain users, and such evidence as we have is, to say the least, confused and by no means one-sided. In the United States it is a particularly hot issue, and courses for teachers and teacher–librarians include units on 'the freedom to read' and 'what to do when the censor comes'; the media centre often has a written policy approved by the school board for its own defence. Many of us have views on such matters, but to claim that we have evidence to 'validate' our decisions is, as far as books and materials are concerned, an exaggeration. We are backing a value judgement, with no follow-up longitudinal studies.

This does not mean however that the selection of materials is a once-and-for-all operation, that an item once chosen is retained, or retained in its original form without emendation. The great advantage of audio-visual items, resource packs and multi-media kits is that they can be added to, amended, altered and revised as the need to do so makes itself apparent. Many of the Nuffield and Schools Council project kits were issued on the understanding that teachers in schools would at least supplement them with local materials, and many schools have gone so far as to replace individual components. The same may be true of commercially purchased items. Filmstrips may be cut up and mounted as slides because some frames in the original are judged less useful, or in order that extra frames locally produced may be added to the sequence. Accompanying booklets may be recorded on cassettes, and sometimes teachers have added entirely different material so that a particular filmstrip is used by the student with a local, specially slanted commentary related to his personal needs. Portfolios of the Jackdaw variety can be amended and supplemented (so long as the results are not re-sold), and the use of books can be at least regulated and co-ordinated by well-prepared work-cards which quietly direct students away from difficult or problematic chapters. Such activities place the teacher in the active mode, enabling him to act creatively in the planning process and freeing him from slavish dependence upon national and commercial sources. 'Those people from London' are more valued now that we can supplement and alter what they produce for us, and rightly so.

We can, of course, welcome whatever information can be obtained about the effectiveness of learning resources in practice, and any research which can be mounted to enable us to make measured judgements of a more specific kind, 'validations' of the kind educational technologists talk about in connection with programmes and lessons, will be most helpful. In the meantime, our safeguard is our productive capacity to improve and amend what we already have. We are not dependent upon outside sources to answer all our needs, fortunate though we are in having so many of them well met for us. It is impossible to consider a school's selection policy without at some point paying careful attention to one of its modes: local production. The resources production unit is one tool or facet of the selection team. We must examine production with more care along these lines.

Before we do so, however, there is one aspect of selection we have not yet touched, and it is one where the teaching and librarianship professions can most effectively work together. We must look at the whole question of selection tools and information sources.

The sources of selection

It is all very well laying down criteria for materials selection, and giving instances of the kinds of resources which might be thought suitable for particular purposes by particular schools or projects; it is quite another thing, if you are a busy teacher in an only moderately equipped school, to find out what is available and get some idea, however nebulous, of its usefulness to your concerns. If an item already exists in a school, the teacher can gain access to it eventually through an index or catalogue or stock register, and by physical examination determine whether it is suitable for his purposes. If the same teacher decides to make an item for himself, he believes he has the understanding of his aims and objectives to at least make a stab at it and produce something which will approximate to what he had in mind. But publishers and commercial agencies of all kinds produce considerable quantities of material with schools in mind, and often these items are devised by eminent specialists with excellent technical facilities at their disposal. It makes little sense to spend lonely hours with typewriter and stencil cutter, or camera and cassette recorder, manufacturing one's own rather amateurish study booklets or tape-slide sequences, if somebody more expert with first-rate skills and equipment has already done the job reasonably cheaply already. The problem for the responsible teacher is that he does not always know how to find out what has been produced, he finds it very difficult to lay his hands on specimen copies, he has no ready access to guidance and critical advice, and very little time to spare on the exercise in any case.

The result in many otherwise excellent schools has been that resource-based learning has proceeded using resource materials of much lower quality than the students have been accustomed to seeing and using in other contexts: hand-outs and duplicated booklets that are illegible or badly typed, photographs slightly out of focus or badly positioned, cassette tapes full of gulps and swallows and background chatter, and even videotaped items that are badly sequenced and timed or have patches of deep gloom in the right-hand corner. Moreover the information content is sometimes less than complete (because there wasn't time to check) and is limited and pedestrian in approach because – well, because none of us is perfect at doing someone else's job. And while the quality of these items in the technical sense might be very greatly improved by the provision in the school of a media resources officer, or even a competent technician, there is still the nagging feeling that Longmans or Time-Life or Diana Wyllie might have been able, because they could be full-time on the job and employ subject specialists, to do a much more telling piece of work.

There are plenty of occasions when a locally produced item is valuable and important, and we will look at these in the next section. But the wealth of provision from outside our schools today is so tremendous that we must all wish to take the fullest account of it. There was never a period, for instance, when the printed book for school use or children's own reading has been more sumptuously and more sympathetically produced. We are living in a great age of children's literature, and the poverty of library provision in all too many British schools in this category is quite deplorable and unnecessary. As audio-visual resources burgeon, it is notable that instructional and other non-fiction books have greatly improved in quality, especially in colour illustration; and the material available in slide form from such firms as Woodmansterne has made a splendid contribution to the learning potential of the library resource centre. There has been close liaison between publishers, curriculum development projects and schools, and although some publishers have jumped on the resources bandwagon and produced so-called 'kits' which are no more than rag-bags of unrelated and irrelevant trifles, a great deal of excellently successful multi-media, inter-disciplinary and thematic material has become available to us in accord with contemporary needs.

One of the major differences between teachers and librarians lies in their knowledge of and attitude towards bibliographic and other sources and selection tools. Much of it probably stems from differences of emphasis in training; and teachers may well still be suffering from the 'make-do and mend' improvisatory attitude which has become ingrown in their profession through long decades of inadequate funding and sub-professional support. The typical school in Britain today contains as selection tools a handful of individual publishers' catalogues, odd copies of weekly magazines for teachers, and an occasional (and usually out of date) handbook issued by one or other of the specialist subject teachers' associations. The teacher–librarian may take *The school librarian* every quarter and make use of its admirable book-reviews, but it is unusual for his colleagues to look at it or to know of its existence. An audio-visual enthusiast may take *Visual education* but it is not often that the English department will ask to look at it. Nobody will have heard of *British national bibliography*, let alone gone to the local public library branch to consult it. The EFVA audio-visual catalogues may sometimes be available, but the majority of the staff will not know of them. Moreover, although quite a lot of assorted selection tools may sometimes be available in at least the better-run subject departments, there is very rarely any co-ordination so that other departments or individual teachers can share, or even know that they exist. The work of the teacher is made unnecessarily difficult as a result.

This would matter less if most areas had good bookshops and

audio-visual centres where teachers could go to examine items themselves before purchase. But even in quite reasonably sized towns in Great Britain, the local bookshop if any is likely to have deplorable stocks as far as items suitable for young people are concerned (though it will probably do quite well for best-sellers and stationery) and where can one go to see filmstrips, slidesets, cassettes and multi-media kits? Few towns and rural areas have the equivalent of the ILEA Media Resources Centre, or Wiltshire Public Library's admirable exhibition service of books and other resources for schools.

Ways of tackling this problem fall into three categories, and none of them will ever be entirely sufficient on their own. Within the school itself, there can be a more systematic co-ordination of selection tools and selection advice, bringing together at one point the major sources of information about what is available and the major reviewing sources so that they may be searched and examined. This is essentially a library-like function and would normally be standard practice in an institution with a professional librarian whose co-operation with teaching staff is at all encouraged. Without the school, but still within the local area, inspection facilities for books and audio-visual items can be offered by a standing or travelling exhibition at convenient points. In the United Kingdom, this is probably most conveniently offered by the public library service; in some areas however the library authority and education authority may not be the same (as in the Inner London Education Authority, which includes a dozen or more library authorities) and in North America it will be normal for the school district to offer its own library services to schools. Moreover, teachers' knowledge of available materials can be reinforced by special teachers' centre exhibitions, by substantial printed catalogues of approved items (as is quite common in USA) and by the advisory service. Local reviewing can be organized on a co-operative basis; this has long been happening with audio-visual materials within county areas, although distribution of the reviews (other than through *Visual Education*) tends to be haphazard, and in counties such as Leicestershire the county library schools service incorporates local review comments in a standard exhibition of new books available for inspection at headquarters. Finally, at national level, the organization of an effective system for bringing about complete and speedy information services on all available items, print and non-print alike, can be and must be improved. We will examine each of these categories in subsequent paragraphs.

Let us begin with the school. I have long argued that support for resource-based learning must start there and that any network of co-operative and supplementary services must be founded upon sturdy and active library resource centre organization. What can the school do for itself? One of the major difficulties for school librarians has always been that the cost of the annual volume of

British National Bibliography, let alone its weekly, monthly and quarterly issues and cumulations, took up an uneconomically large proportion of the slender book fund. British visitors look with awe and envy at American high school libraries able to subscribe to *Cumulative Book Index* and often a whole shelf of other bibliographical tools. Arrangements can sometimes be made with local public libraries to receive the superseded weekly, monthly and quarterly issues of *BNB* once the annual volume has appeared, but this is small recompense. An up-to-date edition of *British Books In Print* may equally be beyond the purses of many, despite its usefulness as an authoritative list of available print-form items; the lack of any subject approach is a decidedly limiting factor, and the volume is normally used for the checking of correct titles, publishers, editions and a clue at least as to possible price. If this is true for books, clearly one cannot expect better for items in other formats; if a non-book version of *BNB* with all its subject arrangement and full indexes appeared tomorrow, it is unlikely that many schools would be able to buy it.

We are here in the area of what librarians' jargon calls 'bibliographic control', a repressive-sounding term which simply means the recording of every item published on some sort of national or international list so that its existence can be traced. *British National Bibliography* does a recognizably sound job here for printed books published in the United Kingdom, enabling us to trace the existence of any such item by its author or authors, editor(s), title, series or specific subject. In the United States, as the previous paragraph hinted, there are several publications offering a similar type of coverage. Until British book funds increase very considerably this type of instant access to the major bibliographic control publications (and to any projected systems of what Mr Shifrin has led some people to call 'materiagraphic control') will not be possible within the school. Access to it will have to be provided elsewhere, as will be discussed in a moment.

What the school can do is bring together as much information as it can and organize it. Teachers are apt to speak glibly about 'keeping a stock of publishers' catalogues', without perhaps realizing that there are several hundred book publishers and as many producers of non-book material into the bargain. A complete file of their catalogues can fill a four-drawer filing cabinet and be hard going when somebody asks for 'something on esparto grass suitable for the third year'. A file of reviewing journals such as *Visual Education* and *School Librarian* can be maintained, and reviews from weeklies can sometimes be cut out and stored in files under broad subject headings. Pupil volunteers have sometimes made laborious but useful card indexes of reviews so that they can later be found by teachers when engaged in the selection process. Lists from outside sources can be kept on file and made available; and where publishers issue their catalogues under subjects, with a separate catalogue for such headings as 'English' or 'Sciences', these are handily maintained in subject groups for quick search.

What else is offered within the school depends not so much on the type (and profession) of available staff, as on facilities available elsewhere which can be tapped. The library resource centre can be a most valuable agency of co-operation and liaison with services and facilities outside, and most professional librarians are accustomed to maintaining a network of telephone contacts with specialist sources and other colleagues, as well as a file of answers. But the resources of an area can be maximized when they are (like the school's) co-ordinated and in ways which make it comparatively easy for teachers and librarians to make fullest use of them. Central collections of books and audio-visual resources are fine, so long as all those needing to inspect them can get in without too much difficulty; the ILEA Media Resource Centre for instance is (as I write) handy to a London Underground Station, although car-parking space is practically non-existent. What may work in London however would provide great difficulty in Devon or Cumberland, and if a teacher or librarian has to make a difficult journey lasting an hour or more in order to visit an exhibition collection he will have to feel very keen before he is tempted to go.

This is another case where teachers centres have a valuable role to play, and the usefulness of travelling or changing collections has been hinted at already. Standard selection tools which cannot be afforded by schools might be provided at the centres, together with specimen collections to illustrate particular series or approaches, and alongside a professional collection of teaching-method books and other literature. Local specialist advisers using centres as bases for in-service courses and for curriculum workshops would use such collections and play important roles in their regular supplementation. Where teachers centres do not conveniently exist, a local public library branch ought to find provision of the basic selection tools well within its scope and abilities; one would not expect a public library as such to be a centre for curriculum discussion, but there is absolutely no reason why its premises should not be used for that purpose so long as its other patrons are not incommoded. Indeed, it is no particular secret that the idea of including teachers' centre facilities in plans for new branch library buildings has been at least discussed by library advisers and others in the Department of Education and Science, and there are many good reasons why such a collocation might prove a useful and productive stimulus for co-operation. Otherwise there are often occasions when library branches are officially closed but available for hire.

Co-operative reviewing has been mentioned, and this is an activity which could well be combined with the circulation of subject lists of new materials, book and non-book, from the LEA headquarters or from the central library. Many libraries already issue 'lists of new accessions', and as audio-visual materials, educational games and kits become standard additions to library stock there is every reason for including them on such lists. To collect the regular opinions of viewing groups and subject specialists in the area, and reproduce these comments in an easily usable form, ought not to be beyond the wit of a competent official or typist, and would make a valuable contribution to the selection information held within schools. There are many educational institutions within any local authority area, including varieties of school, college and polytechnic as well as, in some cases, universities ready to co-operate, and their services could be more effectively combined than is now the custom. The value of personal report (especially if it includes an account of an actual teaching episode) is hard to exaggerate.

The generation of lists of available material is of course a typical librarian function, limited usually only by the tight staffing restraints under which libraries typically exist at the present time. The advent of the computer, and the experiments that have proceeded now for many years with Machine-Readable Cataloguing (MARC), make possible further supplementary information services about available materials, which it would be perfectly feasible for a local education authority or public library service to operate, given the appropriate organization at national level. Already the cataloguing data for new books published in *BNB* and the *Library of Congress Catalog* in the United States is made available on MARC tapes to large libraries and other institutions having the computer equipment to make use of it. From a MARC tape, the computer can, if suitably programmed, produce a variety of lists as required: it can be set to produce lists by author's name, specific subject, publisher, illustrator, or date, and if additional data were added to the present MARC II format, it would be possible to produce lists by vocabulary level or age range. Equally, the tape can generate catalogue cards in any specified number if these are required. A local authority could therefore, using the MARC tapes, produce a very complete information service on print-form publications in English, giving anything from a list of books about polyhedra to a complete set of catalogue cards for all the books in a given collection. There would be a price, of course: and in general the service would be most economic where it generated lists or cards for widest distribution, rather than answers to individual enquiries. There is no reason inherent in the system to preclude feeding into the computer summaries of review opinions, so that when required the computer could be programmed to produce lists with evaluations attached, as well as lists without evaluations when these latter were not called for.

Such a possibility has existed for several years now, in theory, for printed books. It was the joint concern of the British Library and the Council for Educational Technology to investigate whether it was feasible to produce such a system for non-book materials, and a joint study was established which reported in 1975. The study, undertaken by Mrs Olivia Fairfax of CET, investigated all the current ways in which non-book media were listed and recorded, including the services of the Educational Foundation for Visual Aids as well as the producers' catalogues, specialist bodies such as the British Film Institute and the British Institute of Recorded Sound, and multi-media libraries such as the ILEA Media Resources Centre. It looked at, and regretfully discarded, compulsory legal deposit privilege (by which the British Library currently receives as of right one copy of every printed item published) which some people have suggested could be applied in the non-book field as well. A co-operative system was envisaged in its place, drawing together from all current sources the information about new audio-visual and other materials and feeding that information into a data storage unit which could generate a tape on the MARC II model. A university, public library or local authority could then by use of the tape generate its own lists not only of books but of other materials.

It will be several years before such a scheme can be mounted in complete form; it does not help, for instance, that the field of non-book materials production almost totally lacks the traditions and conventions of book publishing, and that many producers do not even think of themselves as 'non-book publishers' at all, but simply produce materials as an offshoot of other activities. None the less, the British Library and CET have sanctioned a two-year pilot project, aimed initially at the education market which probably offers the most clearly identifiable single group of likely users at the present time. Much will depend upon how successful this pilot experiment is; if it catches on, we may see a British breakthrough in the provision of major selection tools for British teachers and librarians. (Fairfax 1976)

It will be observed that the beauty of the above scheme is that, so long as a similar format is used in the entry items, the tapes could be used to generate lists of both book *and* non-book items, giving a complete bibliographic and 'materiagraphic' guidance service on demand. Those of us who have campaigned within the profession of librarianship for all items to be treated simply as information sources without unnecessary distinctions between print and non-print have cause to be gratified.

The virtues of a national scheme for storing catalogue data of all book and non-book items on machine-readable computer tape do not simply reside in the undoubted virtues of tidiness and service to scholarship. It has been shown that copies of the tapes placed in regional or local centres could generate a wide variety of lists and catalogue cards, which could be used at any level of operation within the area. Lists could be updated regularly and provided to all schools, with a consequent leap in efficiency as far as precision of selection guidance was concerned. Catalogue cards generated centrally could be fed into schools as required, freeing the teachers and librarians from housekeeping and recording chores and allowing the librarians in particular to concentrate on subject analysis and utilization rather than descriptive listing. We shall examine this aspect more thoroughly in the cataloguing chapter.

Cynics and sceptics are likely once again to be scoffing at the vision presented here of a unified information service, giving access to data about all available materials in whatever format. The computer, it will be said, has let us down before, and like most wonder machines of its type has had greatly exaggerated claims made for it by its advocates. In this particular instance, however, there is good reason to believe that the vision is entirely practical. The computer is increasing in its usefulness and local authorities already use them in a wide variety of housekeeping and administrative activities. But computers are expensive if under-used; the MARC tapes offer a wholly utilitarian way of keeping the equipment in full use. Already in the United States, such practices are in regular operation, not only with MARC tapes but also with the information on educational materials stored in the ERIC system, as was mentioned early in Chapter 3. The extra expense might turn out to be minimal; the increase in efficiency, and in the ability of the teacher to select well and properly, could be very considerable indeed.

6 Production: the Creation of Resources

Production: one mode of acquisition

Curriculum planning necessarily includes an element of materials creation, either to supply stimulus and source material that is lacking from elsewhere, or to supplement existing resources in order to match more closely the needs of particular students or a particular teaching situation. Teaching is an individual affair and few sets of materials produced by others exactly suit our wishes. Moreover with the rapid expansion and re-creation of knowledge, textbooks and other items become more rapidly out of date than we find comfortable. The resource-based learning movement has brought with it a proliferation of local production and whatever one thinks of some of the products there can be no doubt that to produce materials oneself greatly concentrates the mind on objectives and method.

At the same time it is impossible not to feel some concern. To begin with, a great deal of the production work has been in reprographic form, the churning out of innumerable work-sheets and pamphlets, many of them reproducing what was much better presented in book-form in the school library, and quite often without regard to the necessary requirements of copyright law. In order to break away from the tyranny of the traditional textbook, the teachers produced textbooks of their own on the duplicating machine, the major difference being that their technical quality was very much lower. The child used to seeing admirable graphics on television, and reading splendid books with superb colour illustrations, found himself handed smudged pieces of ink- or spirit-duplication on which grey masses represented what had been excellent half-tone photographs, and in which press cuttings mingled with book chapters and the teacher's own irregular typescript to form a curious and baffling amalgam, the main characteristic of which was the need to carry it grubbily around in the hand during a series of prolonged afternoon sessions until it disintegrated. Leslie

Ryder put it tactfully: 'The latest forms of equipment encourage "do-it-yourself" approaches to materials, but we must guard against exposing our students to an excess of second-rate domestic material no matter how sincere our intentions.' (Ryder 1972: 30) It is a characteristic of good school work with resources that teachers' own productions significantly increase in quality as their experience grows, and this is particularly noticeable in schools where a deliberate in-service programme is in operation (as at Codsall Comprehensive School during the early 1970s) or in areas where a local adviser has been pursuing active programmes of curriculum discussion (as at Dudley Teachers Centre in the same period). One does not wish to stifle the creative energies of the teacher, and a certain amount of initial fumbling and fudging may be tolerated if the prognosis (as it were) is good. The situation of the average teacher is not one that is immediately conducive to high-quality work, and it is unlikely that the courses undertaken during preliminary training, at colleges and university departments of education, contained much consideration of resources production techniques, or of curriculum building in the broader sense. The teacher needs help, advice, guidance, encouragement and support, rather than destructive criticism; but we must still ask ourselves what that support should be, and what kind and level of guidance needs to be given.

Within schools, responsibility for oversight of resources production may be in the hands of a variety of types of person. Many British schools, particularly in the English provinces, have appointed a senior teacher to a post labelled Head of Resources, and we saw in Chapter 2 that this person covers curriculum planning in the school as well as exercising overall supervision of resources production and the activities of the library resource centre. Such a person has a leadership role, and may be appointed at what in Britain is Deputy Head level, implying a senior level of responsibility and a concomitant high salary. The knowledge and background of a Head of Resources will usually be in teaching, rather than in resources creation or librarianship, although he may have gathered other useful experience and even qualifications along the way. A Head of Resources can stimulate good resources production, and can combine helpful criticism of materials with advice and guidance on methodology and lesson planning, with the limitation that he cannot of course be a specialist in all the subject fields involved. That aspect of the work must be left to the Heads of subject departments. The disadvantage of the Head of Resources is not only his frequent lack of specialist design training, but also the very heavy responsibilities he will have within the school, meaning that the amount of time he has available to discuss with individual teachers can be very limited. Within these constraints, there is no doubt that a well-selected person can have a galvanizing effect upon a school's work and make a valuable contribution to raising the level of curriculum planning and materials production; there are some splendid examples at present in posts in Britain.

The Inner London Education Authority has, in Britain, pioneered the training and appointment of Media Resources Officers; we saw that his work has an important element of advisory work on production and also, where suitable, the actual creation of materials themselves. The MRO has special training in graphics, audio-visual materials, and educational design, among other things, and can give informed advice of a kind that the teacher Head of Resources may well be unable to provide. He will know a great deal about layout, about the proper exploitation of sound recording, about the selection of different reprographic processes, and about photography. Some MROs have been teachers, or have undergone courses of teacher-training, although the salary structure usually does not encourage teachers with the length and level of teaching experience typical of a Head of Resources to apply for MRO positions; where an MRO can draw upon teaching experience, it is rarely very extensive or senior. None the less MROs can provide much more than purely technical advice, and teachers consulting them about the planning of courses as well as the supporting materials frequently find they receive helpful comments. A school with an MRO ought not to tolerate the production of second-rate resource materials. Once again, the advice on subject matter remains the province of the Head of Department.

Other schools outside the ILEA have sometimes appointed technicians with art college backgrounds, and many such colleges or departments now include courses in educational design. The purely technical expertise of such people is usually considerable, and where they are fully integrated into the staff planning of the school they have effective contributions to make. The Exeter University Institute of Education Regional Resource Centre found itself able to make very full use of the skills, imagination and time of students from a local college of art and the experience was profitable for both. Few schools in Britain can at present afford to employ them, although it is fairly common for schools in the United States to have a design technician working on audio-visual and reprographic production for the faculty; in some Wisconsin schools, for instance, the production area adjoins the library, both merging in an Instructional Materials Center or Media Center. The Media Technician will often have taken a few credit courses in education at university or college, and may even be required to continue doing so, although he will not normally be required to take the type of balanced course including practice-teaching that would lead to full teacher certification.

While considering ancillary staff, however, we should not overlook the simple but often effective advice given by the secretarial or

clerical assistants whose duty it is to type the stencils and use the
duplicating and copying machines. We found during the Schools
Council Resource Centre Project that previously unqualified ladies
could, when given simple preliminary instruction in the workings of
stencil cutters, heat copiers, offset litho machines and other equipment, give simple advice to teachers (when requested) on choice of
process, reproduction techniques for high-quality pictures, and other
technical matters of this kind which are by no means common
knowledge amongst teaching staffs. Usually these people lacked the
authority, and the temerity, to intervene with unsolicited advice
and guidance (as the MRO or Head of Resources properly can),
nor of course could they comment on content or accuracy. However in in-service training programmes a half-hour with the
reprographic assistant was sometimes a salutary and enlightening
occasion

Other sources of advice and guidance include one's particular
cronies on the teaching staff, some of whom may have artistic or
audio-visual specialisms, and the knowledge that can be gained by
going on courses, either in-service courses offered to teachers by the
local authority, or evening courses offered by evening institutes and
colleges, for instance in photography. Curriculum study groups
linking teachers from a variety of neighbouring schools can also pool
insights. It may be that parents with special experience and interest
can be persuaded to come along and give help for particular
occasions, such as the planning of entirely new and innovatory
programmes.

However the support and guidance necessary for the average
teacher does not only consist of the provision of people who can
advise him when he decides to produce his own learning resources.
What is often overlooked is the rightness or otherwise of the decision
to produce in the first place. The creation of learning resources takes
time, patience, effort, materials and therefore money; the teacher
needs to know, not only what to produce, but when and whether,
and for that matter why. Occasions will differ: for one purpose, and
in one set of circumstances, a teacher may need only to produce an
introductory one-page hand-out, or a work-sheet, or a very simple
set of work-cards needing no very great technical expertise; on
another occasion he may need to supplement existing materials
with a further set of slides, a few separate information sheets and a
local map; on yet another occasion the requirements may be very
much more detailed, because there is so little already available for
the students to use.

The last half-sentence carries part of the clue: what is necessary
must depend, not only on objectives, but on already available
materials. Production is one mode of acquisition and should be
considered as part of the whole process of resources selection for the
school. One creates an item if there is nothing else available that

will do the job, or do it as thoroughly, and the decision to manufacture for oneself should therefore be taken after careful examination of other avenues of supply. It is wasteful of time, materials and
energy to produce what already exists and can be obtained, and all
too often what one produces oneself does not reach the same high
standard of excellence. If we are concerned, as we must be, with the
twin goals of economy and high quality, we must balance our
eagerness to create for ourselves with a readiness to look first for
other sources of provision. As Chapter 2 noted, among the questions
asked by the good teacher when planning a course or a sequence of
class sessions is not only 'What can I make?' but 'What have we
already?', 'What can we buy?' and 'What can we borrow?'

How does the teacher find this out? We have already discussed in
Chapter 5 the ways in which the teacher can be helped with the
selection of materials for purchase, and indicated that this is an area
where further co-ordination of local, area and national activities can
be of great benefit. But of course it is foolish to buy items if one has
them already, or possesses in the school stock materials that will do
a sufficiently good job. It is surprising how often teachers in schools
are unaware of what is around them: not merely what is kept in
other classrooms and departments, for which they can be forgiven,
but what has been regularly on display on library shelves, which
they have not come across or had occasion to find or which they
have simply forgotten. In addition to well-organized and co-
ordinated bibliographic and materiographic sources, therefore, the
school needs to provide, *for its teachers*, excellent indexes to the
materials currently available in the school, wherever they may
normally be kept.

We shall be discussing the nature of these indexes in the next
chapter, but it is worth dwelling for a moment on the purpose of
such indexes and why they should be consulted. The literature of the
resources movement is sufficiently full of discussion of the draw-
backs and difficulties of departmental private enclaves for it to be
unnecessary to labour the point very strongly here, but it remains
true that in present conditions of economy and expenditure cuts we
simply cannot afford the luxury of spending school money on under-
used facilities. Naturally if a particular set of materials is heavily
in use in a particular department or classroom, it should normally
stay there; but any item purchased with public money remains
public property, and if the item is not being used by its major holder
it should be available, under proper safeguards, to others in the
school. The school's indexes should therefore list the existence of
every item in the school, and provision must be made for suitable
negotiations to be entered into for wide use. Thus the teacher may
look in the index to locate material whose existence he would not
normally know of because it was kept in a part of the school he did
not normally use.

Equally, however, the indexes should include the items in the major school collection, which will be that of the library resource centre. These again should be so organized that the teacher is encouraged to cross departmental lines, looking not only in what he regards as 'his' section but elsewhere, bearing in mind the insights which have come to us through inter-disciplinary thinking. We saw when considering the materials on the 'Creation' theme how widely they came from different parts of the field of knowledge, and thus from a variety of places in the Dewey Decimal Classification scheme. The indexes will indicate items irrespective of format, so that a teacher (or a student) looking for material on a specific topic or theme will find what is available in book, filmstrip, slide, audio-cassette, reprographic and film loop form, or whatever else may be possessed by the school. It is up to him to decide what format he might need, not the indexer.

The items he traces may not all be immediately available, but he will wish to examine those that are, so that he can assure himself that they are really what he is after. Does this particular filmstrip really give the detail he wants, and is the colour quality sufficient? How useful is that particular Jackdaw portfolio? Would that book have the approach he had in mind, and what about the illustrations and vocabulary level? The print-form items can be examined easily enough, but the audio-visual materials may need simple equipment for them to be scanned or sampled: a lightbox for slides and film-strips so that at least the general contents and colouring can be tested; a tape recorder or player for the sound recordings; perhaps a viewer or projector. In a library resource-centre where these items are available for use in a private study setting, this will be easy enough to arrange, but if this has not been achieved there may be problems of locating the viewing and sampling equipment. Quite often this needs only a minor re-organization, but it does need advance planning to be effective and to attract the teachers to use the service freely.

Even when he has examined what is already available, and what he can purchase through school funds, however, the teacher has not completed his reconnaissance. Items may perhaps be obtained on loan, under circumstances that would be perfectly acceptable to him and save the school unnecessary expense. We saw with the 'Creation' theme that multiple copies of some books were supplied by the public library, and there may be museum exhibits, art prints, archive specimens and audio-visual materials that can be obtained from one or other of the supportive services. Access to whatever public information is available from these services can be provided through catalogues and handbooks, as well as the experience of colleagues, but if external borrowing is normally arranged by one specific member of staff, this person may well have accumulated considerable experience of the kinds of materials which are readily available and likely sources. A talk with such a person would be an important part of the planning search.

That person could well be, perhaps should be, the organizer of the library resource centre, in other words a person acting as and using the skills of a school librarian. It is noteworthy that in the United States the person who would have been called 'school librarian' in the days of the traditional book library now typically bears the title 'media specialist'. This has sometimes confused British teachers and librarians, reading about or visiting American school media centers. The latest set of American standards, *Media programs, district and school*, jointly devised and approved by the American Association of School Librarians (a division of the American Library Association) and the Association for Educational Communications and Technology (formerly the Department of Audiovisual Instruction of the National Education Association) and published in 1975, distinguishes between media specialists, media technicians and media aides; the media technicians are concerned among other things with materials production, and the media aides with clerical and secretarial support, but the media specialists act principally as fully and dually qualified teacher–librarians, advising on available materials from whatever source. We may quarrel with the use here of the word 'media' (for a teacher or pupil does not simply choose a medium but a specific item within that medium) but differences of language need not hide the importance of what is being advocated and described.

Let us presuppose a well-organized and staffed library resource centre, to which the teacher turns for guidance in his own planning. He has to decide whether materials exist, of the right kind and in sufficient quantities, for his pupils' work, or whether he must buckle to and create some of his own; but he may not have reached the stage of articulating his decision-making in this way. He may well announce what it is he plans to manufacture; alternatively, he may begin in the traditional style, 'What have you got on – – –?' The task of whichever person it is who greets and deals with him is to relate back to the context, and step by step to identify the objectives and the true problem. A specialist in curriculum materials design (by whatever title) would certainly respond to a statement like 'I want to make a project booklet on the treatment of the criminal' with questions such as, 'Who is it for? What is it all about? How are they going to use it?' and 'What is the main purpose of the booklet?' He would probe and analyse, and would be concerned not only to help the teacher to produce his booklet but to decide whether the booklet was the ideal form or whether some other type of material might be more suitable. This is very much the kind of advice a teacher values, because he may well not have hit upon the best solution first time.

On the other hand, the teacher–librarian handling a teacher's request might be thought to be behaving in a totally different way.

This is not so. Let us go back to the teacher who is planning something on the treatment of the criminal. He may come directly to the point: 'What have you got on the treatment of the criminal?' or he may ask, 'What is there on prisons'? or just as likely, 'Where is the crime section?' The basic training of a reference librarian teaches him or her to 'hold the reader in conversation' and to probe the background and context of the request so as to distinguish his real need, which is usually not quite what his initial question asked or implied. What the teacher is basically asking, in fact, could best be phrased as a statement: 'I am planning a course unit on . . . with students in . . . class; I want materials on . . . subject matter which they can use in order to . . . What can you offer?' The librarian first turns to the school's stock, showing the teacher if necessary how to use the indexes and suggesting relevant topic headings or areas of the classification worth searching; if these do not suffice, he turns to major bibliographic and materiographic sources, to identify items that could be purchased (this assumes, of course, that the teacher's enquiry has come in good time), and an experienced librarian is likely to know particular publishers or producers whose individual catalogues are worth examining, as well as specialist lists that may have been produced; even if these produce likely examples, the librarian may still pause, and consider his experience of local libraries, museums, audio-visual departments and so on and the possibility of obtaining items on long loan, as well as looking at film catalogues for materials on hire. It is this sort of advice and guidance that a good materials consultant, 'media specialist' or teacher-librarian can most helpfully offer. The result may be that the teacher decides that production of a project booklet is no longer necessary.

On the other hand, if he feels the booklet is still necessary, or identifies some other production need, again the librarian/materials consultant/media specialist can help, in the identification of contributory material, as well as with discussion of the likely interests and needs of the students in question, seen from the particular vantage point of the librarian's observations. The design of the new material will have to bear in mind many of the points that a teacher or librarian uses in selection of already published material, considering content, level, sequence, format, quality and many other factors. To produce an item, in fact, is an excellent exercise in the principles of selection, and the reverse will also be true if the selector thinks himself carefully into his problems. If a teacher–librarian, in fact, is unable to discuss with a teacher some of the major points he would need to keep in mind in the production of an item for use with pupils, then he or she is equally incapable of taking part in the selection process; the two operations are intimately linked and make use of similar insights and concepts.

This is underlined by the experience and testimony of many

librarians who have in fact at some time or another found themselves producing or acting in an advisory capacity for producers of materials. Mr Bernard Chibnall is one such: a professional librarian with public library and film library experience, who is currently in charge of the Media Service Unit in the University of Sussex. (The Unit is, incidentally, a division of the University Library.) Mr Chibnall's job is to discuss with university faculty audio-visual and other materials they wish to have produced, and in full consultation to see that suitable productions are provided. He has found the basic discipline of questioning and consultancy to be remarkably similar at every stage of his career:

> It is now becoming clear that there is an underlying common philosophy in the work of libraries, resource centres and production units. They are all concerned in one way or another with organising information. In the process of doing this they must be particularly concerned with the attitude of the user and perhaps the most interesting thing of all is that the process of organising materially assists in its understanding. Thus, the resource librarian helping an enquirer is not only providing answers but is adding to the enquirer's understanding. In an exactly similar fashion, a film director, television producer or materials designer, because of the questions he will have to put to the subject specialist will also be enhancing the specialist's understanding. (Chibnall 1976.)

Once again it should be stressed that I am not arguing that the present training and qualifications of librarians in Great Britain are necessarily all that may be required of a teacher–librarian in a school library resource centre, nor am I arguing that other professional qualifications and experiences are unhelpful. It is however not a matter of common recognition or acceptance amongst teachers and media resource officers that librarianship training and experience have so useful a part to play. One of the constant surprises of any investigation of the resource-based learning field is the truly interdisciplinary and inter-professional nature of its implications. Anyone working in connection with resources work will find the training and experience of a librarian relevant and helpful to him; this is, as we shall see later, why the 'dual qualification' increasingly regarded as necessary for a teacher–librarian should be full and complete in both aspects.

Production: methods and media

This preliminary discussion of teacher-support, and the contributions of different types of personnel towards it, is of course only a beginning to an elucidation of the full problem. Having established that production cannot be considered in isolation from either curriculum planning or materials acquisition and guidance, we are still left with the questions of what types of material teachers are most likely to wish to produce, what purposes these may serve in the learning process, and what the most useful media currently are to achieve these objectives. An enormous proportion of the teacher-produced materials churned out to support resource-based activities in Great Britain have been print-form reprographic items, a fact that has been disconcerting to audio-visual advisers as well as to audio-visual propagandists in the library profession. Five hundred years late, teachers have caught up with Gutenberg. It sometimes seems that the so-called 'resource-based revolution' is little more than a revival of the Dalton Plan plus the electronic stencil cutter: replacing 'chalk and talk' with the badly printed handout, and daringly supplementing the old-fashioned book with . . . the old-fashioned work-card. Perhaps we have all misunderstood what is happening?

To begin with, there can be no doubt about the handiness, the comparative simplicity, and the frequent relevance, of duplicated materials. The spirit duplicator and the ink stencil duplicator, not to mention offset lithography, worthily earn their place in our schools. As means of conveying written instructions and guidance, which a student can retain while pursuing individual or small group activities, simple reprography is ideal. How else could one as satisfactorily give students a ready check on the terms of their assignment? Moreover, where information or stimulus is best conveyed in verbal terms, stencil duplication is often the best and cheapest method of carrying it to each member of the class, if each person needs to have it in his or her possession or retain it for later consultation. True, there are occasions when duplication may be unnecessary, or breaks copyright laws in an undesirable way; a literature teacher who wishes a class to consider a poem by a contemporary poet, or a short descriptive passage by a contemporary author, may begin by thinking he must duplicate copies to hand round to the entire class, but the creative writer properly objects to this breach of copyright. If multiple copies of the books themselves are not easily available, or are too expensive, the law in Britain does not preclude the teacher from making *one* copy on an overhead transparency, and in a practical criticism class there may be advantages in such a method of display; the teacher can point to particular words and phrases, link up images and concepts visually, and save all the time spent on telling the class to 'look back now at the second line of the third stanza – no, Sandra, the *second* line . . .'

It is less important to be using the latest contemporary marvel than to be using the right means for the desired ends. However, it is noticeable that there are fashions in formats and that teachers and students alike do not always consider (may not always have time and patience to consider) whether the means they have chosen are the most effective, the least time-consuming and/or the most economical of those available. In universities and colleges, for instance, there is a marked tendency for librarians to assume that the best or only medium for providing self-instructional packages in library orientation is the tape-slide sequence; in many cases this may be so, but not always, and it is rare that other media are considered. The same may well be true of the project pamphlet: not only exemplifying a supposed unreadiness of teachers to consider non-verbal methods of communication and stimulus, but also a possible over-protectiveness in bringing too much together in one small package. Clearly neither of these strictures will always be true ones, and there will be many reasons why some material goes best in verbal form and why in particular circumstances it should be gathered together into a handy compendium; everything depends upon purpose, objectives, intentions. 'I want to avoid students saying, "I couldn't find that map, sir" and thus not doing the exercise, and this really isn't an occasion when the ability to find maps is worth practising' – in this case, reproduce the map together with the instructions, for clearly the main focus of the work is a particular type of problem-solving. Where the main focus includes the skills of research and foraging, however, it may be unnecessary spoon-feeding to include too much in their preliminary hand-out. Equally, information may be reduced to the teacher's own words (or somebody else's) when it would be a useful exercise for the student to deduce it for himself through consultation of pictures, maps, experimental apparatus or the environment.

Moreover, some information carefully included in project pamphlets can as effectively (and with less expenditure of paper) be reproduced in large chart or poster form and displayed on a wall. In some cases this might make it easier for tiny details to be included. Some reproductions from newspapers would appear equally effectively on a wall frieze as in photocopied or stencilled form. Sometimes instead of copying out one account of a phenomenon or opinion and limiting the class to its consideration, one could indicate a variety of sources held in reserve in the library or in a box in the classroom which students could choose amongst and compare. Some diagrams used in exposition in overhead transparency form in the lead lesson could stay in that form, available on request, rather than be laboriously reproduced; or one copy could be made in paper form, again pinned on a notice-board or readily available in a file. Some materials gathered together in pamphlet compendia might as effectively be collected loosely together in topic boxes or folders; if the teacher is worried about damage he can always photocopy them and retain the master, and one copy of each would usually be cheaper than thirty. Schools with vandalism problems will prefer controlled issue, however.

There will still be many who remain unconvinced by these arguments, and the duplicated project pamphlet will retain its usefulness and popularity. Carefully set out, with the right mixture of stimulus, information and assignment, it can include material not available in any other form, surrounded by comments and questions relating specifically to the locality or to the child's interest, and representing the particular stance or approach-point from which the teacher wishes the work to be tackled.

For some schools, the duplicating machine is the major and most reliable piece of production equipment, apart from the fibre-tipped pen, and it is understandable that it should be the first thought of the teacher when he considers materials creation. For other teachers, however, particularly if they have for long been audio-visual enthusiasts and prided themselves on being technically up to date, it is the latest, glossiest and most expensive equipment that their critics claim they always turn to. Tens of thousands of pounds have been spent by some colleges of education on closed-circuit television equipment, sometimes at the expense of other departments of the college wanting a simple pottery wheel or an overhead projector in every classroom. There are many things for which television is an admirable medium, but in considering resources production it is important always to keep in perspective one's objectives, needs and economic guidelines. Videotape can be cheaper than movie film; tape-slide can be cheaper than either; but nothing is a true economy if it is wrong for the job.

Thus the design consultant's litany, which we saw was closely matched by that of the reference librarian or the teacher–planner. 'What are you trying to do – what is your major aim? Can you now clarify this aim in terms of individual components – and if possible can you state these in terms of the resulting abilities or skills or behaviours of your students? Now can you relate these objectives to what you already know about these students? What do you see as the sequence of activities, and how does this sequence exemplify or attempt to carry out your objectives? How can we describe the desirable characteristics of the materials this will require?' At each point the questioning will check back to the objectives to see if they have been correctly articulated or need amplification, and will move forward to the next stage in the sequence to see that there are no missing links. An experienced consultant can ask the searching and disconcerting question. Rowntree, in discussing the controversy between exposition and discovery, shrewdly comments:

> Much of the controversy has always centred around confusion of terms. 'Discovery learning' has proved an ambiguous term in many ways, not least in its implications for objectives. Are we concerned with learning *by* discovery or learning *to* discover? (1974: 93–4.)

It is a question of distinguishing between content learning (covering the syllabus') and 'learning to learn' or as Rowntree puts it: 'acquiring the affective strength that will enable them to adopt the inquiry approach as part of their lifestyle.' (p. 95) Rowntree clearly calls for a blend of expository and discovery learning. Such questioning might not be within the competence of any other but a senior and experienced person, and the typical teacher–librarian, media resources officer or production technician may ask the simpler questions without quite daring to go so far. The resources planning will be a collaborative effort between teachers and resources colleagues in friendly consultation rather than neophyte with guru.

As a result of this detailed questioning and consultation, the teacher should already be better able to tackle his task, but he will then need guidance on the application of his elaborated design specification to available facilities and formats. The careful study characteristic of the background qualifications of an MRO is an admirable basis for the giving of such guidance, and few other individuals will, in the UK at present, have the same advantages. One can baldly summarize some of the points here in order to give an idea of what may be involved, with the caveat that one could spend many more pages on the subject (and a book specializing in such matters certainly would do so) and moreover that new facilities are developed so rapidly at present that much of what is said will certainly need supplementation and even amendment in a very few years.

The teacher will normally be advised to consider reprographic methods when pupils need verbal or diagrammatic information or instruction immediately to hand in their files for continual reference. This assumes the duplication of multiple copies, and that all pupils can read sufficiently well or work with someone who can. An advantage of written material is simply that the pupil is not then dependent on his memory; another gain is that he becomes a little less dependent on the teacher's presence and attention at every stage. It should none the less be remembered that very simple instructions can be written on a blackboard, or even on a large chart which can be resurrected on each occasion, with the consequent saving of paper; this is not always a good solution, but it is surprising how often the obvious is overlooked. The material must be carefully written, well laid-out, and appropriately illustrated, and the more important it is as an information carrier, the more attractive its physical presentation should be. Sometimes the effort of making a really effective booklet is so time-consuming that teachers would be well-advised to consider the alternative, a simple work-sheet directing the learner to a variety of well-produced printed and other sources, made available in classroom or on reserve in the library resource centre.

The choice between spirit duplication, ink duplication and offset litho may seem unreal to teachers in ill-equipped small primary schools, but teachers' centres sometimes possess all three and make them available, and there are many secondary schools which have made a similar investment. Generally speaking, spirit duplication is best for short runs of up to one hundred, where the result is not regularly handled over a long period, and where illustration other than line drawing is not required. Ink duplication is excellent for runs of up to five hundred, gives better quality copies and does not deteriorate so rapidly. Thermographic copiers can produce fair quality stencils for ink duplicators, and electronic stencil cutters produce excellent quality reproductions, not only of newspaper articles (as innumerable humanities and sociology resource centres have found) but also tone pictures. Offset litho seems expensive in capital outlay, but the table models do not need specially trained operators and may often be purchased second-hand. This method produces high-quality duplication, on paper which can be written on afterwards in ordinary ink; for very long runs it works out much cheaper than ink duplication, and is an obvious choice at teachers' centres where materials are produced for many schools at a time. A variety of plate-making equipment is available; for many purposes paper plates are acceptable and inexpensive, though metal ones are better for very long runs and very high quality work. All three systems, in different ways and within limitations, can produce coloured illustration, but except for fairly simple diagrams this is rarely as important as the salesmen suggest.

Sound recording is helpful when the subject matter itself is aural, and this includes the spoken word and language, music, and both natural and artificial noises such as birdsong, heartbeats and the detection of radiation. It may be used when the pupil is required to make his own response, by singing, speaking, playing an instrument or typing. It can be effective in the teaching of reading, both to young children and in remedial work with older or adult students. The sound can be recorded on a strip of magnetized tape affixed to a card, as with Language-master work and the recognition of words; on a strip of magnetized tape attached to a slide (Sound-on-Slide); on the magnetized back of a large sheet (e.g. the Talking Page) on which written or pictorial matter is displayed; and on magnetized tape in reel or cassette form. It is not usual for schools to make their own gramophone records, although this may occasionally be of value for special purposes and effects, but the other alternatives to audiotape should be remembered.

Reel tape is generally preferred where high fidelity is required (and in practical terms this is remarkably rare for school work); it is necessary where editing and splicing are contemplated, where the item to be recorded is very long, for instance, over an hour and without a break, and where a master is required from which copies of whole or part can be manufactured. (For instance, a whole morning's broadcasting for schools – later erased when staff have heard programmes and chosen what needs to be retained.) Cassettes are best for individual pupil use, where convenience is more important than high fidelity, and where the handling of a large reel is not desirable. Cassettes cannot normally be spliced, and poor quality ones sometimes break and tangle. The sound quality can be improved by playing the cassette through high-quality speakers rather than the tiny speakers in the average cassette player. Removal of the lugs in the cassette prevents the contents being accidentally (or ever) erased, but this is an inconvenience if pupil response is called for. All tapes should be played through at least once a year, to avoid 'print-through'.

Music and sound effects can be used imaginatively and attractively even on purely 'information' recordings, and attention should be given to pacing and articulation, a contrast in voices wherever possible, the erasure or avoidance of clicks, gulps, swallows and intrusive background noise. It should be remembered that the attention-span for audio-recordings alone is much less than with visual accompaniment, and it is often useful to provide the student with a break for activity in a long sequence. All who may need to examine the tape will value a typed transcription, with timings, and this is useful also for the producer!

Much information is best or helpfully presented in visual form, either for class display or individual study or stimulus, especially when challenging the pupil to elicit from visual sources facts and concepts he then translates into spoken or written words. If the material is to be displayed for a long time, then charts, maps, posters and large diagrams are advisable; they can be used without equipment, and stored vertically in a classroom corner or library. The material should be legible from a distance, uncrowded, interestingly coloured and attractively lettered; nothing is worse than staring for long hours at an amateurish poster. Overhead transparencies are excellent for lecture-display, and the addition of overlays enables sequences and processes to be built up and explained most effectively. Diagrams, maps, flow-charts, verbal headings and certain illustrations can be presented in OHT form by thermographic or xerographic copying processes. The transparencies can also, with caution, be used individually by pupils later.

When considering photographs, it is worth remembering that they come in different forms, each with its value. Enlarged, they make a wall-display and help to give a classroom atmosphere during a lengthy project; black-and-white is just as effective here as colour. For colour photography, prints are useful individually but slides are the obvious choice for class presentation and can be linked to a taped commentary for individual or small-group use in addition to the mass lecture. All photographs should be well produced, with contrast, clarity and avoidance of extraneous clutter, but slides can also be effectively used for diagrams and for written matter (headings, captions, quotations) on their own or in a sequence. Thus slides can even be an excellent means of teaching the use of a parti-cular reference book to a large class, where multiple copies are not available. Multiple projectors linked together can give elaborate displays without periods of blank screen, either with overlapping images or throwing different pictures on different areas of screen simultaneously, and with some equipment these displays can be automatically repeated.

It is possible, though cumbersome, to make one's own filmstrip, rather than a slideset; this allows one unalterable sequence to be followed. Filmstrip can be linked with sound recording, and some-times commercial filmstrips are improved for school use by the addition of a recorded tape in which the teacher makes his own commentary, including whatever is valuable in the published booklet.

When motion is an important element of the content to be pre-sented, or when still photography would miss out important ele-ments, some kind of moving visual presentation is obviously indicated. It is not necessary always for such items to be 'full-length' or even very highly finished and complete, though they should always be good as far as they go. Filmclips, or short portions of video-recording, can illustrate a process lasting less than half a minute and be effective. For school work the three main processes to be considered are 8mm and 16mm film and video-recording in one or other form. In spite of our economic plight, a considerable number of schools now possess video cameras and recording equipment, and many more have access to it; film equipment is also more widespread than many seem to believe, and many homes make their own movies.

The 8mm film is relatively cheap in capital expenditure, and is the medium used for domestic and family purposes. Instamatic versions exist which, within limitations, are almost foolproof, and have been used by young children under minimum supervision. For outdoor work in favourable weathers they allow tolerable results to be achieved, depending on objectives, though they rarely stand comparison with high-quality work shot by professionals on equip-ment of professional standard. For indoor work their effectiveness depends on the quality of available lighting, an expense which must be remembered when planning cine provision. Something a little better than instamatic will give acceptable quality pictures in average circumstances without any pretence at high fidelity. A film loop can be manufactured in the school, and placed in cassette to play and re-play a single concept. Where very close synchronization of sound and vision is not required, it is usually cheaper to accom-pany the film with an audio-cassette sound track rather than go to the expense and difficulty of putting this on the film itself. Recent developments in synchronization have made this an increasingly good solution even for more professional work. 8mm is the usual medium for the amateur, but it should be remembered that instant replay is not possible (as it is with video work) and the expense of filmstock and the time spent waiting for the return of sequences from the development process can be very discouraging.

The 16mm film is usually for professionals, and would be employed by a school, college or education authority which had trained professionals to hand and was ready to make quality productions for extended use. However, it is worth remembering that some schools and colleges already offer film-making courses, and a useful practical exercise for such courses might be the creation of films to order in support of local teachers. Except when the making of a film is regarded as a learning exercise in itself, as with student-movies, it is normally reserved for the manufacture of high-quality items for wide showing and distribution. Detailed editing is possible in a way not at present easy to emulate with videotape, but it is a time-consuming and expensive process.

Video-recording requires a heavy investment in initial equipment, but once this has been made it offers many advantages over film. In most instances, film is ten times as costly as video, which very much makes up for the latter's inflexibility in the editing process. The image is rarely as precise and fine as a good cine image, and it should be remembered that a video image tends to deteriorate in use, requiring regular copying to maintain over long periods. However, video is ideal for motion recording when high-quality finish is unnecessary, when the activity being recorded is impossible or expensive to repeat (as with elaborate scientific demonstrations involving costly materials and processes), when instant replay is valuable (as with athletes, dancers and teacher-trainees, as well as trainee camera-persons) and when long runs are not expected. When the life of a particular item has run its course, the image can be erased and the tape used again for other purposes, whereas deleted film can only be scrapped. Colour video is naturally more expensive than monochrome, and schools and education authorities are considering carefully how important the addition of colour is likely to be; my own guess is that it will be more important than many now think – in contrast to the situation with stencil duplication. As well as conventional programmes, and school broadcasts recorded off-air, pupil-production has important advantages with video and teachers valuing participation should consider carefully whether the instant playback facility may be the motivating factor he requires. Very detailed preliminary planning is advisable, and this can sometimes be a valuable way of involving a whole group in the discussion of the content of caption charts, locations and angles, as well as the gathering of necessary information. Verbal and mathematical skills can be practised and confidence sometimes improved. It is certainly very different from the experience of teacher-exposition or yet more sessions with work-cards. Because television is already so widespread and accepted, there are some who would be prepared to argue the eventual economy of presenting as much as possible of the visual element in learning resources on the TV screen.

Embarking on work of any kind with these very different media involves the teacher in anxiety-making decisions; the pain can be lessened by discussion with informed people with services and experience to offer. It is clear from the account given in Walton and Ruck (1975) that teachers using the Exeter University Institute of Education Regional Resource Centre services valued them for very much more than simple supply and production facilities. What held the network together was not a postal service of request forms but the availability of informed people – teachers' centre wardens, advisers, lecturers, librarians and educational designers. Teachers needed not only the item but the chance to talk about why they might want it and what to do with it; discussion with a resource designer was more than simple instruction on layout; it might be a discussion of educational first principles, or it might be a personal relationship including emotional support in a professionally anxious period. The account of available media given above does no more than sketch some of the major points about some of the more useful formats, and personal experience shows that the subject is virtually inexhaustible; the more one explores the world of resource production for oneself the more insights, doubts, excitements and new possibilities one discovers.

Production: itself an education

If the preceding pages have shown anything, it might be that the task of producing a learning resource very greatly concentrates the mind. Indeed, one of the reasons for suggesting that pupils may, from time to time, benefit from themselves producing something is that the planning, collecting and re-creating procedures necessary bring into play a variety of intellectual and imaginative factors, not to mention practical and artistic skills, and an emotional commitment important to personal development. The teacher, however, needs to be able to achieve a level of excellence that may not always be necessary in the pupil production. His work will be studied by what one hopes will soon become a classroom full of good critics (just as student teachers find themselves evaluating the teaching performances of their mentors). Even the devising of a series of work cards brings into play intellectual and verbal skills of high quality, alert for vagueness and possible misunderstanding, double meanings and absence of meanings. Some commercially produced work cards contain questions which cannot possibly be answered solely by reference to the information on the card, and yet are planned and sold on the assumption that no other source will be available. When the exercise planned is open-ended and allows a considerable element of pupil choice, the need for thorough pre-planning, careful self-criticism and a clear elaboration of what will happen in the case of all foreseeable alternatives is paramount. As a result, the teacher will learn a great deal about lesson planning, about his own methodology, and about his pupils, not to mention the subject matter itself.

It is because of this that many head teachers, advisers and educational pundits have so greatly welcomed the resource-based learning movement. We saw in Chapter 4 that not only was the teacher the prime mover in curriculum planning, but that the contemporary situation demanded more than ever his profound involvement in the process. Systems of education which depend on superb material being produced at some faraway centre, with the teacher acting as a non-participatory mediator, carrying the can for the mistakes but unable to influence the original design, must surely be mistaken, and this was the thinking behind the normal Schools Council method of close relationships between curriculum projects and teachers in pilot schools. Educational publishers have often tried to promote similar liaison. The more the teacher can be drawn into the planning process, the more insights he gains into the nature of the systems with which he is working and the necessary concomitants of improvement and change. If education is to be brought closer into accord with the demands of our time, if schools are to be guided or accompanied or dragged into the last decades of the twentieth century, then the understanding and commitment of the individual teachers is of paramount importance. This may, indeed, be a reason for the disappointing results in some schools in the USA, where very elaborate and remarkable media centers were provided but with minimal results in terms of changes in educational attitudes.

Few teachers have time to create more than a few resources themselves in the course of a year, and it would be unfair and impractical to expect anything else. Moreover, because of the limitations of teacher-produced materials, it is probably desirable that most items falling into the hands of pupils should come from other sources. None the less it is impossible to consider meaningful curriculum development discussions and in-service programmes in which an element of resources creation does not take place, and no teacher can devise resource-based activities to suit the special needs of his pupils in their own locality and with their own special interests and mixture of aptitudes and abilities without some measure of resources production or resources adaptation. In the process, the teacher himself will learn more about his subject, his pupils and the process of education. Production is itself a means of in-service education for the teacher.

The 'educational technology' movement was characterized, as we saw, by a coming together of the programmed learning and audio-visual movements at a time when teacher-production of programmes and materials was excitingly and newly feasible. Their heavy concentration on such typical elements as strict definition of objectives and a carefully systematized series of operations (full of self-checks and capable of being reduced to a conceptually neat algorithm) may well have been influenced by the necessities of production. Programmed learning sequences and audio-visual sequences, as well as more loosely organized work-card and pamphlet exercises, are relatively unfamiliar activities for most of us and we need at each stage to ask ourselves questions about what we are doing. The lists of procedures, the algorithms and the how-to-do-it chapters have sometimes seemed unnecessarily rigid and unimaginative, and it is worth remembering that they are a general guide to the average person, that like all rules and regulations they exist to be broken when they cease to be helpful, and that to the experienced and practised person they become so fully absorbed that they function below the conscious level. Moreover for some people they do not function at all so far as the initial creative process is concerned; students, for instance, are always told when writing essays to draw up a schema first, a framework to act as a guide to later performance, but some of our best essayists do nothing of the kind, and the best tape-slide sequence a student has yet produced for me at Loughborough was created in quite the 'wrong' order according to all the pundits. For some people the rules apply afterwards, as a way of criticizing what they have done. The children's author Helen Cresswell often tells audiences that if she planned in advance what was going to happen in her stories, she would no longer have the incentive to write them; but of course when we read the stories afterwards we look for logical construction, balance and a sense of purpose – and in her novels these are exactly what we find.

What the experienced teacher ought to be able to do, therefore, is state clearly and simply the factors involved in judging a resource, of whatever kind, and relate these to the process of production, and to the process of lesson planning. We often have an instinctive feeling that 'this would be excellent for the third-years'; systematic thought, and the kind of judgement that comes from *considered* experience, helps us to be sure when our first instincts are correct (and for most of us a 100 per cent score would be exceptional). True, we read books and watch films and television, we look at film strips and slides and listen to music and the radio, but we are not always critically involved when we do so and we do not always know what factors we should be particularly looking out for. Audio-visual literacy does not come automatically, and it is clear from the average family photograph, tape recording and overhead transparency that most of us have quite a way to go before we have really mastered it. The average teacher remembers from his training days the so-called 'rules' of lesson preparation, but although he has regular practice in it as far as the teacher-directed expository period is concerned, there is insufficient experience among average teachers in both USA and UK of all the niceties and implications of resource-based extended work. For these reasons it is necessary, not only that teachers should be fully involved in the actual planning of curricula on resource-based lines if they are to proceed with them, but also that they should take part in the resources production side in a quite explicit way: not 'Will this resource be interesting and is it accurate so far as it goes?' but 'Is this precisely what we need for this specific situation or programme?' And this is not going against the view earlier expressed, that the collection of book and other resources in some depth was an important activity not only for now but for later; what is being asserted is that when materials are acquired *by production*, it is better that they should be produced for a specific purpose immediately to hand, so as to limit the expenditure of teacher-time to first priorities, and link the production effort with the generation of insights into the entire process of curriculum development, resources collection and specific production.

In planning a resource item, of whatever kind or format, the two underlying questions are: 'What is its purpose?' (which means what should it do *to* and *for* the learner, and what will the learner be expected to do *with* it) and 'what must it therefore contain and consist of?' Content is related to purpose: it is not just a matter of the information to be included and conveyed, but the effect that information is to have on the target audience, the student, and the activity he will be undertaking while, or after, he uses the resource. The information content will usually be presented together with, and perhaps interspersed with, a required student response; it must be presented at student level, and bear in mind how it will seem from his point of view. Thus it is foolish to produce (as one occasionally sees) a major resource for ill-motivated 13-year-old poor readers presented in the form of many solid-looking pages of ill-duplicated typescript, with a set of instructions for activity right at the end, and requiring the reading of the entire pamphlet before any work can be begun. The teacher trying this out will find 'it doesn't work', and one hopes that he has the understanding to see why, or that a head of resources or some other colleague will be at hand to advise him. Equally, one sometimes comes across the production of admirable but lengthy audio-tapes, perhaps discussing between several concerned individuals some interesting but difficult matter of principle or social justice, and requiring no student response or intervention for as long as twenty minutes. Other teachers over-ambitiously record wholesale the week's school broadcasts from the BBC, admirable though these are, and expect them to be always as suitable for individual study as for group listening and stimulation.

Thus part of the analysis for production focuses attention, not only on objectives and the nature of the information concerned, but also on the learner and what is known about him. 'What do we learn about by teaching History to Johnny?' Answer, in part: 'Johnny' – if we keep our wits about us.

Because much of the rationale behind resource-based learning is concerned with the affective domain, with catching the student's interest and involvement and building up his self-confidence and enjoyment in intellectual pursuits, much of our resource planning will be concerned with presentation, enticement, and the structuring of positive response. This does not mean, and it must not mean, that we neglect proper intellectual standards or seriously lower the level of truth and accuracy. It is one thing for Professor Samuel Postlethwait to begin his audio-tutorial tapes on freshman botany with a casual, 'Hi. I wonder if you've ever thought about . . .?' It would be quite something else for a tape to descend into the level of bathos and inarticulateness that characterizes much adolescent speech.

Unfortunately this is not the only way of standard-lowering. The drafting of work-sheet questions, though in standard or received English, can exemplify a similar sloppiness of thought and lack of awareness of alternatives. Even more so, the pictorial level is very easily neglected. Most of us are still verbal in our responses, our higher education has been primarily verbal and we tend to think that literacy and grammar are only related to the word. Charts, photographs, slides, diagrams, school movies, can descend to levels of visual illiteracy which school pupils themselves are aware of and respond against, though they are not always able to say why. Audio-tapes can be crude and uninteresting, not because the content is inaccurate or verbally dull, but because the sound presentation is tedious, and the teacher's own voice monotonous and over-concerned with message rather than with the attraction of interest to it.

This must not be taken to mean that the teacher retires defeated from the field, leaving all production to specialists who will produce gleaming and highly professional examples. Quite often pupils react against such items, and respond favourably to the personal, amateurish touch. They will happily accept Sir's accent, or slides that are not quite perfect, but they will react against slurred articulation, monotonous speech rhythms, and slides in which the teacher's wife and family block the views of the geological scenery presented, or in which the close detail is lost because of focus or distance mistakes. Tactful advice from specialists, whether teaching colleagues, AV technicians or media resource officers, may be called for, and one has heard tell of some polytechnics where the AV director will not allow items to be projected or played in class that do not meet exacting standards. One applauds the intention but not the execution; guidance ought to be possible without diktat. Given the minimum of help and advice, most teachers will find the designing of transparencies, the planning and taking of photographs and the recording of a short audio sequence an immensely stimulating and educative process, and the next hazard is sometimes that it is enjoyed for its own sake rather than for its results with the students.

It may be objected at this stage that there is much more to the educative value of resources production than simply an improvement in graphic layout and camera technique. This is perfectly true, but we must begin with simple things. Instructional materials on the planning of resource-based sequences and the design of learning resources sometimes amaze the beginner with their flow-charts and chains, their lists of questions and discoveries of unsuspected complications and traps. These are matters that are often best learnt not only in practice but through and after practice; like our pupils we learn by doing and we must start from where *we* are. It is only during the lengthy process of designing a series of resource-based units and the materials to go with them that we begin to grasp the true meaning of the theorists' instructions and codifications. Rowntree (1974: 81) produces an excellent analysis of the behaviours that will be necessary for a student to be able to state the time as so many hours o'clock, one glance at which would (as Rowntree hints) somewhat alarm a newcomer to the methodology. Ten levels of activity in six or seven concurrent columns seem an awful lot to be planning at one time with what will normally be quite young children, yet Rowntree admits: 'If figure 4.2 already looks so complex that you wonder how anyone ever learns to tell the time at all, remember that even now the analysis is incomplete, or at least the objective is fairly limited.' (p. 80) Yet the exercise was not pointless, as Rowntree goes on to explain: 'whether they recognize it or not, the hierarchical principle does enter into their students' learning; and difficulties in learning may well be attributed to neglected steps in a hierarchy that has not been recognized.' (p. 82)

We learn to grasp such apparent complexities, and begin to be capable of our own advanced analyses, when we have experience of grappling closely with the problems at first hand, and although most teachers experience this in the process of their ordinary teaching, there is a sense in which the production and setting of a learning resource becomes the opportunity for a more precise testing of the factors involved.

This is because there may be so many different factors present in an average class teaching situation that it is hard to tease out the key elements that went wrong or needed revision. A learning resource, on the other hand, is a microcosm of a lesson; it is the teacher in little. Producing such a mini-lesson enables us to assess how much information or stimulus we in fact have to give to the students in our own personal presentations, how much we can leave to a resource, and how we can devise ways in which we can be sure that the requisite knowledge is achieved. The resource is an important focus of our attention, and when we have learnt some of the key factors in its designing we shall also be better able to look at somebody else's work, including commercially produced items, and assess their usefulness. The educational effect of production is thus many-sided and has important relevance to other parts of the teacher's work; not only does he learn better how to produce quality items, but also to plan better lessons and learning systems, to select items for the school's collection, and to think his way into the student's predicament and mentality.

Thus the very justifiable feeling (which I share) that, in Shifrin's words, 'there is far too much unnecessary production of materia within schools' (1973: 248), needs to be set against other benefits. L. C. Taylor is perfectly correct to calculate the amount of time necessary to produce a good 'package' and to deplore:

> the ratio between the time taken to produce resources and the time taken by children to get through them ... Willing but burdened teachers cannot provide from their spare-time labours (and without a questionable diversion from other more important tasks) a regular and reliable supply of materials in all the main academic subjects, for successive age groups, designed properly for the direct understanding of children. (1972: 149–51.)

This does not mean that no teacher-production takes place, and it should not mean that the amount of production any one teacher undertakes in any one year, especially when he begins planning resource-based exercises, is minimal. On the contrary, production is an important part both of course planning and in-service education. Ron Mitson from his experience at Codsall and elsewhere concluded:

> What wastage there is in teachers creating their own materials and making mistakes in the process is entirely compensated for by the insights they gain into material production; and their increasing ability to discriminate between high and low quality commercial items, is in itself an investment. (Mitson 1972: 48.)

The aim of school organization must be to make this time problem less without taking away the advantages of the teacher's personal involvement.

The argument has been that teachers, like pupils, learn by doing. We conclude this section by reminding ourselves again that active creative work in the various media formats can itself be a feature of resource-based learning for the pupil. Paul Collis describes in simple terms 8mm film-making by the pupils in a school for the educationally sub-normal in the London borough of Newham. 'The main point I wish to make is that this is not a particularly difficult task, even with children (and teachers) who have little or no experience of film making.' (1974: 10) His objectives were straightforward and unpretentious:

The first intention was that the children should have fun and enjoy the experience. It was hoped that the confidence which comes with success would carry over to other school activities. Apart from the skills acquired in the actual filming and editing the preparation involved a lot of useful thought, discussion and ordering of ideas. Perhaps it is not too much to hope that children who have made films, of whatever quality, will learn something of the film-maker's art. Consequently they will view professionally-made films with a more critical and attentive eye because they will have greater understanding. (ibid.)

In Mr Collis' case, the costs involved were comparatively small; the camera, editor and splicer were all borrowed from the local education authority's supplies section, and the school had only to purchase film and, for one film needing a sound accompaniment, audiotape.

The first film, made by a group of children aged between 8–13, lasted about five minutes and explored the theme of 'Water' without attempting any real 'story'. The group drew up a list of uses of water and situations in and near the school that could be employed; in the process they visited Woolwich Ferry, the ponds at Wanstead flats, fishmongers and fire engines (among others) and this gave them experience in seeking and gaining the co-operation of strangers and the public. They viewed, edited and spliced their shots (re-arranging from the original script because of the results) and made a tape of 'watery music' to accompany the film. The film won an award at a local film festival.

The experience encouraged the school to persevere, and a second, older group made a story film ('Foul Play at Fairplay') where the challenge of having to tell the tale purely in visual terms drew together the first, rather impractical suggestions into something more possible of achievement. The children wrote a full shooting script, including indications of types of shot, and after rehearsals the film was eventually shot, edited and completed. Mr Collis commented:

> The actual film deviated considerably from the script and a lot of editing was required, but the children can now proudly say they scripted and made an entertaining film . . . No-one expects everything a pupil puts on paper to be worth preserving. The same applies to film. (op. cit.: 11–12.)

Still photography and cine photography can be valuable ways of teaching a child to express himself through visual images, which includes not only training the ability to see but also to respond and then create. Where this can be linked with subject study, the two activities can valuably reinforce one another. Nor is visual imagery the only possible area for development; sound and its creative use can be excitingly explored through instruments and tape recorder, and recorded sequences produced which link music, non-musical sounds and spoken language to explore experience and communicate knowledge and feeling. If resource-based learning is only an extension of the old 'library project' on the one hand and a more elaborate version of work-card activity on the other, it is missing a dimension which can itself add greatly not only to learning but to motivation, involvement, confidence and a sense of personal worth. Too often creation is linked to a level of physical co-ordination and talent (for example, the ability to draw well) which many students are painfully aware they will not achieve. Moreover, it tends to be an individual, solitary process. Film-making, photography, sound recording, video-taping, can be achieved happily by smallish groups and involve in the process much more than one set of skills. Determined teachers like Mr Collis are now showing us what is possible – and often with students for whom it could never be said that they began with all the advantages.

7 Information Analysis as an Educational Tool

Nothing sounds duller than cataloguing. It conjures up images of antiquarian pernicketiness, tedious listings of titles and editions, and obsessive concern with collection and stocktaking rather than utilization and promotion. For students of librarianship, it is apt all too often to seem the preserve of those with legalistic or bureaucratic minds, an impression often fostered by an unmotivated reading of some of the major codes which seek to regulate and coordinate cataloguing practice. These rules, overwhelmingly tedious to the non-librarian, are crucial to practice in a library of any size and age, and to a person faced with the responsibility of providing access to such a collection they will become not only relatively comprehensible but a matter of active interest. Cataloguing, indexing, and the whole complex of activities coming under the general heading of Information Retrieval, are vital to the organization and dissemination of recorded knowledge. None the less it would be a safe assertion that for most librarians it was not this type of activity which first motivated them towards their chosen profession.

It is so much more exciting to get at the material, to work with enquirers, to plan buildings and room layouts, to mount displays, to run story-hours and even to have a good chat with borrowers at the issue counter. For teachers, students, and the general public, it is not the catalogue that attracts but the books, the resources, the information, the enjoyment. Few people, certainly few teachers, enjoy looking up in catalogues; they want to get at the materials themselves. More than once I have found, when talking to headmasters and college principals who have sought advice on 'how we should have our resource centre catalogued', that what they secretly hoped for was a system of shelf arrangement which would enable them to do without any intermediate stage between wanting the item and finding it sitting there waiting for them.

The aim of all systems of classified arrangement of course is to make this increasingly possible. Sets of slides on birds, fishes, reptiles, insects and mammals can reasonably be grouped in a section labelled ZOOLOGY or ANIMALS or LIVING THINGS or whatever synonym is most likely to match the terminology of the users, and probably most of them will find them. But if some of the animals are farm animals at least some users will expect to find them in a section for AGRICULTURE, and if some of the pictures of animals are by famous artists, some other users will seek them in the ART department. Some animals have a special religious or mythological significance, and material about them will therefore be sought under those headings. Some animals are eaten for food, some animals are used in sporting events, and some are useful in road transport and military engineering. Most educated people learn to cope with this problem, and the technique of research includes the ability to foresee and articulate the many different possible subject relevances of any specific topic. Any physical arrangement or display is, must be, arbitrary: an administrative decision based on experience of the ways in which enquirers typically approach their problems and upon a view of the supposed 'consensus' of informed individuals. This, whatever their many faults, is the reason for the continued existence of schemes of classification such as the Decimal Classification.

Classified display is helpful, and those resource centres which keep large quantities of material in mere accession number order (that is to say, a purely random numbering dependent on the accident of date of purchase) are denying their users one very effective road to finding what they want. Despite the limitations of the Dewey scheme, a grouping of materials based upon it will reveal at least some items relevant to most requests, and the skilled user who has developed an imaginative flexibility of approach will find more. A librarian who provides a classified collection with a simple classified catalogue of the stock is doing a useful job (so long as he remembers to add an alphabetical index of subjects so that classification numbers can be quickly found) and many librarians have been loudly critical of any suggestion that more help might be possible or desirable. The observed habit of most library resource centre users is to go direct to the shelves; the second is to turn to the librarian for help; by the time we reach the stage of turning to catalogues and indexes, many users have given up or found some other solution.

Yet let us take the example of the teacher coming into the library resource centre to look out material for a project on CATTLE. He knows something of the classification scheme and goes direct to the shelves in the AGRICULTURE section, where quite probably he finds some material that will help. Some of it is specifically about cattle, and some of it is in books and other items about agriculture in general. He is an astute library user, and remembers that not all items are the same size and shape; therefore he checks the oversize books section, and the pamphlet collection, and (if there are separate sequences) the various audio-visual formats, and this results in the location of several more items. (If he is not so astute, he will already fail at this stage to find resources relevant to his quest.) Cattle can however be considered in other contexts; books and other items on individual countries may well include sections on their agriculture and livestock, so he turns to the various sequences (books, oversize, pamphlets, audio-visual . . .) under each major geographical area in turn. Cattle were domesticated in earlier cultures, so he turns to the history sections. Cattle have come under religious taboos, or had special religious significance; bulls are killed for sport in the bullring (and were also killed for ritual purposes in ancient civilizations); cattle were depicted on cave walls at Les Eyzies and other very ancient places, and have been depicted by artists from Constable to Picasso. Moreover, he stops to wonder whether veterinary medicine would be found under FARMING or under MEDICINE itself. And in each case he has several different sequences to consult, even in a library resource centre where as much as possible is interfiled in one integrated sequence, because differences of size necessarily enforce *some* separation of (say) large charts from (say) filmstrips in cans.

Such a search takes a considerable amount of time, something a teacher has little enough of at best, and in many cases he will find no item actually there on the shelf. Is this because there is nothing, or has someone taken it out? Has it been misplaced? Are there other sections he has overlooked? For all these reasons he must look in a catalogue, or index, and the simpler the index the less likely it is that he will find the kind of help that will encourage him either to look at a catalogue again or to develop the imagination to pursue library enquiries, and certainly his time will not have been saved. If this is so for the teacher, relatively well educated and motivated, it is even more so for the pupil, and failure to find answers to his problems may be disastrous to the development of confidence and interest in further study. It is not that the pupil must not, at various stages, be confronted with temporary failure or frustration, particularly in an information search where in the end failure may be a necessary spur to further initiative; but there must be sufficient expectation of success, and sufficiently regular experience of it, to provide some kind of incentive to further effort.

For all these reasons, library resource centres provide indexes and other information tools, and recent years have seen much experimentation in forms of indexing within school centres. The Schools Council Resource Centre Project was partly founded on the assumption that such techniques were important enough, educationally, to warrant investigation in practice, and this was undertaken in the case studies reported in *Organizing resources*. This report did not entirely still the debate, nor was it possible to examine all aspects of the subject within the parameter of the project's brief. Behind the controversy over indexing (which aroused for a time astonishingly fierce passions) lies a subject that deserves much fuller discussion and even experiment. Many people believe, or act as if they believed, that indexing and information analysis can and should be an *educational tool*, with implications beyond the mere convenience of the user. At least one head teacher has been known to instruct his librarian on the method of indexing he should employ adducing educational objectives, and overriding the librarian's protest that his professional territory was being invaded with the tart retort that it was the purpose of the library to carry out the objectives of the school and the function of the librarian to see that his system fulfilled those objectives.

Because resource-based learning places heavy demands on the teacher, including the need to research the availability of suitable materials at every stage, and upon the pupil, calling for his active involvement in enquiry and his acquisition of the relevant enquiry skills, the question of classification and indexing, and other approaches to the discovery and retrieval of information, must be examined afresh and re-thought. The eventual conclusions may not be very different in practice from what has been for some time the standard convention, but at least the interpretation of that convention should be, as a result, more informed, knowledgeable and imaginative. For too long all those involved have been allowed to get away with half-statements and unexamined assumptions (this, indeed, was the reason for my own tongue-in-cheek needling of many of my librarian colleagues over the optical coincidence issue). I drew many conclusions relevant to the specific issues then under examination in *Organizing resources* but now is the opportunity to broaden the discussion and introduce themes it was not then possible to include.

Teachers and learners in search

It is characteristic of research themes that in terms of library enquiry they vary considerably in difficulty and complexity. 'A study of verse forms in sixteenth-century English poetry' will take us to perhaps two, fairly closely related sections of library shelves, and is unlikely to involve any AV materials other than (perhaps) gramophone records; the serious student, and certainly the university teacher, will also turn to critical journals and the indexes to them, and that will be that. Other themes, as we saw when we analysed CATTLE in the previous section, may take us through quite a lot of the collection and require a certain ingenuity in the enquirer. This is not simply a matter for the teacher to remember when he is setting about his own searches; it ought to be in his mind when planning which students would be encouraged to do what, or when planning different but equal tasks for individuals or groups in the class. Clearly if one topic or facet is easy in retrieval terms whereas another requires much more searching time this is an important factor to keep in mind in assessment. Differences of difficulty are one reason why geographers and social scientists (for instance) usually require more practice and understanding of library skills than do students of literature, and why the traditional relationship of the English teacher with the library is often a misunderstanding.

One key element for quick success in search is the size of the stock, and a major reason for establishing as rapidly as possible a broadly based and substantial collection is to give to the pupils the encouragement of finding at least something when they begin their activities. A fairly obvious reason why the resources collections at Heywood and Fakenham were not greatly used during the life of the Resource Centre Project was that they had not had the time to collect enough items; and many schools have held back from attempts to promote resource-based work while their major enthusiasts built up a substantial 'bank' of materials. The Rawlins School, Quorn (Leicestershire) is an example, where the Head of Resources has steadily developed a collection of reprographic and audiovisual items (admirably seeking copyright clearance wherever necessary) and only begun encouraging his colleagues to develop resource-based patterns as the collection (in particular subject fields) justified it. There is no doubt that timing is an important part of educational innovation, and that schools who tried to move too quickly too soon generally came a cropper: 'it didn't work' – and nor did it deserve to.

This may well be one reason why American librarians have been much less interested in problems of information retrieval than their British colleagues; where you can give the enquirer at least something to get on with, it may not seem to matter that your system has not picked up the excellent alternative which for good reasons you have classified in another place. In the UK, the General Studies Project at York was greatly excited to find a book in York Public Library on the history of football which also contained material on Florentine architecture, a Gloucester cathedral misericord, and the history of styles of dress. We commented on this in *Organizing resources*, but it is worth pointing out that this discovery is part of the richness of library collections and the pleasure and excitement of library use. Just as the enquiring mind does not stay convergently upon a narrow theme: just as the world of knowledge does not relate together in one single dimension: so the world of books and resources is multiple and various, leads the enquirer in many directions, and adds enriching detail to the simplest investigation. To say that a book on the history of football may include a picture of a misericord is similar to saying that life has depth. It does not mean that a general public library must therefore abandon its practice of trying to help at least some readers by grouping items together in a tolerably helpful way, nor does it necessarily mean that we must be so struck by this blinding revelation that we choose it as the first out of a number of possibly conflicting objectives and priorities. If the collection is well chosen and reasonably stocked, there ought to be other, less recondite sources for information on costume and Florentine buildings and cathedral misericords, assuming that these are part of the curricular pattern, and their existence in a book on football is a happy if accidental bonus. Whoever notices the bonus would do well to record it in some way, and this is in fact the kind of useful information that a reference librarian notes in his own files for future guidance.

The question is one of balance: of asking ourselves what the most important tasks are that we should try to perform. A library resource centre could, if it chose to and had enough staff, index every page of every book and every frame in every filmstrip or slideset; a computer can have the entire contents of books fed into it word by word, and could be commanded to print out pages or chapters where specific words occurred more than a certain number of times. In the one case, it would mean that the busy staffs of library resource centres in the UK or even the USA would never do anything else but index, and would almost certainly never keep up with the flood of materials coming in for attention; in the other case, the cost not only of the computer and its software but also of the staff required for in-put would be totally prohibitive for educational institutions of any foreseeable kind. This does not mean that we therefore abandon the question of multiple or depth indexing, and fall back on the kind of simple listing that has been typical of British school libraries run by non-librarian teachers; it does mean that we cannot expect to meet the question head-on and elevate it to a major preoccupation.

For the General Studies Project, of course, the great revelation (for which they recommended the adoption of post-co-ordinate indexing) was the breakdown of subject barriers and the development of an inter-disciplinary approach on the part of teachers. By guiding teachers outside the limits of what they tended to regard as 'their' sections of the library shelves, the index was to reveal relationships hitherto unsuspected and possibilities hitherto unexplored. This was an admirable objective, and it was a pity that more librarians did not take advantage of this opportunity to make their own point. Use of traditional library collections has always required much more imagination than is immediately apparent to the average reader, and any college tutor-librarian accustomed to working with students at research level, however modest, will have racked his brains to find new and more effective ways to bring home to his clientele the variety of places and sources to which they can and should turn. The research unit staff working with the General Studies Project found the experience of using a post-co-ordinate index immensely exciting because it broke down some of their preconceptions and released their imaginations, and it happens that this form of index is admirably suited to the varied but finite collection a Project maintains and to the demands made upon it by a particularly motivated team.

Any collection of materials, in whatever formats or media, if organized and arranged for subject retrieval, must be seen, not simply as an aggregation of broad clusters ('Where are all the Religious Education items?') but as separate groupings of very small and specific subject units ('Here are the materials on the journeys of St Paul') whose relationships to each other are sometimes ex-pressed by physical contiguity ('You'll find the Picasso slides in the Art section') and sometimes only by a cross-reference in an index (under Physical Education, a note: 'for Athletics, see 796; for Human anatomy and physiology, see 611 and 612'); indeed, on many occasions the relationships are so varied that the librarian must leave it to the ingenuity of the enquirer to articulate to himself likely areas of further search. This is the collection as the good librarian envisages it, where as much as is practically possible has been prepared for and guided and where the rest is left to sensi-tivity and intelligence, but where *every topic* is individually collocated and provided for.

Closely sequenced and directed exercises in resource-based learn-ing do not (for good reasons) leave the student any scope for further enquiry, and it is only when the work broadens and includes ele-ments in preparation for his own personally motivated researches that it is important for the teacher to remember these insights in lesson planning. But they are the kind of insights most successfully developed in *practice*, and for the teacher even to be able to envisage the problems his students may encounter and learn to tackle he must have plenty of experience himself in preliminary search. This is another reason for a strong element of on-the-spot involvement in curriculum development, because the involvement of the teacher in such preparation is (as we saw with production) 'itself an educa-tion'. Where work-sheets are beginning to broaden and prepare the student for his own discovery, it is important to build in these insights so that the learner is not simply dropped unnervingly in at the deep end. Use of equipment, understanding of the experi-mental method, practice in the framing of hypotheses to test and some idea of the type of possibility that may be before him are all important factors; so, also, must be use of the library resource centre, its indexes and other routes to successful exploration.

Life would be very simple for resources organizers if teachers and students used a common terminology with classifiers and indexers, or with each other, and were practised in articulating their wants. Sometimes it is simply a matter of the differing terminology of disciplines: 'What is there on cells?' means one thing if the questioner is a biologist, quite another if he is interested in prisons. This is the kind of discovery that does no harm to the student enquirer, who learns from it (one hopes) to be more specific or aware of possible confusions; it is the kind of confusion however that is frequently unpredicted by teachers, making their own amateur subject catalogues on an alphabetical basis without reference to skilled advice. On the other hand, 'Which is the section on creation?' can be more than just a confusion of homonyms; the enquirer needs to disentangle what sort of creation he is concerned with (Divine, continuous, literary, artistic, scientific . . .) but may also need to be clear about his phrase, '*the* section', because examples of what he wants may be found in any number of possible subject areas. Other questions need considerable re-phrasing. A college lecturer once asked me, 'What have you got on Peace?' and the subsequent discussion led him to put instead a series of sub-questions – 'What have you on Pacifism?' (which led us to look under Religion, Philosophy and Politics as well as Military Science), 'What have you on International Agreements? What have you on the League of Nations and the United Nations?' and finally, much to his surprise, 'What is there on War?' We looked out material on human aggression, and delved for information about inter-group battles among certain species of ants. We looked at the policy statements of major political parties on international relations. We suggested looking at the causes of specific wars in human history, and recalled the Marxist doctrine on human conflict. This sort of exercise is, one likes to think, a fair example of the way in which discussion with an experienced readers' adviser in a library can help the enquirer not simply to find material but to clear his mind and understand more fully what he is thinking about and seeking. Yet to have tried to anticipate all these problems by putting a comprehensive entry in the index – 'For PEACE *see* PACIFISM (CHRISTIAN), PACIFISM (BUDDHIST), PACIFISM (INTERNATIONAL RELATIONS), WARS (HUMAN), WARS (ANTS), WAR (PREVENTION OF), WAR (SCOTTISH NATIONAL PARTY POLICY ON) . . .' – is clearly out of the question in a busy general library, and particularly if the subject is peripheral to the normal concerns of the institution (in this instance, rightly or wrongly, the subject was to be considered for one hour in one option subject in a three-year programme).

There must always be a considerable element of thought and analysis in an informal search, and no one tool can be expected to give the answers to all problems. The computer index would only help in the exhaustive retrieval of all relevant items on the 'Peace' enquiry if the original input into the computer had made exhaustive allowance for that sort of query coming up, and practically indexed every topic and sub-topic of every item; and the 'natural language' search (by which the computer would be set to scan titles or contents for the appearance of certain key words: PEACE; WAR; CON-FLICT; TREATIES . . .) would not only result in the discovery of masses of irrelevant material but quite possibly miss significant items which worked on a different vocabulary. There is a practical limit to what can be, and should be, expected of an index, even the most sophisticated kind.

The truth of this will be apparent when one considers other immediate sources to which an enquirer habitually turns. Quite often, the simplest help one can give him is to suggest a dictionary; defining what the subject actually is, or what the term means and comes from, clarifies the search strategy very greatly. An encyclo-pedia gives fuller treatment, and the best encyclopedias include the names of prominent experts and other figures, and give sugges-tions for further reading. Atlases sometimes solve problems without recourse to anything else. Directories, biographical source books, year books and similar 'reference sources' are excellent starting points. Moreover, much of the most valuable information may well be very recent, and only be found in magazines and journals. The UK lacks the superb 'Readers Guides' to periodical literature avail-able in the USA and stocked in most media centers, and indeed the economics of a smaller population mean that fewer journals suitable for schools use are published in Great Britain. However, for older pupils and certainly for teachers in planning, 'British Humanities Index', 'British Technology Index' and 'British Educa-tion Index' (to name but three) give valuable information on recent journal articles which if not in stock can usually be obtained, often in photocopied form, from elsewhere. One hopes that pro-fessionally run school library resource centres may see greater use of such sources in the future.

Having gone through the major reference sources, the enquirer can still find a considerable amount of information in a well-classified collection by going, as we saw, direct to the shelves and filing cabinets. The value of the index therefore may well be as a catch-all at a later stage of enquiry. Even the LRC must define its objectives and priorities, and it may be better to release a teacher–librarian for work in the centre with enquirers rather than drive him or her into the backrooms to produce laborious indexes. One important job, indeed, which the teacher–librarian or any other knowledgeable adviser can often do is help the enquirer to recognize those parts of his problem which are not solvable by information resources at all. Quite often one tells students, 'This is not a problem you can read about, nor solve through audio-visual resources: you have to think – or experiment – or go and find out for yourself.' The expression 'mere book-learning' is not entirely foolish or unconsidered; books and resources are valuable and it is possible greatly to exaggerate what can and should be learnt by practical discovery, but it is obviously far better to confront many problems practically rather than copy down somebody else's words on the subject.

Readers at this point may be wondering whether the author has drastically changed his opinions in mid-book, and particularly wonder whether the paragraph in *Organizing resources* (page 53) still holds true:

> Some teachers and some librarians have expressed the view that one can concentrate too much on an indexing system. They rightly point out that much information is gleaned from encyclopaedias, from consulting the librarians, from the advice of the teacher, even from random browsing. The usefulness of charts giving lists of likely classification numbers has been proposed, and in all these comments the value of the personal contribution has been stressed. Our feeling is that it does matter, and that, indeed, the major contribution of a retrieval system to an LRC is that it brings together all these admirable personal factors and pools their knowledge, saves their time and encourages their activities.

It will emerge that this is still my view, but in expressing it and trying to bring out its further implications the reader must first be aware of the other part of the case. An enquirer can go direct to his sources, and it will not always take him very long to find satisfaction; once we have admitted that, and admitted also that sources may not be what he needs at all, we can insist that there are times when he desperately needs help, and when direct approaches to shelves and to sequences in filing-cabinets and cupboards not only take up inordinate amounts of valuable time but may still lead to unnecessary frustration. This frustration is not always something of which the enquirer is directly conscious, except to feel that he has not been very greatly helped or encouraged; many people using libraries, resource centres and indexes have no very great expectations, assume that many things will be quite unfindable, and merely have these intuitions reinforced by what happens. Others are more articulate, know that the information or material is there somewhere, and are therefore greatly excited when some system or other appears to offer them greater flexibility and more chances of success. It was this feeling that contributed to the 'great OCCI boom' (Optical Coincidence Co-ordinate Indexing) in the early 1970s when many schools were developing resource centres and investigating retrieval systems.

Post-co-ordinate indexing, using optical coincidence cards (or for that matter the computer), appeared to teachers to be offering something which no other index could (in their experience) provide, and which they felt to be valuable. We concluded in *Organizing resources* that the case for it was not, in fact, proven, and that although there were many times when the system performed admirably and did exciting things, there were many disadvantages and many occasions when the system performed very badly. Other systems of indexing were then examined and compared, none of them seemed to provide the perfect answer, and there (because we had many other things to describe and points to consider) the matter so far as the Project was concerned rested. But it would indeed be sad if this was the end of the story, because this is an almost classic case of everyone in the argument having some right on his side. Many teachers misunderstood what it was proper for an index to attempt; and many more had clearly not investigated what was possible with any other system. Many librarians had not understood the dilemma and difficulty of the teacher/student enquirer in the new circumstances of resource-based learning, and were therefore unnecessarily hostile to what seemed to them a gimmicky and pointless novelty. If we are to bring both groups together we must be clear that what is at issue is often a matter of emphasis, of conflicting objectives, and of choice of priorities.

One misunderstanding can perhaps at this point be cleared out of the way once and for all; one hopes, indeed, that it has been resolved already, but it is best to be certain. Any problems arising about indexing and information retrieval in school library resource centres arise from the fundamental problems of all information collections, and not from the novelties of the so-called 'new' media formats. A tape-slide sequence presents no fundamentally different problem to the indexer from those he is accustomed to facing with books; the amount of detail he may need to include in a catalogue entry, the number of subject references he may wish to make, the physical problem of where the item will be placed in the resource centre, are all resolvable by the same principles that would be applied to books and other documents in the most traditional of libraries. Codes of practice for cataloguers of audio-visual materials may specify unfamiliar details which the book cataloguer does not deal with, e.g. for films, but these are mere technicalities entirely comparable to those which would be noted about an item of incunabula in a Rare Books Collection.

What is different about the school library resource centre situation is the needs of the clientele, and perhaps the limited nature of the organization which may allow some specific needs to be met in more thorough fashion than is possible in a large library with an unpredictable range of demands. The predicament is that of all information collections, but with an extra urgency:

1. The world of knowledge is multi-dimensional and rapidly changing, and any physical arrangement in one dimension (i.e. along shelves, in a file, in a cupboard) must necessarily favour one

type of approach over another. In the Dewey Decimal Classification, for instance, it is very easy to find all the collections of poets of the eighteenth century, but very difficult to find *everything* in the collection relating to that period unless you have previous knowledge of all the facets it is possible to search.

2. The teachers are searching, with limited time at their disposal, for material in a variety of formats and often relating to a wide variety of ways in which a particular topic can be treated. This must take them through a number of different sequences and to many different places within each sequence, so that the length of time taken by the search is sometimes prohibitive.

3. The pupils are searching, with both limited time and limited technique, for material on subjects which they have sometimes themselves articulated in open-ended situations, or which the teachers have devised in order to increase the degree of pupil involvement, and which therefore crucially depend upon success in search as a motivating factor. The pupil's vocabulary, the way he articulates his problem, may well differ sharply from that of his teachers or from the consensus of (middle-class oriented) library indexers; indeed, the pupil may not, in this exercise, have gone through the period of initial verbal conditioning that represents much of his teaching in more formal situations.

To many teachers, teacher–librarians and chartered librarians, the problem is simple; the enquirer will come to them and they will help. We saw a few pages back how useful this can be, and it is a valuable and important part of the facilities offered by a library resource centre. However, as a solution to the problem, it presupposes the quiet, untroubled world of the teacher–librarian in the days when the research use of the school library formed a very small part of the school day for any child. In a busy session with teams and groups of students in urgent search, the teacher–librarian may spend many hours at the centre of a clamouring mob. Moreover, it presupposes the regular presence of the teacher–librarian (or somebody equally skilled) in the library resource centre at all times. This is an ideal we are all at one in urging; in the present economic situation in the UK, we shall be fortunate when we achieve it. (It *can* be done, by sympathetic timetabling, as well as by the appointment of an extra person; Codsall Comprehensive School's library resource centre was always staffed by a teacher throughout the school day, illness permitting, and no extra appointment had to be made. A headmaster who sees this as a timetabling priority is essential, however, and we have not yet succeeded in convincing all present incumbents.) Part of the solution to the problem of the enquirer is finding ways to release those who act as librarians in library resource centres from unnecessary chores, and perhaps increasing their numbers. It helps, again, if the teacher or teachers

who have initiated the resource-based enquiry exercise are themselves available to help; but seeking resource materials and information may be only one type of activity called for by the class
exercise as a whole, and the teacher may have to remain available
in classroom or practical area to supervise other students.

We must consider, therefore, whether systems of information
retrieval can be improved, in the particular context of the schools,
to make truly independent research more readily possible for the
student without discouraging delay and difficulty, and to save the
time of the teacher in preliminary search and preparation, so that
he too can have more time available for student help and creative
thought. The solution may not be to meet the situation head on;
the users of OCCI attempted this and the results were not altogether
convincing; moreover, sometimes they took up an inordinate amount
of somebody's time. There are still schools, none the less, which have
persisted with OCCI and it should not be dismissed entirely. There
may be a modified use which would meet some needs without too
great an expenditure of effort and without making extravagant
claims. I do not believe there is any one perfect solution, but it may
be that library resource centres can make their own selection from
a variety of possibilities.

Let us, at any rate, take a further look at the problem: not to
solve it (for this is not a how-to-do-it book) but to help further
illuminate the implications of resource-based learning.

The revelation of dimensions

Among the many temptations facing the ambitious resource centre
organizer two at least relate to information retrieval. The first is to
believe that what is needed in a school must, because of the pupils,
be kept excessively simple; the other is to fly in the face of all professional advice and try to devise a completely novel system oneself.

> School librarians ... sometimes argue that the finding mechanism
> employed by large libraries is unnecessarily elaborate for secondary
> school library purposes, or that it is too difficult for their pupils to
> grasp. They contend that a 'simple' arrangement of the books under
> the 'subjects' that the pupils know, with a 'simple' list or two, are most
> easily constructed and quite enough 'for all practical purposes'. The
> fact that secondary school pupils, whatever their limitations, are prob-
> ably at the height of their power of learning new things does not seem
> to occur to them and they do not discover for some time that the do-it-
> yourself mechanism they have devised – often with some trouble – is
> by no means simple to apply as new subjects arise, or simple subjects
> begin to need subdivision. (Morris et al. 1972: 48.)

This is sound advice, and it is worth adding that a system which
sounds very elaborate for staff to set up in the first place is often

very simple in practice for the user. Teachers blench at the pages of schedules for the Dewey Decimal Classification, or the lists of alphabetical subject headings necessary for a good subject index, and think that a simple, home-made concoction must be simpler for a pupil to find something in; it probably is not, and if the pupil is really to be helped there is no substitute for the kind of professional skill in index compilation that is typical of those chartered librarians who have paid particular attention to that part of their professional training. (Employers should note that this is by no means true of all chartered librarians, and if indexing skill is what they are after they should question applicants and their referees with care.) Moreover, one must not be tempted to assume that no one else can ever acquire these skills, although the task is not an easy one without guidance.

There are two tasks which need attention, apart from the simple ones of helping the enquirer to locate items by a known author or compiler, and helping him to find items on subjects for which the Decimal Classification (or whatever is in use) provides an unequivocal place. The first is to allow the enquirer to find items relevant to any *facet* of a subject; and to explain what this means we can take (say) a short film on 'Pollution of British beaches and coastlines by oil: effects and treatment' (this is not, as will be seen, a title, but an analysis of its subject content). It is likely that for classification purposes (finding a single place on a shelf) the item would be seen as a special development of the subject 'Pollution', and it breaks down conveniently into component parts ('facets') thus: 'Pollution': 'Beaches and coastlines': 'Great Britain': 'Oil': 'Effects': 'Treatment'. Although for shelving purposes we decided to regard it as being 'about' pollution, it can certainly be argued that it is also 'about' oil (what it does to beaches), 'about' beaches (how they can be affected by oil pollution), 'about' British beaches (ditto), as well as 'about' the treatment of an environmental disaster (in this case, oil pollution). An enquirer might well begin his search having articulated any one of these facets, and not necessarily the one that was chosen for prominence. Moreover, it is likely that the 'effects' would include an examination of the ecology of the beaches and coastlines concerned, and that the relation of the topic to the oil industry, to North Sea oil, and problems of international law, would be discussed. We need to examine our indexing system to see whether these individual facets are picked out in any way, and what can be done to see that they are.

This is not the same problem that the General Studies Project raised; all the facets listed above cluster round and make up the total subject of the item in quite a conventional and specific way, just as 'audio-visual methods in the teaching of French to mixed-ability classes in the secondary school in Wales' includes 'teaching methods': 'audio-visual formats': 'languages': 'French': 'mixed-ability classes': 'secondary schools': 'Great Britain.: 'Wales' (among others) in a perfectly ordinary way. The GSP, on the contrary, was bothered that in the book on football there was information that would *not* be expected. This brings us to the second task, which is to allow the enquirer to find items of major importance which are part of or included in resources where that information would not necessarily be normally sought. This is what is technically called 'analytical indexing'. The photograph of the miserére, if sufficiently important, is given a separate index entry, and this was explained with illustration in *Organizing Resources*.

What will be immediately clear about these two tasks is that they involve a major policy decision; they are, in fact, properly a management problem, and must relate to available resources of staff, etc. and to major objectives. How important is it, and how does this affect our choice of indexing system or our use of it in practice? In some cases, for instance, the articulation of each facet is provided for by the application of 'chain indexing', applied to each successive stage of the classification number. 'Audio-visual teaching methods' has a Dewey number 371.33, which can be broken down into its components as follows: 300 Social sciences; 370 Education; 371 Teaching and school organization; 371.3 Teaching methods; 371.33 Audio-visual teaching methods. Each step of this chain can be separately included in an alphabetical index, so that each new facet as the number gets longer and longer is independently accessible to the enquirer. Unfortunately, there is no Dewey number which represents the whole string of facets 'audio-visual methods in the teaching of French to mixed-ability classes in the secondary school in Wales', and one would therefore have to make secondary index entries under (for instance) 'French: Foreign language teaching'; and 'Mixed ability classes: Teaching'; as well as 'Wales: Secondary schools'. Similarly, the oil pollution example in the previous paragraph is capable of receiving a Dewey number, but this number does not include every step of the chain of facets (including some intermediate steps) nor the full elaboration of 'effects' *and* 'treatment'. This means that we could not rely on a simple and automatic procedure being followed by a semi-skilled person once he was presented with the item duly classified for him. Full indexing of this kind requires the presence of professional skill, somewhere or other available.

The last phrase was deliberate, because we need not always assume that our indexing must be done in the school itself. It is possible to conceive of a completely centralized service available to school library resource centres, either from a regional centre or from a national source. In the United States, where the dictionary catalogue is practically universal, printed catalogue cards are available from a number of different agencies, including the Library of Congress itself. One can, if one chooses, simply order one card for each item; alternatively, some very large libraries order the entire catalogue as it is serially produced in book format, and produce multiple copies of individual entries by photographic or xerographic means. Normally, however, one buys a 'set' of cards for each item, and this means cards for all the individual entries which the Library of Congress cataloguer (or his equivalent in one of the other card services) decides are required; this would include an entry for each author, an entry for the title, and specific subject entries under alphabetically arranged headings. American catalogue agencies do not employ facet analysis of the kind we have instanced above but the result is usually to have rather more subject entries than are typical in most British libraries using the classified catalogue in its simplest form.

A centralized cataloguing agency established in the UK could itself specify, not only the classification number of an item and its full catalogue description (as *British National Bibliography* does today) but also the nature and number of other entries to be provided and the alphabetical index entries to be included in the subject index; one would then order a 'set' of cards which would simply need, as in USA, the typing in of the extra headings and their filing in order. It would then be possible to buy, as it were, a standard indexing 'package' from the central service, and one would not need to provide the same level of professional expertise in one's individual school. However, this service would not normally include the school's own productions – the teacher-produced materials we examined in Chapter 6 – and it would be necessary, if these were to be added to the collection and indexed in the usual way, to choose an indexing system that could still be followed if no centralized provision was available. However, a local authority service might still be envisaged, getting the bulk of its cataloguing data from computer tapes of the MARC service but undertaking also individual cataloguing of school's own products as an extra.

Whether a national agency would provide the indexing service we are considering is another matter. Public libraries, who might provide at least an important part of the custom, would certainly find it unnecessary to pay for a package which included alphabetical subject index suggestions, as they have well-established catalogues already and trained librarians to check that the index contains what it should. Only schools, among educational institutions, lack the professional librarians required, and are likely to be sufficiently short of staff to need to concentrate as much as possible of their activity on reader-guidance rather than cataloguing. But without a thoroughly professional alphabetical subject index, access to each facet and each step of the chain cannot be provided with a classified catalogue.

Is this important? Check most British school library resource centres at present, and you will find that whether or not there is a fully qualified librarian to run the catalogue, the indexing is rarely as thorough as we are suggesting. Chartered librarians habitually chain-index from their classification number, but if that number is imprecise, misses out intermediate facets or is broad rather than specific, important links and entries get missed. The LRC still runs, the librarian is satisfied, and no third-former comes up and says, 'Miss, I didn't find this item on oil pollution of beaches and coastlines because you hadn't specified the beaches facet!' It is a characteristic of pupil-failure in enquiry that normally nobody hears about it unless the pupil is unusually persistent. We simply do not know how many enquirers fail to find what they might, and give up long before they should, because our indexes were imprecise or unhelpful. My own observations simply suggest that the number is considerable, and that the usefulness of our indexes is a key subject for continued investigation if more and more pupils are to be finding themselves involved in individual searches to encourage confidence and autonomy in learning.

If this is so for pupils, I suspect that it is also true for teachers, already harassed and short of the time for detailed research. The item on audio-visual French teaching would probably be placed by librarians under the number for the teaching of the French language, and its relevance to studies of audio-visual methods in general, or to mixed-ability classes in Welsh secondary schools, ignored. This is not because librarians are very wicked or thoughtless, but because providing a variety of extra entries in a catalogue is expensive of their own time as well as of materials, with extra cards to type and file and cross-references to insert. If this is the case with attempts simply to specify the full range of subject-matter covered by the item's major focus, it is certainly true of attempts to bring out contents which fall outside that area, in other words the 'analytical entires' such as the miserére. Can expense of time and materials be justified when there is so much else to do?

It was here that post-co-ordinate indexing had proved so tempting to many in the field. R. P. A. Edwards, himself a chartered librarian and writing as School Libraries and Resources Adviser to Leicestershire, concluded about card catalogues:

> A point is reached, however, even if the labour and money is available, when a multi-media catalogue with a large number of added entries to cope with multi-subject material becomes unwieldy. The effect upon the reader of serried ranks of cards is intimidating and counterproductive. (Edwards 1973: 97.)

He then turned to examine a 'typical example':

> An illustrated article about life in the slums of a particular city, say Liverpool, tells of economic conditions which lead to such housing being in use, the social effects upon adults and children, and of the efforts to overcome the problem, perhaps stressing the official efforts in terms of education of Dr Midwinter's team and the unofficial efforts

of Shelter and squatters' groups. The pictorial element might include
evocative pictures of children playing among rubble, pathetic old
people and, perhaps, someone lying sick because of the bad, damp
housing. (*ibid*.)

For Mr Edwards this item could easily be handled, in retrieval
terms, by post-co-ordinate indexing, which he described as follows:

> He underlines or circles all the terms on the Features List which he
> thinks are needed to describe it and its potential users. Under FORM
> he will underline *Article* and *Illustration*. Under LOCATION he will
> underline *Class-Set File* . . . He may decide it is unsuitable for first and
> second year students and underline under APPLICATION *Third
> year*, *Fourth year* and *Staff*. The TREATMENT, he decides, is *Docu-
> mentary*, the DATE heading may be *1969–*. Under PLACE he may
> underline *Great Britain*, *England*, *Lancashire*, *Liverpool* . . . Then he
> would come to TOPIC, and first he thinks of his own use of the article
> and underlines *Environmental Studies*, *Housing*, *Slums*, *Vermin*. These
> might be sufficient from his point of view but he may feel that the
> R.E. staff would be interested in Shelter as an organization and in the
> social and moral implications of the article and underline *Charities*,
> *Secular*, *Deprivation*, *Hunger*. Knowing that the English teachers like to
> use strong emotional stimuli as a means of getting children to talk,
> write and act he might underline *Unhappiness*, and because it is likely
> they would hope that the children might identify with the miserable
> plight of the children in the pictures he might also underline *Children*.
> (*op. cit.*: 104.)

We must immediately ask questions about this, but it is clear from
Mr Edwards' account that he envisages the teacher doing his own
indexing for the benefit of his pupils and his colleagues. It must be
re-iterated that teachers in practice vary enormously in their
aptitude for such work, and that there appear to be personality
differences in the number of entries suggested under the above
system rather than differences related to the item and its likely use.
Mr Edwards believes:

> All this would not need great leaps of imagination on the part of the
> teacher since those headings are in the list of topics, having been put
> there by teachers who have decided they are topics they would like
> the children to study. (*ibid*.)

But in fact the larger such a list becomes, the easier it is for a very
busy person to miss headings, or to underline compulsively every
heading that seems in the least relevant so as to miss nothing. The
number of headings in the list from a Leicestershire school given
as an example to Mr Edwards' chapter was nearly 700, and included
only three of the topic headings Mr Edwards suggests as necessary
for this particular item. How long must a list be to cover all the
necessary headings, and are teachers the best people to forecast
what might be required? Who, in fact, will draw up the headings

list and what guarantee have we that it will be more efficient and inclusive than the professionally compiled Dewey Decimal Classification?

It will be remembered that the Schools Council Resource Centre Project concluded that no single indexing 'best buy' was available. One factor in this was the time involved in compilation. Mr Edwards believed, and many agreed, that:

> ... a system which enables a seeker for information to combine a string of terms chosen from a simple list so as to spell out his specific needs ... can be done, and without great labour or expense, by using post-co-ordinate indexing and, in lieu of a card index, a punched card system. (*op. cit.*: 99.)

The punched card system does not involve, so far as equipment is concerned, expense significantly greater than the cost of catalogue cabinets and cards for conventional catalogues; but the operations listed by Mr Edwards do involve a significant expense of time. The compilation of a headings list itself is a lengthy procedure. Once it has been drawn up, the teacher-indexer might expect to take perhaps ten minutes examining his articles and the headings list and underlining appropriate features. The head of resources would take about the same time in 'editing' (that is to say, checking that the teacher had done a satisfactory job, and adding new under-linings or erasing unnecessary ones as he felt fit). The task of extracting punched feature cards and punching holes in twenty-two of them would take an average ancillary about fifteen minutes, assuming reasonable care was being taken. Add the time taken to produce an accessions card and you have spent forty minutes on one fairly short item. Have you then solved retrieval problems? The enquirer looking for information on the activities of Shelter must still search, apparently, through all the items revealed by combining the features cards 'Housing', 'Charities' and 'Secular'; the enquirer wanting the item and looking for it under its title or its author has to follow the subject approach (which he has to remember) unless an additional author/title catalogue has been added; and the enquirer starting his search from 'Liverpool' may well find that a large number of item numbers stare up at him from the card on the light box, which he can only differentiate by experiment (laying a series of other punched cards on the top) or by examining every accession card in turn.

At a price in time, and with a rather clumsy and long-winded process of search, the OCCI system does turn up information from *any* facet if items exist relevant to it, and the only reason conventional catalogues take less time is that they do not offer this useful facility. Moreover, once the teacher has thought to tell people of his interest in themes like 'Unhappiness', it is possible (with OCCI) for indexers to keep the theme in mind. The theme might, of course, eventually be abandoned, and just as, before it was chosen, no one was selecting item⸱ for it, so after it has passed to the land of all good themes there might still be indexers beavering away on its behalf. They may not do it equally well; not every teacher of sociology is good at choosing material for thematic work in English. However, a pupil looking for something to illustrate an 'Unhappiness' theme, or a teacher looking for stimuli, could well take the feature card for it and perhaps add to it the card for 'Housing' to retrieve items that linked the two concepts. This is splendid; but the reader should note that the enquirer could also take the 'Illustration' card and add to it 'Vermin' and expect to retrieve a picture of (say) a rat, when the vermin themselves might only have been mentioned in the text and not included in the pictures.

In considering what, in fact, a system of indexing for retrieval should attempt, Mr John Hanson of Oxfordshire produced a useful summary which is worthy of study at this point:

It should not divide books from non-book material but show the availability of both in one system.

It should be efficient and not difficult to operate.

It should make teachers and students aware of related topics.

It should facilitate the degree of cross-indexing which is genuinely required.

It should show sources, ideas, information, people and places which are readily available to the school and educationally helpful.

It should not isolate the school as a system but should be part of a network with certain standardised procedures so that wider communication is encouraged, materials may be easily exchanged, and links established with area or regional agencies loaning and giving material to the school. Such a service is likely to be based on five-by-three inch cards for these can be printed and sent out with material from, say, a regional centre. (Hanson 1975: 69.)

It will be seen that Mr Hanson believes strongly in some form of centralized cataloguing service, and he is correct in assuming that this must mean the adoption of 5 × 3 cards rather than punched cards of any variety. For Mr Edwards and others of his persuasion this will imply accepting limitations of performance which they regret. This section has argued that any ordinary centralized cataloguing package is likely to require (if the classified catalogue form is used) a degree of skill in the accompanying alphabetical subject index which is not normally found among non-specialists and which many professional librarians themselves do not possess. As the proponents of fully faceted classification systems have long made clear, the conventional classification schemes are imperfectly constructed for thoroughly efficient retrieval purposes; and indexers must therefore exercise ingenuity and skill in bringing out the full subject content of the items before them. Without such indexing, pupils and teachers in search will be less likely to experience success, and in the case of the ill-motivated pupil this may be a considerable disincentive to further effort. Yet Mr Hanson is correct in reminding us that there are other objectives we must keep in mind, including communication with other agencies and schools and economic use of regional facilities and manpower.

It is possible that part of the answer to this dilemma may be found if we examine other ways of achieving what the post-co-ordinate indexers try to achieve through their system. Perhaps not every one of those multiple feature headings is equally important. It is pleasant to be able to limit one's search to those items kept in the 'Class-Set File', but at the search stage does it really matter where the item is held? Does not this arise after the item's existence is detected? Can we be sure that everybody interprets 'Documentary' in the same way, and is this a facet which might be fairly obvious from the item itself? If we had classified Mr Edwards' item by the Dewey scheme, and stored it in classified order, would not many of the possible seekers have found it by a process of reasonable logic? The very concept 'Slums', for instance, includes within itself the related concepts of 'Housing', of 'Deprivation', and perhaps of 'Unhappiness'. Perhaps we need, not an indexing system which takes up a lot of staff time in adding extra entries, but a system of linked headings to guide the enquirer in search? Post-co-ordinate indexing proceeds by means of what it calls a 'Thesaurus', a grouped list of subject headings showing chosen terms and with cross-references from related terms and synonyms; perhaps such a thesaurus could be used in collaboration with a conventional catalogue, drawing attention to the multiplicity of possible areas and carrying out Mr Hanson's direction to make enquirers 'aware of related topics'. This would certainly be very much more useful than the rather unhelpful lists of major Dewey Decimal categories which are pinned up round all too many libraries under the completely misleading title, 'How to Find a Book'!

This is not the answer to all the problems we have raised. Some of them can only be answered by indexers who will, whatever classification number they give for convenience, meticulously analyse the item's subject content in terms of its string of facets, and devise ways in which these can be separately indexed for retrieval. We cannot afford analytical indexing, but we ought to be able to provide indexes which at least reveal main contents. The job of an index is not simply, as some British librarians seem to think, to provide a simple shelf list to reveal items out on loan; it is to be an extra spur to the enquirer, allowing him to question and probe the collection through the eyes of a skilled information analyst and organizer. One of Dr Ranganathan's 'Laws of library science' was to 'save the time of the reader', and this is the index's job as well. Despite the general antipathy of most of us towards the activity, indexing is one facet of reader guidance and reference service. Its task is more than recording and describing, more than listing and stocktaking: it is concerned with the revelations of dimensions within the stock.

Education by index

Many readers who have struggled through this chapter to this point may well be ready to ask what possible relevance it can have to anyone except the poor person or persons charged with the tedious or (it may seem) awesome task of indexing. Is this not a by-way off the main subject matter we are supposed to be exploring, resource-based learning? Ought not this chapter to be reserved for the pages of some specialist periodical, to be perused by cataloguers over their coffee-break or students of librarianship facing their bleak exams? Surely it would have been more appropriate to have spent more time on curriculum building, or production techniques, or the use of particular types of audio-visual equipment!

I believe the opposite is in fact the case. Indeed, it hardly needs more than a brief glance along a shelf to convince one that questions of hardware and production are being busily and competently analysed elsewhere. Equipment and facilities change, and the biggest problems for any educational planner today in this area are obsolescence and incompatibility. The mystiques of format occasion lengthy disquisitions and much headache, but they are well researched and the newest models are best left to the more quickly published periodical article and the INTERNAVEX conference exhibition, or its overseas equivalent.

Curriculum planning is another matter. Involved in the design of curricula is analytical insight into topic relationships and subject fields in relation to the development of understanding. Part of the equation is the awareness of student learning strategies; just as vital must be the ability to see links and counterparts and resemblances and stages, to grasp conceptual structures and be aware of universes of knowledge (in the plural) seen from related or contrary vantage points. This is exactly what the discipline of indexing is concerned with, what discussion of indexing as a practical concern in relation to education can generate, and what good indexing systems seek to promote. We will begin our curriculum planning by considering the subject X; in our library resource centre we have an organization of recorded knowledge whose arrangement offers us a plurality of materials in a particular order, and our index probes and if necessary disturbs this order so as to reveal dimensions of relationship to X that we might have overlooked, or the existence of relevant materials we might not have suspected. This is why we spoke of information analysis as being an educational tool: not only for the student, but for the teacher in planning.

The teacher dissecting the various facets and relationships within a topic area (particularly in the case of a broad inter-disciplinary project) needs to consider the divergent paths along which the topic can be explored as well as the narrowly convergent track he may have been conditioned by his previous training or inclination to concentrate on. The weakness of all conventional subject groupings, whether in initial courses for qualification, departmental structures and external examination syllabuses, or sections of library classification schemes, is that they lead the teacher and the school librarian to overlook directions along which student thinking, interest and motivation may travel, and ways in which the work of other colleagues can interact with one's own. It may be that we shall not all wish to employ themes with the broad integrated approach advocated by team teaching converts, but at least we can remember to check whether a related aspect is shortly to be covered, or has already been examined, by other colleagues teaching other subjects.

More than this, however: the teacher planning any work that is open-ended, that will lead the student to undertake his own modest exploration of information sources, must anticipate not only what directions this may take but what help and hazards may be met on the way, and how these will be tackled. It is wholly proper for him to notice, and point out, that some subjects are easier to research than others in the traditional subject catalogues common in school libraries. By convention, it is easier to find items on a time aspect of a given subject (COSTUME – FRANCE – NINETEENTH CENTURY) than a subject aspect of a given time (NINETEENTH CENTURY – COSTUME – FRANCE); it is easy to find material on modern fire prevention, but not easy (through an index) to find material on specific fire disasters in history (Alexandrian library, Rome, London, Dresden) unless one happens to know already which ones there were and where and when they happened. Schemes of classification, and published lists of subject headings for the dictionary catalogue (so popular in North America), are based on needs and practice in large traditional general libraries, and are usually a century old in essential structure no matter how much tinkering there has been in later revision. There are good reasons why this is so, but not only has the whole of human knowledge dramatically changed since those times, as we have insisted earlier, but also the approach of modern schools has made traditional schematizations unhelpful and irrelevant.

We have been urged to look for the 'hidden curriculum' in social pressures, organizational structures and teaching approaches. It cannot be idle to look for the same subtle influences, the message within the medium, in library resource centres. To put it at its crudest, teachers who are trying to break down the distinctions between 'fine' and 'useful' arts are not helped by classification

practices that insist on retaining them; female students whom progressive teachers are encouraging in accordance with modern law
find their whole sex (half of human-kind) related to a tiny subsection
of 'human problems', and usually in relationship with *minority*
groups (!) such as immigrants, homosexuals, and the like. But this
is not the only type of bad message the conventional systems are
subtly transmitting; more insidious is the suggestion that there is
one 'proper' organization of knowledge, just as there is one 'correct',
BBC-endorsed pronunciation, and that retrieving information
through its use is an arcane discipline only grasped by the few, the
bright ones, the successful, the academic stream, or the mysterious,
indispensable trained librarian. Teachers and librarians have pro-
tested that this attack is unjustified, that to criticize traditional
indexes is irrelevant because 'most pupils never use the index
anyway'. Regretfully, the reply must be, 'Exactly! Most school
library resource centre indexes are so comparatively unhelpful that
semi-random browsing is a better solution.'

For some the conclusion that the case for OCCI was far from
proven came as a great disappointment, and not only because they
thought it might be a more efficient retrieval system. Many teachers
were impressed with post-co-ordinate indexing as a mental discipline
for the student; it seemed to many of them that to look up in the
classified or dictionary forms of catalogue was less 'educational'.
After all, a student using the classified catalogue simply has to
specify his subject to himself and seek it, or a synonym for it, in the
alphabetical subject index, from whence he is directed to a section
of the classified file arranged according to the classification number.
A student using the dictionary catalogue thinks of his subject
heading and opens the drawers, and if he has chosen wrongly
there ought to be a cross-reference direction to the form of heading
actually chosen. It sounds very simple, almost spoon-feeding. On
the contrary, the student enquiring through a post-co-ordinate
system must first analyse his subject into its facets or features, and
then seek the optical coincidence feature cards for each; combining
them, he finds whether material exists on the subject, and by with-
drawing one or other feature he can vary the subject spread. He has
to make an intellectual decision from the start, which sounds more
demanding and more in line with research methods than simply
following a see-reference. Many teachers wrote to me on these
lines.

Whether they were correct to think so is a matter for debate. The
classified catalogue is not an easy tool, and the way many school
librarians have organized them hardly helps to make use any
easier, but it is possible to construct, for instance, an alphabetical
subject index which takes account of varieties of terminology, which
sets out clearly hierarchical structures, and shows relationships
and linkages. This can be in itself an occasion for learning by the

student, in that he sees unsuspected dimensions to his subject and is forced to choose; in so doing, he confronts and works through the ordinary difficulties of a linear subject arrangement, and one may hope that regular practice in this way will give him the insight to browse more usefully and see the word of knowledge with more enlightened eyes. Equally with the dictionary catalogue, the so-called syndetic references linking related and subordinate subjects can be constructed in such a way as to increase insight and convey information, however exasperating they sometimes are at the moment of search. The OCCI system arguably placed too much strain on the student in his early experiences with it, forcing him to articulate headings before he had enough knowledge to guess what possible headings there might be; although it must be noted that this did not seem to be its biggest drawback in practice, and many quite unacademic youngsters used it confidently in retrieval.

The interesting point is that we should be discussing indexes along these lines. Yet if the aim of resource-based learning is, among other things, to develop the autonomous individual learner, we must surely take into account all the various learning experiences which the student will undergo on the way, and check on their educational effect. Once the learner has mastered information analysis and the keys to the retrieval of source materials from a collection, he has arguably taken a major step forward in his own ability to learn by himself and to enquire of his own volition. In the process, what he learns is relevant not merely to the struggle with catalogues and indexes, but to the devising of research strategies, the analysis of problems, and the verbal re-statement of his needs, not to mention his improved understanding of the whole universe of knowledge.

Many teachers may here interject that most indexes, catalogues and retrieval systems in the out-of-school world are not devised in the careful manner or with the fullness of treatment that has been generally advocated in these pages. In the UK, most library cat-alogues are of the classified kind, and for economic reasons tend to be sparing in the number of entries or the provision of references; in the USA and Canada, and often in Australia, the dictionary catalogue reigns supreme, and although superficially it may contain rather more entries per item than its classified equivalent, many of these are rather simply repetitive and do not probe and question the subject content of the items very profoundly. Ought not the student to be prepared for the real world, rather than molly coddled and spoon-fed by an indulgent school library resource centre indexer? It is worth making the point that, in the first place, such cataloguing is not necessarily the only kind the student will come across in his adult life, and that industrial and special libraries are increasingly using the post-co-ordinate variety, or other relatives of it; indeed it was in such libraries that the punched card really developed as a retrieval tool, and for which it is very well suited.

Moreover, the use of the computer as a retrieval tool increasingly requires the use of faceted and/or post-co-ordinate methods, and we can expect to see computer indexes more frequently used in tomorrow's world.

A further point however comes across by analogy with the teaching of reading. Whether or not the initial teaching alphabet is the best possible tool for the purpose is no doubt open to discussion, but there are many teachers who are convinced not only that it works very well indeed with children who find difficulty with traditional orthography, but that transition in due course to traditional orthography is no great problem. One can think of other areas of education where a specially adapted version of something used in adult life is employed for the initial learning, requiring a transition at a later stage. I suspect that students who have truly grasped what an index is all about, and how it can be used in information searches, and who have developed confidence in the use of indexes and other retrieval devices, will transfer with relative ease to the necessarily more awkward catalogues of general adult collections, and be more ready to follow up their interests in a research mode. Early confidence, and sympathetic preparation, is the key to so much learning that it is hard to believe it is not so in this case, and I recall limited but suggestive experience in this regard with day-release building workers just out of compulsory school.

The information retrieval system of the school is therefore a matter of concern to the teaching staff themselves, and not simply a private professional matter for an imported librarian. This does not, however, mean that teachers can or should make arbitrary decisions, instructing their minions accordingly; they rarely have the right background to do so. Teachers can, however, lay down what they regard as desirable characteristics, aims and objectives which the librarian is requested to consider. He may reply that he can achieve such objectives through traditional methods; he may have to explain that he could only give the type of service required with a considerably increased staffing budget; he may bring forward objectives of his own which he feels have been overlooked and are equally or more important. But the dialogue should wherever possible be there, and the good indexer is the person who consults with his clientele, remembering in this case that their objectives may not only be to find material, but to find it in ways that are educationally stimulating and helpful.

Not all the objectives laid down may be suitable for an index to attempt. It may, finally, be useful to remind ourselves that there are other ways in which students learn, and other paths by which particularly insightful experiences can be brought to them. Shifrin has pointed out that indexing systems may simply be changing one orthodoxy for another:

Instead of getting rid of the old rigid subject divisions such as chemistry and physics, history and geography, and allowing children to discover that knowledge is a multifaceted thing, he is merely replacing them with new, but still rigid, subjects such as WORK or POVERTY, as though the child needed blinkers in case he discovered peripheral knowledge. (Shifrin 1973: 141.)

He explains that as well as the index, the teacher himself may well have something to contribute:

All that is required is a large chart, illustrated perhaps, displaying aspects of the major theme and using subject headings from the index to the library's permanent classified catalogue to point the way and guide the child.

When topics change, new charts can be made and the choice of component subjects to be signposted can itself be a guided group activity with intrinsic educational value. (*ibid.*)

This is by no means an adequate alternative to thorough indexing, but whatever one's doubts it does remind us that other things are going on. The preparatory pamphlets setting out the parameters of the new resources theme for the students can contain much useful guidance on search strategy. The class themselves, as Shifrin imaginatively suggests, can themselves discuss that strategy and make their own contributions to it. This may not be 'all that is required' but it is an important element. In planning for the student's active participation in his own learning we must, it is clear, take much more into account than any of us anticipated.

PART THREE

Three Professions Together

Introduction

The ideas and developments we have been investigating require organization for their achievement. This organization involves the professional skills of what have until recently been three separate and distinct groups: teachers, media production specialists and librarians. We have seen that these three groups have become more and more inter-related, not only bringing their complementary skills to bear upon joint problems, but also acting in very similar ways. Mr Chibnall's recognition that both as a librarian and a production consultant he was operating in the field of information and communication echoes the discovery by many teachers that in planning resource-based activities they were often acting like media producers and librarians, and the recognition by librarians that in their reference and guidance work with students they were very much acting like teachers and needing to bear in mind educational considerations.

In some parts of the world, and typically in North America, all three professionals were involved in schools before the resource-based movement made its full impact, and it is interesting to study the subsequent history of their relationships: the careful tiptoeing around (and sometimes across) demarcation lines, and (at national association level) the increasingly close co-operation in planning and development. There are signs that such top level co-operation is developing in the United Kingdom too. Producers and librarians were each poised to enter the schools field, after already becoming active among the colleges, and were initially suspicious and self-protective in their interaction with others. It is good to feel that this is disappearing, and that in schools themselves there is growing exploration of the implications of new learning patterns on their work and relationships, by people broadly involved in one or more of all three professional areas.

The British educational system, including its approach to personnel appointments as well as day-to-day organization and approach, is significantly different from North American patterns, and it is by no means certain that we can import without amendment what they have found works best for them. Moreover, the economic crisis without much doubt precludes the wholesale appointment of extra personnel, whether teachers, production specialists or qualified librarians. Some pessimists fear that these constraints will hasten the swing of the fashion pendulum, and that the impetus behind resource-based learning and other similar breakthroughs in educational methodology may be lost. This need not happen if we keep our heads and use our intelligence, although we cannot expect the way ahead to be anything but difficult. Yet the immediate availability of heavy funding did not make the dramatic changes in American education that were hoped for, and it may be that the need to consolidate on present achievement will give us the incentive to assimilate what we have already learnt and build on it, as well as persuade our natural allies of the next set of priorities as we see them.

The realities of our world, indeed, are not different from those we analysed in Part One; they are only more difficult, and the needs they expose remain the same, but very much more urgent. If we feel we are financially crippled, we might consider the fact that my postbag continues to include regular approaches from the developing countries, few of whom can muster anything like the financial and other resources which we in the UK bemoan as inadequate. Many of the mature students in my own university department come from such countries, and their combination of eagerness and scepticism matches exactly, for all the differences, the approach of undergraduate and mature students from the UK itself. 'Resources' remains relevant.

If we cannot expect, in the immediate future, to see the three professions separately represented in every school, this need not mean that resource-based learning cannot proceed, nor that a resources organization cannot be developed containing important elements of the activities we mentioned in Part Two. It will be more difficult, but schools have already demonstrated that it is not impossible. We must know what we want to do, and what we might need to do; we must know what we have, and what we lack; and we must plan with care so that our objectives can be attained and our deficiencies made up. Among the variety of patterns found in British schools, no one solution will be applicable to all, and many schools will make arrangements that are perilously fragile, dependent upon the enthusiasm and availability of particular individuals, the goodwill of volunteers, and timetable re-arrangements that necessarily collapse during stress and epidemic.

And the solutions will not only be at school level. Arrangements between institutions, extensions of service from particular points, the development of co-operation and the deliberate planning for it, are all (as we saw) important and necessary. At association level, the professional groups will need to maintain constant discussion, and arrangements for professional education, and re-education, must be kept under review. The final chapter will try therefore to sum up the argument and point towards directions for action.

8 The Resource Centre as an Economic Necessity

If one were set the task of planning a system by which schools made the fullest possible use of their existing monies, their existing staffing, their existing materials and the equipment already in their possession, one could do much worse than devise an organization of resources based upon a resource-centre, and suggest the adoption of methods of teaching and learning strikingly like those described in these pages and the sources from which much of the information therein was drawn. In recent years, it has been common for heads of resources and teacher–librarians to stumble upon this truth and propound it at courses and conferences, often in tones of great surprise. For many schools today the resource centre is as much an economy measure as a consequence of educational objectives, and a primary school headmaster once told me, 'Please, we've done this sort of thing for years, only we didn't know it was called a resource centre. *We couldn't afford to do anything else.*'

Thus this book is far from being an attempt to terrify ratepayers. Some readers may well have begun to feel that it suggests a concept impossibly beyond their grasp: offset litho machines, videotape recorders, media resources officers, full-time librarians, not to mention space within schools for all these items and individuals to be put to best use – at a time when social services are being run down, hospitals are unable to afford their full quota of nurses, unemployment stands high and is rising, and the battle for jobs and against inflation preoccupies press and politicians alike. Curriculum development, resource-based learning, educational technology, team teaching, all belong to what we now nostalgically call the 'bonanza years of the sixties', and we are now, in deference to the oil moguls, having to cut back. It does not help to remind ourselves that even in the 1960s we thought we were in economic crisis: that 1968 saw Britain facing devaluation and cutbacks:

that we have never had, in the UK, anything like those funds we read of in the American journals for building, staff and materials. At the moment of writing this, we see teachers unemployed, teacher-education courses cut back, new building at a virtual halt, book-funds slashed and equipment funds completely erased – and yet here comes another book on resource-based learning, as if we were millionaires! This is, I hope to show, a misunderstanding.

Look inside a typical classroom cupboard; locked away there, among the sets of textbooks, exercise books and mysterious (and often empty) containers left behind by the previous teacher, are what were thought of as 'audio-visual aids' (i.e. to teaching): filmstrips, little boxes of slides, rolled-up charts and maps, a heap of colour supplements, perhaps a few specimens, picture postcards, models, or examples of last year's project work from students. They are, as we saw, carriers of information and stimulus. We store printed information already in our school libraries; placing the 'AV aids' (if they are of good quality) in the library, instead of (for large parts of the year) in a locked cupboard, gives students an extra information source without any further expenditure at all. When the teacher needs it, he asks for it. One does not need to be a convert to a resource-based doctrine to see possibilities here; it is simply a sensible measure of economy to maximize use. In the case of cas-settes and audiotapes, more regular use actually decreases the danger of print-through, and may therefore increase the potential life of the item. Centralizing of this kind helps to reveal uneconomic duplication of purchase (three departments each buying the same item unwittingly), allowing more rational selection policies that actually allow for the purchase of extra items.

Of course, the materials may need equipment for their use, although this is not true of posters, models, mounted pictures, photographic prints, specimens and many other stimulus and information materials found lying around classrooms and desk drawers. But let us ask the question again: what do we have at present that is under-used? One often finds audio-visual and other equipment lying idle in classrooms and departmental store-areas. It can be co-ordinated and, where suitable, centralized; a booking and control system allows for easy access by teachers with a mini-mum of planning, and meanwhile some of the equipment may be suitable for student use in the library situation. Moreover, not all viewing and listening equipment is expensive; simple slide-viewers (using natural light), cheap filmstrip viewers, cassette players with inexpensive headphones (or if you lack the headphones, used in easily supervised offices or storerooms) take up only a modest proportion of even a mid-1970 budget. Centralizing equipment often makes it easier to plan for inspection and first-line maintenance, even if this is achieved only through detailing a teacher to keep track of the machines and inspect them regularly.

Economy need not stop there. Production work, of one kind or another, proliferates in schools, from the school secretary duplicating timetables and circulars to the assistant RE teacher beavering away making maps of the Middle East on the spirit duplicator. Co-ordination of production equipment and effort often leads to dramatic economies; and where the results are less startling, there is usually a more thorough and economic use of equipment and ancillary staffing, an improvement in techniques and materials produced, and beneficial effects in the damage rate to machines. The ancillaries economy is often quite chastening, underlining how re-arrangement of duties and priorities reveals previous waste (can somebody keep an eye on X while doing Y?).

Thus a school can, with a little ingenuity, make greater use of the resources and staff it already possesses; financial allocations can be re-arranged to match priorities with the minimum of heartache; and the result can offer new dimensions of possibility to the students. This does not only result from the mere placing of materials and equipment in (say) the library; it results from the fact that by organization of this kind one can offer new possibilities in teaching strategies to the teaching staff. Talk-and-chalk-and-textbook will only be supplemented and replaced when this is supported by organization. A school which does organize can make innovation possible, and a school wishing to encourage innovation must attend to the necessary backing of organization. It is precisely because resource-based learning so often concerns itself with the examination of objectives (prompted by curriculum developers and believers in educational technology) that its adoption in contemporary economic circumstances in the UK has tended to lead to saving rather than extravagance, and at least to a thorough utilization of *existing* provision.

Of course it is easy enough for a university lecturer and travelling pundit to say such things, apparently insulated from the harsh realities of life at 'the coal-face', 'the front line', the stark awfulness of school. But so many schools have now proudly shown me the quality of their achievements under economic duress that not to draw attention to this vital and heartening aspect would be to do a great injustice to them. During the 1960s, many British teachers and librarians visited the United States, to see what media centers could do when given huge injections of federal money. In a modest way, one begins to hope that there may soon be pilgrimage the other way, to see what library resource centres can do without it. I suspect also that in a few years' time, both countries may begin to visit the resource centres in schools in non-electrified African rural villages for even more surprising revelations.

The resources unit in dream and reality

We begin from where we are: what we have, who we have, and what we plan to do. Some schools have, by any standards, superb premises, adequate or lavish staffing, and a clear idea of the needs of their pupils and the ways in which these can most effectively be met. Madeley Court, in Telford, Shropshire, was given an admirable series of buildings, including a pleasant if smallish library room, with linked production and audio-visual area on a mezzanine level above, and satellite resource areas in different parts of the school to which audio materials could be relayed on command. The school exemplified a clear philosophy, appointed a Head of Resources, borrowed a librarian on secondment from the public library service, and embarked on an ambitious programme. Not all the initial provision was used as thoroughly, or in the way, that the planners had forecast, but the school was very much an act of faith, a pioneer development at a time when little information was available from UK sources.

Similarly, in Leicestershire, the famous Manor High School at Oadby was virtually built around the library resource centre, with activity areas from which pupils could easily move into and use the collection, the carrels and the audio-visual booths. The LRC became rather too much of a necessary corridor for ordinary traffic around the school, and the planners did not foresee the extent of reprographic production or the future use of TV and videotape recorders, but there can be no doubt that the building acted as a spur to innovation and to the development of resource-based and enquiry work. In Countesthorpe College, however, in the same county, unforeseen developments in school organization and the response of students led to a drastic re-arrangement of the library resource centre area, which has only recently begun to re-emerge as a unity.

The point to be emphasized is that no building can be wholly successful and no planners can infallibly foresee trends and requirements even five years ahead. The designers of John Smeaton School, Leeds, did not foresee the fashion for a unified library and audio-visual area, but placed the two so conveniently together that a joint unit was in fact easy to achieve; however, the school enrolment multiplied more rapidly than expected, and the carefully provided 'informal areas' outside many classrooms had to be used more formally than was planned. In the USA, Monona Grove High School, Madison (Wis.), created a fine library media center with four subject-based 'resource areas' leading off each corner; the intention was to encourage free flow from subject areas through the resource areas into and out of the library, but it was clear on a visit that some subject specialists felt threatened by this arrangement and arranged partial barriers of shelving and other furniture to re-establish demarcation lines.

We all adapt our premises, and few of us find everything ideal. Some of the most active resource-based work has taken place in what would be thought relatively unhelpful settings. At Codsall Comprehensive School, the unity of organization between the library resource centre, the production centre and the teachers' preparation room was maintained and emphasized despite the fact that they were physically separated by two flights of stairs and a long corridor; when a new extension allowed audio-visual preparation rooms to be added to the library resource centre area, these were in fact less used than the rooms downstairs. Many of the schools in ILEA have been unable to arrange any physical contiguity between production work and the library, yet where the Media Resources Officer and the Librarian are in harmony a high level of fully co-operative activity is maintained.

For some types of work, of course, there are certain accom-modation pre-requisites. Few schools in Britain or America have the enviable facility of some of the newer schools in Nottinghamshire, where over half the lower school can be accommodated in the library at any one time without conflict of groups. The Library Association's 1970 standards, requiring that one-tenth of the student body should be able to use the library resource centre at any one time, were thought by many to be unduly lavish and optimistic, yet obviously this depends on how completely the school has decided to make use of resource-based and enquiry strategies. We have to go back to objectives, and if we are faced with a building already in existence, we have to use those objectives to see how and in what ways we should try to modify that building or our use of it. In this connection it will be interesting to see how the Abraham Moss Centre develops in Manchester. This ambitious project brought together in one building a secondary school, a further education college, a com-munity centre and a branch public library. The library ran upwards through the centre of the building, serving a different clientele on each floor, although it was intended that all floors should be acces-sible to users of any one of them. The economic factors in favour of collocation of resources and staff, together with the educational objectives of developing community involvement, may well give us an interesting new model for future development, but planners will be impatiently awaiting the results in practice.

Physical accommodation is so intricately bound up with the organization of a resource-based learning support unit that it will repay consideration at some length in relation to the various stages where support is required. For the pupil it begins at the point where his or her sequence of activities is initiated: usually the classroom. When team teaching is in operation, involving a number of classes combined, this 'classroom' may well be the school hall, if it has one, or some other large area, for instance a series of classrooms turned into one by the pulling back of folding walls. If the subsequent activities take place partly in the hall, partly in a series of different classrooms and laboratories, and partly in the library resource centre, then there are immediate implications of timetabling, activity planning and supervision to be attended to. In many schools it is unwise to allow older pupils to wander along school corridors unattended, and unless the teacher–pupil ratio is unusually favourable there will have to be careful consideration and preparation for when separation into groups takes place, how and at what point pupil choice is operative, and how and when materials are sought, located and used. Some of these implications are for the timetabler; if it takes several minutes to get from a classroom to (say) the library, fifteen minutes to find assorted materials on a self-chosen topic, and several minutes plus to get back again, not very much will be accomplished in a forty-five minute period, especially if the materials have to be returned to the library at the end. On the other hand, careful anticipation can (as we saw with the 'Creation' theme) provide considerable basic collections of material beforehand, perhaps on book trolleys or a 'resources table', and where the element of pupil choice is limited to a few prescribed alternatives (as may often be the case with younger pupils) it is easier to include both the provision of basic materials and a pre-planned library visit in the design of the whole sequence of class meetings.

In a school with many buildings on a large site (and even more in those unfortunate schools on split sites) the planning problems of using particular facilities, whether library, laboratory, craft-room or audio-visual room, are much greater if these facilities only exist in one of the buildings. Much more devolution is necessary: the provision of scientific apparatus on temporary loan to another classroom, perhaps, where this can be arranged with due safety, as well as the provision of craft materials, AV equipment and learning resources. Multiple resource areas (somewhat after the Madeley Court model) become more necessary, although it must not be overlooked that such areas, like departmental collections, are usually more expensive and less efficient than centralized ones. The fabulous Oak Park and River Forest High School, in northern Chicago, had a series of separate subject 'resource centers' away from the main instructional materials center (the library), with smaller collections which with planning could be supplemented from the central source, but the amount of duplication of standard materials like encyclopedias and viewers was considerable. The more we have to think about economy, the less we can afford to think about devolution. However, as Keith Evans (1971) insisted, much resource-based work will fail if it poses undue difficulties for the pupil, and distance from the necessary materials is to be avoided wherever possible.

Where the activity is confined to one classroom, and to one specific subject area or department, an *ad hoc* collection of materials is readily organized, including press cuttings and other similar ephemera where relevant. The example given in *Organizing resources* of the special index to such materials produced in duplicated typescript at Redefield School, Oxford, shows how a class of pupils can work away in a social studies context, each with his or her own copy of the index for materials of first resort; this index did not, of course, include materials from collections other than the departmental one, so that for further reference the pupil would still have to proceed to the library. Project loans from the public library or elsewhere can, as we saw, supplement the school's own stock, and while we are thinking of economy it is worth noting that in some circumstances these borrowed materials can be useful to other groups, under careful supervision, as well as the group for whom they were primarily intended. This is a reason why it is useful for such external loans to come through a co-ordinating point, for instance the library resource centre, so that maximum use can be planned of any materials arriving. One has only to think of how a project collection on Tudor Britain could include (say) a model of a Tudor house, a film of 'Henry V', a set of prints showing Tudor costume, some portfolios giving examples of Tudor documents, as well as books on the period, to see that these might be used both for history classes and, by arrangement, by pupils beginning the study of Shakespearean drama.

Librarians naturally believe that as much time as possible should be spent in the library, learning to use library tools and becoming familiar with the various sections and collections therein. However, some of the work faithfully performed by teacher–librarians in 'library periods', such as teaching the different parts of a book, how to use contents pages, chapter headings and indexes, and how to take notes, can just as readily be carried out by teachers in the classroom, and be a prepared element of some of the resource-based exercises of the lower forms. The pity has been that so few teachers have bothered to do this, and to tie it in with other aspects of study including the ability to draw information out of visual and aural sources. Few school library resource centres in the UK are large enough to allow more than a couple of classes at most to use it at one time, and some are much smaller. (Some, indeed, are in use for non-library-related classwork for much of the day, and may even be form bases to which pupils revert at the beginnings and ends of periods. This is of course to be avoided at almost any cost.) Such limitations make spontaneous use of the LRC less easy, imposing the need for elaborate booking ahead by the teacher, or at least a quick preliminary check that the coast is clear before descending upon the librarian with another thirty students. However, this may have the beneficial effect of stimulating the teacher to anticipate, to plan ahead, even perhaps to consider his basic objectives, rather than persist on the level of day-to-day improvisation to which most of us descend at one time or another.

Some material, of course, must be used in the LRC itself, either because it is quick reference material that the librarian needs to keep there for the benefit of all users, or because the equipment for viewing or hearing it is kept there and should not normally be moved. In the USA, considerable back files of the major newspapers and periodicals are commonplace in school media centers, and this may include the *New York Times* on microfilm. British schools rarely have room for such holdings, and few have even considered the possibility, so that although periodicals such as *Geographical Magazine, New Scientist, New Statesman, New Society* and *Spectator* are often taken, they are discarded or cut up, as are any national or local newspapers which may be displayed. Where back files do exist, most librarians would probably prefer pupils to go through them on the spot. Similarly, it is probably easier for an individual or very small group to hear an audio recording in the LRC, through headphones, than in a classroom, but this may depend on the capacity of the LRC and what else is going on in the classroom. At the Rawlins School, Quorn (Leics), team teaching activities often take place in the school hall, and a projector is set up in a corner pointing at a suitably blank area of wall for individuals and small groups to consult the slides that may be part of a particular assignment. If such material were stored initially in the LRC, and fetched from there by the pupil, the centre would need at the least a hand viewer or light box, to make sure that the slides were in fact what he required, before he took them away. If a pupil is following up a theme through a variety of sources (for instance, finding a series of quotations from many different poets) he may need to remain continually in the LRC, changing his books every five or ten minutes; if however he is making detailed notes which will last him the rest of the available period, it does not matter whether he is back in the classroom or not.

Thus whether the pupils are able to spend long spells in the library resource centre may not be the crucial factor for planning. The point is which pupils need to remain there, and must therefore be provided with seating space, and which will require only ten minutes for search. The layout within the LRC will try to anticipate such questions as far as possible, separating 'quiet reading' areas from catalogue areas, shelving and equipment areas, and perhaps 'consultation' areas where teacher or librarian handles questions. Equally, the layout of the classroom may have to be reconsidered, allowing for a variety of materials once found to be consulted with the minimum of disturbance to others. Proportions of those seeking material to take away and those seeking material to consult on the spot will of course vary in every instance, and although the physical difficulties of particular schools may impose constraints of their own, one hopes that the main criteria will be educational.

Schools which have made a conscious decision to encourage resource-based and enquiry strategies as much as possible may have to reconsider as a result their disposition of physical accommodation to match this objective. The library resource centre may be in a relatively inaccessible part of the school (architects often place it at the end of a top corridor 'for quietness', thus creating a remote and irrelevant area) and it may pay dividends to move it nearer to the heart of things. Moreover, if this learning strategy is to be more frequently employed, it may make good sense to assign an adjoining or nearby classroom or series of classrooms for use in such activities, something which can be achieved by a simple act of timetabling. This could mean that on Tuesdays at 2.0 the second year were based within reach of the LRC, and would be able to use it spontaneously at least for information search, no matter where they normally found themselves at other times. Some schools have found this a helpful practice. For those who lay down guidelines for new buildings (and in the UK this certainly includes the Department of Education and Science) it may be important to remember that changes in teaching/learning modes have their effects on the proportion of space required for different activities. We may need to provide more room for learning, and less for teaching: or at the least, provide areas which can be used flexibly for either.

The importance of teacher-preparation areas seems to be reasonably well understood in such new American schools as I have seen, and in such showpiece establishments as the Stantonbury complex at Milton Keynes (Bucks) a very substantial provision for reprographic and audio-visual production is included. (The plans for Stantonbury envisaged a library resource centre serving a number of individual schools on the same campus, each of which in turn would have its own more modest LRC for everyday purposes. Completion of the whole scheme will not be for many years, partly depending on the growth of the new town which it is planned to serve. As at Abraham Moss and Madeley Court, the Stantonbury complex embodies the community school ideal.) Attitudes in British schools towards a co-ordinated production unit have varied considerably. For some this has been what was *meant* by a resource centre (i.e. a resource for the teacher), and visitors were proudly introduced to a white-hot stencil cutter and duplicator. Elsewhere there has been a noticeable de-emphasis; such schools as Keyworth in Nottinghamshire give the impression that resources production is something not to be very much encouraged. Yet for ILEA the MRO was often the catalyst for change.

An important element in the success of a resources support

organization will inevitably be its popularity with teachers. Malcolm Holder has argued strongly in many papers the importance of winning, indeed almost of buying, teacher involvement and co-operation. We saw in Chapter 6 how much the production element was bound up with the educational development of the teacher as a professional and his understanding of curriculum design and mat-erials selection. In physical terms this involves a focal point, a production co-ordinating centre, even if much of the actual work takes place in odd parts of the school. 'I look for the MRO or the Head of Resources or the reprographic technician and I know where to find him or to make contact with him.' This may be a splendid suite of rooms, as envisaged in the Library Association standards supplement (1972); it may be a cubby-hole where he keeps his filing boxes and notes; it may be a converted office, now holding dupli-cators, heat copiers, a radio and a linked tape recorder. The import-ant thing is not what it is, but that it should exist, be well known to teachers and offer them an immediate service. Even a small table with four labeled in-trays (say, 'Reprographic', 'Photographic', 'Audio' and 'Overhead Transparencies') can do the job if the in-trays lead to quick and valued action.

However, an important element must be teacher involvement, and this is more likely to be achieved when the teacher has something to *do* as well as hand over some diagrams and scribbled instructions. For this reason, an area where simple heat copiers, photocopiers, spirit duplicators and the like can be available for teachers to use, together with felt-tip pens and Letraset, is useful, and many schools have such equipment in various places and might gain from bring-ing it all together. In schools with wide geographical spread, local areas for simple reprographic work probably serve a valuable func-tion, particularly for last-minute work or to save a busy teacher a ten-minute round trip to a central point. In a large school, any head of department would expect (in UK) to offer advice and guidance on resources production and related matters, but an MRO, Head of Resources or similarly committed person has a key role in continuing development, and should have a room wherever possible where teachers can consult, discuss and plan co-operatively with him. Schools which simply hand over all reprographic work, unedited, to the school secretariat are losing a dimension of oppor-tunity even though they are doubtless producing efficient copies.

Previous chapters have argued the link between what we may call 'resources library' and 'resources production', and a physical expression of that link is undoubtedly a contiguous or combined library/production unit, where the joint insights of all members of the team can focus. (We will say something more about that team in the next section.) Sufficient understanding of this joint service is now current for it to be unnecessary to labour the point unduly. However, quite apart from the economy aspects and the value to the teacher of a many-sided resources team, there is a further consideration for which we should all be planning. A BBC television series has pointed out that for many young people today it is as natural to work with a camera as with a notebook; and one can add that the number of teenagers with their own cassette recorder is impressive. Previous chapters have mentioned the considerable value many teachers place upon the pupil's own creative use of the range of communication sources available. The Library Association standards supplement (1972) said: 'Pupils will also wish to communicate their ideas in non-print formats, and, therefore, facilities for this will have to be provided.' (Library Association 1972: 5) Where a combined library resources unit deals with the related activities of software provision, resources creation and hardware co-ordination, such facilities are all the easier to provide. With the right staffing, the facilities can even be provided with supervision.

Staffing is indeed the major focus of this entire book, and before we come to the next section of this chapter, which specifically looks at the question in the everyday circumstances within which most of us will be working during the years immediately ahead, it is worth recalling again the point made a few pages back. All buildings are temporary, and almost all buildings are less than ideal; it just happens that some are even less ideal than others. We have to amend our buildings as we go along, adapting them to changed possibilities as well as to changed needs and demands. This is so with staffing, with any structure of internal resources support, and with curriculum itself. Teachers who sit back and say, 'We cannot do this until we have new premises – extra colleagues – more equipment – much more money' are avoiding the perpetual challenge of the real world. There is never enough, and we never do a perfect job, but we have a stab at it. Who can say that support for resource-based learning is more important than better hospitals, improved housing, an unpolluted environment, the conquest of famine, or any other of the many causes on which public money is properly spent? None the less, with ingenuity and planning, an organization can be built up within the school which can make an important contribution towards meeting six major objectives which are important to innovation:

1. The teacher will be able to identify materials within the current school stock, available to him and/or his pupils, and relevant to his objectives and their needs.
2. The teacher will be able to establish the existence, and sometimes the usefulness, of other material which can be bought and added to stock, relevant in the same way.
3. The teacher will be able to find out what services exist from teachers' centres, galleries and museums, libraries and audio-

visual centres, as well as hiring facilities of commercial companies, and have his requests supplied via one agency within the school.

4. The teacher will be able to make for himself or have made for him, materials in reprographic, audio-visual and/or other formats, similarly relevant.

5. Teachers and pupils will be able to locate and use suitable equipment in a suitable place at an appropriate time in accordance with overall objectives and within the constraints of the typical school budget.

6. Pupils will be able to use materials and undertake units of work in physical circumstances that operate to maximum advantage to them with minimum of disturbance to others.

For all these services, accommodation is necessary, and British schools have shown considerable ingenuity and persistence in adapting unsuitable premises to new ends, as well as designing excellent new facilities when funds have been available. But as well as accommodation, schools need, crucially, people: people with skills, people with time, people with patience, people with experience, even people with little else to offer but their warm presence. Let us consider them in the light of all that has gone before.

Staffing and skills in a decade of economy cuts

In all organizations, there comes a time when what they are doing no longer adequately matches the staff available to do it. Methods change, facilities available improve or at least alter, and overall aims and objectives are modified to suit new needs. This must be so with schools, and in some ways the profession is intensely conservative, even though teachers are now surrounded by dinner ladies, caretakers, lab assistants, secretariat and others. However there have still been significant changes: elaborate hierarchies of faculty, department, subject specialist and assistant teacher; appointment of teachers to administrative, advisory or counselling posts; the growth in British schools of teachers specifically concerned with pastoral care; the employment of ancillaries in quasi-teaching roles. Services clustering around schools have also proliferated, including psychologists, careers advisers, remedial therapists and social workers, as well as inspectors, subject specialist advisers, technicians, librarians and many others.

One suspects that British education has undergone so many changes and seen so many burgeoning trends and fashions that only the most persistent, the most publicized and the most officially supported have left their imprint on staffing, apart from some accidents which need not be specified here. In discussing the staffing implications of a continuing commitment to resource-based learning, we clearly cannot ignore the competition (if that is the word) from other interests and developments. A headmaster has to balance his staff, looking as much for personalities as for skills, and eventually relating his decisions to what he or the school regards as priorities. It would be very nice if every school had a staff of clerical workers for every teaching department: a reading aide for every ten primary children: a team of audio-visual projectionists and technicians: lab assistants for home economics: one teacher for every religion represented in the school (e.g. Moslem, Hindu, Sikh, Buddhist, Jew, Bahai and varieties of Christian): and so on. When we look narrowly it is such requirements we come up with; but it may be just as important to look more broadly at the structure of school staffs as a whole, to see not only how particular tasks are to be performed but also how improvement in education (which is presumably the overall aim of the exercise) is to be encouraged.

Lawrence Stenhouse, discussing 'the curriculum problem', commented:

> As a minimum, a curriculum should provide a basis for planning a course, studying it empirically and considering the grounds of its justification ... In fact, when we apply these criteria, it is clear that neither traditional nor innovatory curricula stand up very well under close scrutiny. *Education is not in practice very sophisticated or efficient.* (1975: 5, my emphasis.)

There are a number of simple bread-and-butter reasons why particular curriculum strategies fail in particular instances, and we will look at some of these in a moment, but Stenhouse's last sentence is uncomfortably convincing. If behind our overt aim of encouraging and developing resource-based approaches and learner participation is the basic aim of improving the efficiency of educational processes in general, then we must bear in mind when planning our staffing structures the need to see that change is controlled and subject to evaluation, and that teachers receive in the process experienced practical and theoretical guidance.

Teachers are, all too often, less concerned with measuring their efficiency than with surviving. They are very concerned with problems of control (their classes are, generally speaking, conscripts), they rate order higher than efficient learning in their list of priorities, and understandably fear that changed methods may threaten it. This may well have been one of the fears behind those teachers who (as the Exeter Regional Resource Centre Project found) turned to resources personnel as much for emotional support as for materials and information (Walton and Ruck 1975). When a teacher changes his role and becomes guide rather than instructor, organizer of learning experiences rather than their performer, the threat to his survival appears to increase. After all, if his class presentation isn't achieving its object, he can change it as he proceeds by brilliant improvisation, and enjoy doing so; but if the work-card or project booklet or tape-slide sequence is flawed, much of his planning falls away, he looks a fool before the class, and it will take a lot of time to put right. The kind of advice he most needs in this regard therefore is that which cannot be given by a media resources officer or a librarian, but by an experienced teacher who is a specialist in curriculum design. In practice, outside ILEA, one of the key factors in the development of resource-based learning has been the appointment of a Head of Resources, and within ILEA, by the appointment or promotion of a key member of teaching staff to a deputy head role in curriculum planning.

Such a person needs to have a sufficient authority. The best educational practices doubtless come from teachers who are united in conviction, but such unanimity does not come all at once nor is it necessary to wait until it is achieved. It arrives as the result of a dynamic process; the management of innovation is a question of skilled use of authority and leadership.

> Change most often comes through conflict within a staff; but it is important for the leadership of the school to recognize squarely what is happening and to manage conflict within the school rather than pretend that it does not exist. (Stenhouse 1975: 169.)

So far as educational efficiency is concerned, one of the biggest problems may be the enthusiast rather than the conservative. As we saw earlier, it is all too easy for a teacher or a group of teachers to jump on a bandwagon without consideration of its effectiveness in their practice. This, in fact, is where another useful concept of Stenhouse's should be mentioned, what he describes as: 'A particular kind of professionalism . . . research-based teaching.' (1975: 141) Teachers have often been sceptical, and rightly so, of much of what counts as 'research' in education, partly because it so infrequently seems to relate to the situation as they themselves view it. At the same time, it is difficult for the teacher on the spot to put himself in the research frame of mind when he is also coping with problems of order, of materials production, of materials identification, and with guidance and marking. He needs the encouragement of being part of a school project of research and evaluation, with agreed guidelines and the spur of discreet authority. This is not easily achieved, as Stenhouse agrees:

> I believe, however, that it is worth facing these tensions and attempting to resolve them. For in the end it is difficult to see how teaching can be improved or how curricular proposals can be evaluated without self-monitoring on the part of teachers. A research tradition which is accessible to teachers and which feeds teaching must be created if education is to be significantly improved. (1975: 165.)

Stenhouse does not say so, but this would appear to tie in well with the view of the Head of Resources as a curriculum developer, stimulating not only planning and discussion but also in-service training within the school. We come back continually to the recognition that resource-based learning is concerned not only with the participation and educational development of the learner, but also with that of the teacher.

Within a school framework of curriculum renewal, the planning of material support becomes easier to manage even in a decade of drastic economies. Ideally, the appointment of full-time individuals with a production brief and a librarian brief should be considered, and even in this decade there are sometimes ways in which headmasters or local education authorities can achieve such staffing, maybe at the expense of other types of individual; the question of priorities must obviously be considered in the light of local needs and decisions. But let us put that thought to one side and consider what must take place rather than the types of individual who would be ideal to do it.

1. The learning resources of the school must be organized for retrieval, i.e. they must be identified and centrally listed with locations, and also suitably marked so that the person finding them knows that they are the particular copies of the items sought and not (say) someone's personal property. Clearly the ideal person to do this is a librarian, in the school vacations when pupils are not around; but up to a point the task can also be performed co-operatively. Items in classrooms and departmental cupboards can be duly listed by the teacher whose responsibility they currently are. Without co-ordination there will be wild disparities of description, and any librarian's heart will sink at the thought; therefore an agreed format and style must be adopted, and preferably an actual form on which the information is to be copied, directing the teacher's attention to all the elements required, such as joint authors, publishers, correct titles, series, number of slides, playing speed, and so on. Teachers will only do this if they must, so a decision is required by an appropriate person or committee after sufficient discussion and explanation. The information would be duly co-ordinated and added to the listing of items in the library resource centre, i.e. the catalogue. This will be a considerable task in itself and require not only a dispensation of time to the teacher–librarian but also the provision of some kind of clerical help: paid, voluntary or pupil.

So far this sytem would give only a simple author-title listing. Subject indexing and classification is handled at present in most schools either by teachers and pupil-helpers who have picked up the technique by trial and error (and a little reading around the subject) or by centralized processing through the local schools library service. For commercially produced printed items, this is relatively easy to organize, and one may hope that, in future, developments towards a British Media Record may help on the AV side; however, there is still the problem of locally produced material and one may again have to hand the problem over to a centralized processing unit – if the local library service can still afford to offer it. Simple and basic classification and indexing will provide at least some access to the school's stock of resources, but the indexing chapter tried to show the inadequacies and limitations of this and the extra services that could be offered by something more professionally advanced.

It would, of course, be possible in theory for teachers concerned to attend evening classes in information retrieval, if any were available. These are conspicuous by their absence, and one prominent author on cataloguing for school libraries has announced that he will not give lectures on the subject to non-librarians. Fortunately teachers are still able to borrow his book from libraries and will find it an admirable introduction to the elements of descriptive analysis, though not to the subject approach (on which topic there are many other sources). Further professional training of all kinds will be considered however later in this section. It is sufficient at this point to stress that the acquisition of such knowledge and skill takes and requires time.

2. The selection and acquisition of learning resources (book and non-book, classroom and library) should wherever possible be co-ordinated, with the general oversight and particular help of one person, logically the school librarian. The task is not to tell people what they may or may not order, but to relate orders to each other so that unnecessary duplication is avoided, overall school policy is pursued, and all possible bibliographic and selection assistance given. We saw that external borrowings were also related to acquisition, and it is helpful therefore if the person co-ordinating acquisition also undertakes external liaison and gets to know what other sources of supply are available. This is not difficult, nor does it require any very special preliminary training, although a thorough understanding of the range of educational and children's publishing in all formats is extremely helpful. It takes time, and requires that the person concerned be available for consultation by teachers. He or she will also be a key figure to have in on curriculum discussions, both the general discussions affecting the whole school and discussions relating to specific subject fields, because of the need to relate what is being planned to available resources and those other items which can most economically be purchased or otherwise acquired.

3. The co-ordination of resources production on the grounds of economy alone can be well defended in most medium-size schools, and even in multi-building schools of larger size it is usually possible to plan some sort of co-ordination, even though it will be necessary to establish sub-units and allow for more devolution of certain types of production work. The relevance of resources creation to, on the one hand, acquisition in general, and on the other hand, curriculum planning and lesson design, establishes further reasons why the Head of Resources should build into his organizational unit the means to co-ordinate and participate in learning materials production. Initially, there is the simple question of whether to produce one's own items, which involves a discussion with the teacher–librarian or whoever else is in charge of materials selection and cataloguing, to see whether something already exists or can be purchased or borrowed. Secondly, there is advice on format, layout, and other technical matters, which can be discussed with ancillaries, as well as with teaching colleagues. Thirdly, and crucially, there is the educational design dimension, which can only be instigated by the Head of Resources, although once he or she sets up a continuing process of discussion and evaluation (the foundations for Stenhouse's 'research-based teaching') it may be that consultation will not be necessary every time.

4. The co-ordination of audio-visual equipment for most economic use can also be easily defended, and even in a multi-building school some kind of rationalization is necessary. This should result in equipment being more readily available, and allow most advantageous policies to be followed in the purchasing of further equipment as finances allow. (An education authority will look with more favour on an application for extra capital expenditure if it is given clear evidence that the school has thoroughly documented its case and shown that it is making the most efficient use of what it already possesses.) The organization need not involve a heavy use of staff time as such. An important element however is that the equipment should be under continual surveillance, all defects being reported at once and checked, and servicing and repair being co-ordinated and arranged. Basically this requires a person sufficiently skilled to give an initial diagnosis, effect very simple repairs where necessary, and arrange (perhaps through the school secretary) for such outside help to be sought as may be available. Where trouble is promptly tackled, delay and inconvenience is kept to a minimum. The responsibility of the local education authority for audio-visual equipment maintenance will be considered in the next section.

5. We finally arrive at the pupil, whose need (so far as staffing is concerned) is for access to a supervised resources collection, with indexes and other research tools, at all times of the school day when he is involved in individual or small group resources work of his own. Where the school has a chartered librarian, such provision is available to the pupil; where the library resource centre is in the care of a teacher, however, there is the question of how much time this teacher has for LRC work, including physical presence therein. Some schools have tried to get round this problem by timetabling successive teachers into the library for such a purpose, on the grounds

that by spreading the load widely amongst the staff the burden on any one person is not very great. This is true, and there is the un-doubted advantage that the system brings teachers into direct contact with library supervision and the guidance of pupils therein. In practice, however, their interpretation of, and temperamental fitness for, such duties varies enormously, and it is much better that the task be limited to a very few, and if possible mostly to one or two.

This brings us to a consideration of the work of a teacher–librar-ian. So far we have only been considering the demands of resource-based learning, but the work of a teacher–librarian is broader than this and broader even than the mere support of the curriculum in its various forms. Libraries now contain non-book media, and con-cern themselves much more with the needs of teachers and pupils in project search and other similar activities, but they have always been concerned as well with the development of the enjoyment of the habit of reading and enquiry, the stimulation of the love of good literature, the provision of recreational and hobby reading and the giving of pleasure. Many school librarians get to know individual pupils informally and well, and play a role in the child's personal affective, imaginative and social development which a class teacher in a position of more apparent authority cannot. Such aspects must not be neglected because we also find uses for the library in the study of sociology, or the history of science, or as a follow-up to geographical field work.

The report of the Bullock Committee (1975) made plain their view that part of the task of developing children's reading and language skills rested with the library:

> There should be no time in a child's school life at which books become more difficult of access. The reading habit should be established early, and should receive unqualified encouragement from that point on-wards ... We shall be going on to discuss resource centres, but we must emphasize at this point that many secondary schools fall far short of satisfactory basic library provision, let alone more sophisticated facilities ... Even when the library is not used for teaching, lack of facilities for constant supervision can result in the locked door ... We believe that every secondary school should have the accommodation and staffing facilities to ensure that this kind of question does not arise. The library is at the heart of the school's resources for learn-ing, and it is simply unacceptable that this kind of weakness should exist. (1975: 303–4.)

The Bullock Committee did not recommend formulae for num-bers of librarians, assistant librarians and ancillary staff, but a note drew attention to the Library Association standards (1970), and it will be remembered by those who saw this document at the time that it recommended for schools of 800 or more a minimum of one chartered librarian plus one clerical assistant; the numbers increased on each count as the school grew in size. The 1972

Supplement added at least one production/technical assistant, recognizing that the 1970 document had given insufficient attention to non-book resources. No reader of the present book will be likely to underestimate the work that such members of staff would be faced with; however, the Bullock Committee did not have the power to commit local or national government money. In a decade of economy cuts the task of persuading anyone to sanction the appointment of extra staff on this scale is formidable. But this need not mean that schools give up; if a greater proportion of the school's work is resource-based and involves a greater use of a library resource centre, then staffing use must be readjusted accordingly. The teacher–librarian, for instance, should be recognized as playing a teaching role *in the LRC itself*, and (as the School Library Association has long urged) timetabled full-time within it. We saw already that at Codsall Comprehensive School the teacher–librarian spent three-quarters of her time in the LRC, and that the remaining quarter was covered by another teacher closely associated with the LRC's work. There would seem to be much to be said in favour of increasing that proportion, with the only caveat that some teachers actively value the chance to keep up their ordinary classroom contact, and may conceivably gain from it as school librarians.

Making sure that the teacher–librarian is in the library resource centre all day (and not always involved with his or her own classes) is of course only part of the answer to problems. The work involved in materials selection, for instance, scanning bibliographies, publishers' lists and journal reviews, and checking back with the LRC index, cannot easily be done when the centre is busy with teachers and pupils, and neither can indexing, classification, stock-appraisal, correspondence and filing. Moreover, we have already suggested that the librarian should have other contacts with teaching staff in their planning, and the Bullock Committee agree: 'In our view he should have a seat at all head of department meetings, and departments should involve him in their own internal planning.' (p. 305) This will involve altogether a considerable commitment in what are called 'out-of-school-hours', i.e. those parts of the day when pupils are not scheduled to be in the building; evenings, perhaps early mornings, and much of school vacations are therefore tied up. It is unfair to expect a person so heavily committed to give long hours to lengthy lesson preparation and particularly detailed marking of exercises and homework, and it must be recognized therefore that the kind of teaching a teacher–librarian does is that which takes place in face-to-face discussion and guidance of pupils in the library situation, either individually, in small groups, or in collaboration with other teachers in the team situation.

The Bullock Committee welcomed resource centres as having 'potentially a considerable contribution to make to the teaching of English,' (p. 305) and saw that:

... their implications for staffing, accommodation, curriculum planning and timetabling are considerable ... A school should feel the *need* for more elaborate and far-reaching resources, and its development of them should be in response to the requirements of its own curriculum planning. (p. 306.)

Those who have accepted the argument of the present book will be ready to agree that the Bullock Committee's concern for the professional training of the school librarian is even more relevant when resource-based learning bulks large in the strategical practices of the school. In paragraph 21.14 on page 305, the Committee consider the various routes open to those who wish to qualify in due course as both teachers and librarians: 'Ideally, all school librarians should be doubly qualified in teaching and librarianship, and we hope this will be the pattern of future development.' This is a growing development and many people have already reached 'dual qualification' by their own initiative. Schools who are prepared to use the school librarian in his or her teaching role *as* a school librarian should begin to seek such dually qualified people, and it is only fair that such exceptionally well-prepared people should have their merit recognized by an appropriately senior salary scale.

Meanwhile there are those other schools who find they are able to manipulate their 'points system' for ancillaries in such a way to gain themselves a qualified librarian on the administrative and professional scales. Such a person ought to be full-time, to encourage a professional to apply, and to make use of his or her services in the important work that takes place in a school library during vacations.

Chartered librarians already working in schools on a full-time basis, in such local authorities as ILEA, Nottinghamshire, Cheshire, Somerset and elsewhere, may at this point ask, pointedly, whether I wish them to be phased out in favour of the relatively rare dually qualified individuals commended above. Any system of appointments which places, full-time in the library resource centre, a person who is fully qualified in every sense as a librarian is to be applauded. It is the general experience that chartered librarians make a great difference to the schools in which they work and that their impact has almost invariably been positive. The Bullock Committee's repetition of an old *canard*: 'The only disadvantage has been where it has led to teachers taking less interest in the library,' (p. 304) was not supported by any evidence, and in most cases the librarian takes it upon himself (or herself) to increase the participation of teachers rather than decrease it. Where the appointment of a chartered librarian increases the total staff of the school (in other words, is additional to the teaching strength) it may well be a better solution than taking away from the teaching strength by seconding a teacher full-time to the LRC. However, there can be no doubt that to add to a chartered librarian's qualifications the training and experience of the qualified teacher greatly adds to the depth of understanding the librarian can bring to all the tasks awaiting him (or her) and increases considerably the already excellent contribution to be made, as well as career options.

An extension of opportunities for obtaining further professional qualifications, either by part-time study or by full-time study on leave-of-absence (seconded if possible), is desirable for anyone working in the educational field, and one hopes that more courses giving librarians an opportunity to gain a full teaching qualification, and teachers an opportunity to gain a full librarianship qualification, will multiply. In the early 1970s the Library Association felt that the Teacher–Librarian Certificate, which it offered in co-operation with the School Library Association, should be phased out, and discussions began to consider a higher quality replacement. If any such future diploma can be built into a scheme that enables the teacher eventually to reach chartered librarian status if he or she wishes, this will be splendid. My own observations in the United States, where school librarians are often content with a postgraduate course which gives them approximately half a teaching qualification and half a librarianship qualification, only one part of which they subsequently top up, convinced me that if a teacher–librarian is regarded as being 'neither one thing nor the other', or is regarded as only half a professional by one side, his standing and morale will suffer. The advantage of any system giving full dual status is that there can be no question about it.

However such courses should not be limited to teacher–librarians. Schools which cannot afford a Media Resources Officer or similar professional on the ILEA pattern must again look mostly to their teaching staff for much of the skilled work. Probably it must be a teacher to whom such a school gives the task of advising other teachers on design characteristics, technical considerations and the uses of different media. The supervision of repair and maintenance may also be a teacher-responsibility, although it is surprising how little use some schools have made of the goodwill of lab assistants and other technicians on their staffs. Courses in all aspects of this work (including the excellent ones which have been offered from time to time by the National Audio-Visual Aids Centre) should be used to full advantage, and in particular local colleges or departments of art should be approached to see what is available in the important field of graphics. (The Exeter University Institute of Education project has made excellent use of art students in training, who have come to the Regional Resource Centre for short periods of practical work to the advantage of both the students and the Centre. It may be that such opportunities can be offered by other schools in a similar way.) Mr Leslie Ryder of the ILEA has informed me that many MROs have sought opportunities of studying education and gaining a teaching qualification, and this is to be applauded.

An MRO does not at present have the same opportunity a librarian has of working in a teaching role with pupils, but as courses in audio-visual communication burgeon at pupil level and as young people themselves seek to communicate their ideas in non-print formats this may be a side of MRO work which will develop strongly.

In re-organizing its attitudes towards the teacher–librarian and to the teacher with overall responsibility for audio-visual and reprographic work, the school should also remember that neither of these people will get very far without some considerable help and support. One of the advantages of a co-ordinated resources support unit is that it often makes possible a more economic and helpful use of ancillaries, technical and clerical. Typing, copying, duplicating, packing, unpacking, recording, collating, stapling, developing, sorting, filing, are all laborious and time-consuming and also unavoidable. It is a pity if the skills and experience of highly qualified people are dissipated on repetitive and purely physical tasks. Parent volunteers, and pupil volunteers and conscripts, have each played their part in many library resource centre developments in recent years in the UK, and some schools have taken a hard look at their use of non-teaching personnel in the office, laboratories and other areas. Much innovation work in resource-based learning has depended on the enthusiasm, and readiness to co-operate, of ambitious or dedicated teachers, but we cannot plan on the assumption that all schools, or even most schools, possess such paragons. A system that cannot be run by the average school staff will quickly fail.

But in this regard, the services provided by supportive agencies in the authority area and beyond it have much to contribute, and we must summarize in the next section some of the lessons that have emerged from the analysis of this book. In the meantime, let us not forget, in discussing the ways in which producers, teachers, teacher–librarians and others can help the resources unit and sustain the development of resource-based learning in the school, that the unit should see itself in the curriculum development context, co-ordinated and led by the Head of Resources/Deputy Head or his equivalent. A resources unit will not produce its full potential in the school situation if it concentrates simply on administrative efficiency; it is here that the limitations of such otherwise excellent publications as the Library Association standards are necessarily revealed. None of the members of the resources team is any the less the professional for being part of an organization which aims to go beyond his immediate professional skills. The aim is not a tidily run library resource centre, or a neatly efficient educational materials production unit, but the better education of young people.

Support services for maximum efficiency

Although some local education authorities have been active promoters of resource-based learning and sought to make administrative arrangements to encourage and support its growth, a great deal of the impetus behind the 'resources' movement came from the grassroots. Codsall Comprehensive School was only the most famous of many other schools which tried with varying degrees of success to lift themselves up by their own bootstraps. My admiration for the achievements of such schools will have been evident from the earliest days of the Resource Centre Project. However the movement has had time to consolidate, and local education authorities and others now have plenty of evidence of the ways in which their support can most effectively be directed.

The major lesson of the 'resources' movement has been the importance of co-operation and co-ordination. At local level, co-operation between schools sharing a neighbourhood has been a valuable way of maximizing use of current resources, and the ILEA has promoted a number of encouraging experiments aimed at developing and institutionalizing such co-operation. A largeish secondary school can make facilities available to nearby primary schools, and in return receive useful help with materials for the younger forms. A polytechnic (particularly where a college of education now forms part of it) may be able to provide facilities and develop mutually useful schemes with primary and secondary schools in its area. In particular, teachers' centres in their support of teachers in all types of school in their catchment area can provide equipment and exhibit materials, as well as stimulate discussion and instigate courses and conferences, and be a curriculum materials production agency, even (as is the case in Oxfordshire) forming part of a network of such centres communicating ideas and good materials throughout the county.

Such developments may, in the first instance, cost very little to develop, and in the process not only stimulate maximum use of facilities but actually prevent unnecessary purchase or unnecessary expenditure of teacher-time. The amount of hidden waste in schools by both these practices is quite considerable, and the taxpayer may reasonably require more accountability for his money. Moreover, it is not only in such fairly traditional areas that help to schools can be cheaply provided. It would be interesting to have the figures of under-use of electronic stencil copiers and offset litho machines in county halls, and to work out how much the provision of a service to (say) the smaller schools without such production facilities would cost.

The provision of audio-visual and reprographic equipment in

schools and other educational institutions has not been matched by
the development of a genuinely efficient system for ensuring that it
remains operable. Servicing of equipment and appliances is of
course a subject of complaint nationally and internationally, and
companies themselves could do more to ensure that the machines
they market are speedily and easily put back into service when they
break down. Education authorities sometimes provide a servicing
system, but years of insufficient funding and staffing have left many
with a situation where the fitting of a new drive-belt on a recorder
or the repair of a worn-out projector puts the gadgets themselves
out of service for many weeks. Teachers complain that they sometimes have to prepare two sets of lesson notes, one for if the equipment works, the other for when it fails, and this can have disastrous
effects on the morale of otherwise innovative professionals. Some
education authorities insist that no teacher may use a specified piece
of equipment until he or she has attended a short course in its
handling and received a certificate of competence, but although this
may sometimes have a marginal effect upon the life of hardware and
(especially) software it is insufficient for the occasions when the
machinery breaks down for reasons other than incompetence.
Nowadays, equipment is increasingly easy to load and handle in
any testable way, and most damage is caused by habits of careless-
ness which no course can reveal or easily cure. In resource-based
learning, moreover, the equipment will often be used by pupils,
many of whom pose less threat to its effectiveness than some of their
mentors.

The previous section suggested that in each school one person
responsible for a co-ordinated and supervised equipment collection
could initiate a system of rapid reporting of defects and regular
examination of individual machines, so that at least those items
whose batteries have slipped, or into which someone has introduced
chewing-gum, can be quickly identified. Education authorities
would in addition be well advised to look again at their systems for
servicing and repair, checking on how many weeks a much-needed
item has to be out of use before it can be returned, and what can
be done to speed things up. Prevention is also important; the
National Audio-Visual Aids Centre will gladly advise on sturdiness
and LEA audio-visual advisers usually have good recommendations
to make.

Various types of institution and department now offer services
to schools, and it may well be that a closer co-ordination of their
efforts would not only cut costs but increase facilities. Many public
libraries offer a schools library service; some museums offer a schools
museum service; some archives departments have a schools section;
some authorities maintain an audio-visual supply service of one
kind or another. We saw that Richard Fothergill (1973: 123)
envisaged the public library service offering indexing, co-ordination

and van services for all these departments, and any local authority seriously interested in cutting costs will have been examining possibilities with care. Wiltshire's service might well be a useful stimulus to emulation and improvement. There are many public librarians who agree in theory but explain that nothing can be done during this period of cuts in funding. However, simply to say, 'We cannot yet afford even the print materials we need, let alone take on additional audio-visual items' is to compound many decades of misunderstanding about the nature of librarianship. As Louis Shores put it in June 1955, a person with a modern viewpoint might just as logically feel that '"I am so over-worked now with books that I haven't time for magazines" . . . Fundamentally he does not believe his profession is a mission of formats as much as it is of ideas.' (Shores 1955: 286-7) There is rarely a convenient moment to take on new responsibilities. In the first place, it may be that much could be achieved with only the slightest extra expenditure, by co-operation, re-scheduling and yet another look at priorities. A local education authority may not always turn down out of hand a proposal that might be able to yield an overall saving.

Chapter 7 indicated ways in which area or regional provision of centralized cataloguing facilities might ease the provision of indexes and release teacher–librarians for reader-guidance on the one hand and subject analysis of materials on the other. It is sad that here the ILEA, so often the leader in the resources field, has not taken advantage of its own considerable investment in professional librarians, and the services of its own Education Library and its Media Resources Centre, to provide a catalogue card service to all its many schools. Some other counties, including Hertfordshire, offer such a service for books, in a simple form, but not for other learning materials. As we hinted in Chapter 7, a full catalogue-card service might well pay for itself if it was aimed at a wide enough range of customers, including public libraries. If however the local and regional picture is sufficiently uncertain to make a projected service insecure, it may be that a national system would be more practicable, co-ordinated by the British Library with the encouragement of, among others, the Council for Educational Technology, with whom the BL undertook the feasibility study on the bibliographic control of non-book materials.

The Nuffield Resources for Learning Project believed (and to a great extent correctly) that it would never be economic or sensible for teachers to do most of their own resources production, but that packages and kits would none the less have to be produced specifically for schools' use based on widely agreed curricula. The materials produced by Nuffield and Schools Council curriculum projects were experimental attempts at filling this need, and often succeeded admirably while they were in operation. The difficulty has been that all such projects were of limited duration. When the Nuffield

Junior Science projects came to an end, many schools felt stranded and abandoned, and this has also been the experience of schools who responded enthusiastically to some of the Schools Council curriculum projects which eventually terminated. (The General Studies Project tried to surmount this problem by a continuing agreement with a publisher.)

Two key experiments perhaps point the way forward. We met the first in Chapters 4 and 5: the Curriculum Resources Development Project which was based at Thurmaston Teachers Centre during the educational years 1968–71. The project was headed by Emmeline Garnett, whose absorbing and entertaining account of the three years is required reading for anyone concerned with resource-based learning (Garnett 1972). The Thurmaston Project set out to identify subject areas, themes and objectives which schools were particularly concerned with and where help could most sensibly be given. There was no question of providing an on-demand service of materials; as Miss Garnett put it:

> Excessive amounts of material would have to be researched and stored – a ratio of 50:1 is a guess, but probably a conservative one. We suffer here from the magnificent freedom and individuality of our teachers – it is quite impossible to estimate what they are going to want next ... after three profitless telephone calls to the Resource Centre, teachers would lose confidence and give up trying. (1972: 79.)

(This is worth remembering in connection with increasing the autonomy and degree of choice given to the pupil; it is impossible to anticipate by production alone what pupil choices are going to be, and the teacher must plan his strategies to allow for the many occasions when information material is not immediately available and the problem of its acquisition becomes part of the learning process.) The Centre did not seek, nor was it able, to compete with the public library service or the museums service; it was supplementary and complementary to them.

An important function was to act as a clearing house or dissemination point for information about good work in progress, available materials on tape, and other similar matters, and the stimulation of co-operative groups. It was able to provide practical in-service training, to work co-operatively with the advisory services, instigate useful links with teacher-training departments. The axing of the project on economy grounds in 1971 may well have been a false economy if the time spent by other agencies, within and without schools, on the provision of substitute services is taken into account. Dudley Teachers Centre, and many others about the country, have meanwhile learnt considerably from the Thurmaston experiences and added to it their own modest but still considerable contributions to the support of resource-based learning.

The other example is the Exeter Regional Resource Centre project, now well into its second phase and funded from non-governmental sources. The Exeter RRC has been able to explore different types of need. As R. F. Farndon put it:

> Emmeline Garnett in Leicestershire worked with bands of teachers to produce project kits of local interest which mostly followed on the lines of commercial packages and landed somewhere halfway between the national and the individual. What we have tried to do at Exeter is to serve the individual first and extend to embrace others where the subject matter has been appropriate. (Walton and Ruck 1975: 63.)

In the process they found themselves engaged in much more than production:

> In the example above we have assumed that the teacher's mental picture of the finished item is the same as the designer's and that the only problem is one of production. This is far from the truth. Most teachers have no idea how to write a design brief. It is only after exhaustive discussion that the designer gets the full picture of what is wanted . . . (*ibid.*)

This had the disadvantage that it almost depended upon the teacher being able and willing to come into the centre. Subsequently, networking arrangements made it possible for initial filtering of requests to be done by teachers' centre wardens well versed in the centre's requirements – and also in other possibilities nearer at hand. The centre provided a range of resources, from simple photographs, slides and models to sophisticated packages; it also formed a valuable link between a university institute of education and the schools in its area, acted as a clearing house for information and exchange of ideas and sources, drew together a wide range of other institutions such as teachers' centres, the polytechnic, other teacher-training establishments, supportive services in the new Devon authority, and individuals with special knowledge, skills or interests. There can be no doubt that it has made an important contribution in itself to the development of educational innovation in the south-west.

Equally as important, however, is the contribution both these projects have made to our understanding of what an area or regional or local resources centre might be able to provide, at no very great expense, to a large number of schools. Jack Walton's analysis of costing led him to believe that a teachers' centre with one full-time warden could provide quite extensive resources production services of reprographic, audio and photographic materials for an initial capital cost of £1,257 maximum (assuming the centre had no equipment at all, which is unlikely), and for recurrent expenditure of about £1,800 a year. Within a year, the costs would be less because schools would be paying the cost price of items received. (Walton and Ruck 1975: 142–3.) Walton goes on to suggest that much of the initial finance could well come from relatively small contributions from schools themselves – sums that might be almost painless in view of the very substantial benefits that might be expected. He draws attention to an account (Netscher 1973) of the planning of a co-operative resources centre for a comprehensive school and four very close neighbouring primary schools. The Link committee representing all five schools not only planned liaison and fund-raising activities, but drew up proposals for joint financing of a resource centre on a simple *per capita* basis of 25 per cent per pupil per annum. This would clearly not solve all its financial problems (it amounted to between £800 and £900 a year) but it is an interesting prod to speculation. Smaller contributions than that to a neighbourhood teachers centre would make remarkable things possible from which all contributors would benefit out of all proportion to their initial donation. (These figures are 1975.)

A more radical approach would re-appraise the proportions of total expenditure on books and on teachers, in British secondary schools. It is not the purpose of the present book to encourage propositions likely to increase unemployment among qualified teachers, nor to arouse union hostility towards resource-based teaching methods. However, L. C. Taylor drew attention to the fact that the amount spent per pupil on all kinds of learning materials was a very small percentage of the amount spent per pupil on teachers. This represented the degree to which secondary education was, in Taylor's phrase, 'teacher-based' (Taylor 1972: 204). He went on to remind us that the wholesale adoption of packaged resource-based learning materials in IMU maths teaching in Sweden resulted in 'an overall *saving* of 16 per cent over conventional teaching when a team of two teachers and a teacher's aide is used for each group of ninety children rather than three teachers.' (*ibid*) After drawing attention to the increasing scarcity of qualified science and mathematics teachers in the UK (and elsewhere), he continues:

> So long as our model of the classroom is one person *teaching* a group of children it is essential that the solitary teachers should be trained. But keeping track of what is being done by children working independently, seeing that materials are there when needed, carrying out reprographic chores, running tests of a routine kind and recording scores – such jobs can be handled for a teacher or a team of teachers by someone less well qualified academically. (*ibid*.)

Rather than lose one-third of their teacher strength, schools might be willing to look at other solutions, especially if they promised to increase the flexibility of teaching strategies, improve the production of locally originated curriculum resources, and give opportunities for individual teachers to enrich their skills and understanding. If a school of 800 pupils seconded one teacher a year (or even for one term of one year) to a teachers centre or area resource centre for curriculum materials work, it would lose perhaps one twenty-fifth of its teaching staff and greatly enrich the resources available to itself and other schools in the area. Smaller primary schools might be persuaded to second teachers on a one-afternoon-a-week basis for similar purposes. Taylor's point that a 'marginal saving' in a boy's share of teaching would permit a 'dramatic increase' in learning materials is well taken. Schools in the Inner London area were offered a certain flexibility in the appointment of teachers or ancillaries by the 'Alternative Use of Resources' scheme, and in appropriate circumstances welcomed the opportunity to employ staff for supportive work rather than for 'direct teaching'. (Briault 1974 gives an account of this scheme, pp. 19–21, 47–9.) This will not be popular reading in schools whose teaching staff is well below strength, but so long as the genuine interests of teachers and their pupils are safeguarded there is much to be said for radical re-thinking here. Some teachers might even welcome the opportunity to exchange, briefly, classroom pressures for those of another kind. The experience of teachers in the ILEA who have been seconded for a period to do such work at the Media Resources Centre has been that it constituted a time of intense professional re-invigoration – although its own pressures were such that many were content to return to the familiar problems of school when the secondment was over.

It has not been possible to do more than sketch in a number of broad areas of investigation which others more closely involved in the supportive services and in educational administration can explore (and in most cases are already actively developing). To do more would require a book in itself, and perhaps a different kind of author. However, the area and regional scene is not the only one where contributions can usefully and co-operatively be made. Anyone with any experience will wish to praise wholeheartedly the efforts of the Council for Educational Technology of the United Kingdom (as it is now called) to encourage, stimulate, promote, develop and support activities, programmes, conferences, investigations, committees, working parties and publications in any way related to its area of interest. CET has itself initiated research into resource centres; it has worked closely with the Library Association to develop a cataloguing code for nonbook media; it has investigated staffing and training for CCTV; it has investigated the contribution audio-visual media can make to the education of the disadvantaged child; it has studied, and promoted further discussions into, questions of copyright; it has examined bibliographic control of non-book media and collaborated with the British Library in a feasibility study; it has convened a working party to look into the best ways of helping those concerned in the education of librarians in implications of AV media; and in many other ways too numerous to list has made its distinctive contribution. All this work has been done with a tact and diplomacy that is quite remarkable, and which is in sharp contrast to many of the trumpetings and self-advertising posturings of other associations and individuals in the field on both sides of the Atlantic.

A small but telling example of this work was the Windermere seminar on 'Learning resources in teacher education', Spring 1975, which brought together the Library and Audio-Visual Communications sections of the Association of Teachers in Colleges and Departments of Education, with representatives from the Library Association and the advice of Her Majesty's Inspectors. Joint discussions of this kind, representing the three professions examined in the pages of this book, can do nothing but good, and very often are best initiated at first by an outside body not itself involved in demarcation disputes or professional suspicions.

The Schools Council, as the major curriculum development agency in the UK, has been very active in the stimulation of curriculum discussion and the development of resource materials, but the limited life of a Schools Council project has led to considerable disillusion amongst teachers in schools. As Jean Ruddock has warned:

> Curriculum innovations that are left to make their own way may for some time travel comfortably on the passport of their sponsors' prestige . . . but without adequate structures for communication and support, innovation is unlikely to survive. (1973: 145–6.)

It may be that some different model is necessary, exchanging the three- or five-year development project for a more permanent team, whose members are regularly changing, but which continues to promote and monitor curriculum renewal in a broad subject area, updating materials at intervals and perhaps also allowing for the interchange of ideas through a series of regional filters. The present links with educational publishers could well be extended, and the overtones of national direction which may already be sounding in some readers' ears could to some extent be removed by careful organization and wording of the brief. An important element may well be grass-roots participation on a wider scale and with the possibility of the national promotion of oustanding local work.

One hopes that the British Library, as it comes to grips with its responsibilities in an era of financial stringency, will none the less be able to develop an increasingly full information service in all formats, and by working through existing organizations eventually achieve the same comprehensive coverage of non-print information materials as its predecessor the British Museum Library was able to achieve for the printed book.

Finally one hopes that the professional associations, the Department of Education and Science, and those in the universities and polytechnics (and a few remaining colleges) concerned with the professional education and in-service training of teachers, librarians and media resource officers, will take note of the increasing inter-dependence of what were once separate professional skills and people. Old boundaries no longer make the same sense, and few in any profession today can expect to go through an entire career without considerable periods of additional and supplementary re-training and experience. In some cases it may be helpful and necessary for professional development for a teacher to seek, not only courses but professional practical experience in an associated activity, be it librarianship or materials creation or whatever; this is an area where present salary scales and in particular super-annuation regulations impose quite unnecessary barriers, and this is a type of restrictive practice which for the sake of educational advance should be rapidly phased out.

9 A note in conclusion

If this has been a long, and possibly difficult, book, it was because of the complexity of the relationships to be disentangled and the contributions to be made by so many different individuals and practices. It is always easy, in a book on education, to gloss over the detailed implications because 'schools must work these out for themselves'. This does not, in my view, preclude someone else trying to offer them a hand, nor are the daily circumstances of a busy school always the best basis for prolonged and analytical thought. Moreover, the implications of resource-based learning are not for schools only, or for the education profession; librarians, media resource officers, commercial suppliers, equipment manufacturers and many others have their contributions to make and may need to be re-thinking their attitudes. Advisers and officials in local education offices, as well as the Department of Education and Science, are engaged in constant re-examination of the requirements of the education scene, and those concerned with the educational pre-paration of teachers, librarians, media resource officers, design technicians and many others will have much to re-appraise as new needs and methods arise and new pressures develop for change.

No single author can hope to have got it all right. There are many librarians, for instance, who will dispute passionately the implications of many of the previous chapters, both as they regard information retrieval and the attitude towards the necessary pro-fessional qualifications for library resource centre work. Teachers will possibly bridle at the amount of attention paid to ancillary workers, and argue that too much emphasis was placed on matters of comparatively minor importance. Media resource officers may complain that their role has been insufficiently analysed. Many schools and local authorities may feel their own achievements should have been written up more fully. Enthusiasts for the opinions and attitudes reflected in the *Black Papers* will not be impressed, and it is hard for one person to know how thoroughly he has digested the implications of the present economic decline. I look forward to comments from all concerned.

What cannot, I believe, be controverted is that resource-based learning implies the interaction of co-operating people, at least in the spirit of this enquiry if not precisely to every letter of it. We cannot in education afford an attitude of improvising amateurism, especially when trying to deal with the challenges of our time in circumstances of sharp financial restriction. As social workers and welfare officers know only too well, when we have no money to spare our problems don't go away. The aspirations of the curriculum development decade were not the playthings of the affluent, but responses to urgent needs that we will have to try, somehow or other, to tackle.

To this end, every one of us involved must necessarily think and plan harder, and preceding chapters tried to help by analysing what there was to plan and think about. Moreover, because of the interlocking contributions of different people with different skills, it is impossible any longer to separate off and say, 'This is only your concern, and this is only mine.' A teacher cannot plan for resource-based work without an understanding of his colleagues acting in the media production and media librarian modes; equally, neither of them can proceed meaningfully without an understanding of the teacher's purposes and practice, and those of each other. I hope very much that, in correcting the mistakes and misunderstandings of this book, all three groups will find themselves in closer concert with each other and with an enhanced understanding of themselves.

References

Ahlers, E. and Sypert, M. (1969). 'The case for decentralization: when multiple resource centers work – and when they don't', *Library Journal* 15, Nov: 41–4.

Albert, Tim (1975). 'An injection of enthusiasm where it's needed', *Times Educ. Supp.*, 6 June: 27.

Amaria, R. P. and Leith, G. O. M. (1969). 'Individual versus co-operative learning', *Educ. Research* 11 (3), June: 193–9.

American Association of School Librarians and Association for Educational Communications and Technology (1975). *Media programs, district and school*, Chicago: American Library Assocn.; Washington DC: Assocn. Educational Communications and Technology.

American Library Association (1960). *Standards for school library programs*, Chicago: American Library Assocn.

American Library Association; School Library Manpower project (1974). *Curriculum alternatives: experiments in school library media education*, Chicago: American Library Assocn.

American Library Association and National Education Association (1969). *Standards for school media programs*, Chicago: American Library Assocn. Washington DC: National Educ. Assocn.

Anglo-American Cataloguing Rules (1967). British text, Library Assocn.

Ashton (1578) *see* Great Britain, Dept. Educn. and Science (1964). *The use of books*, Educ. Pamphlet No. 45, HMSO.

Audio-Visual Instruction (1970). 15 (4), April: 89, 92, 94.

Averch, H. *et al.* (1972). *How effective is schooling? A critical review and synthesis of research findings*, Santa Monica, Calif: Rand Corpn. (R-950-PCSF/RC).

Bagley, C. (1972). 'Why withdraw the race pack?' *Times Educ. Supp.*, 11 Feb: 4.

Beeby, C. E. (1970) *in* Howson, G. (ed.). *Developing a new curriculum*, Heinemann for Centre for Curriculum Renewal & Educational Development Overseas.

Benn, C. and Simon, B. (1970). *Half way there*, McGraw Hill.

Bennett, N. (1976) *Teaching Styles and Pupil Progress*, Open Books.

Bernstein, B. B. *Class, codes and control*, Vol. 1, 1971; Vol. 2, 1973; Vol. 3, 1975, Routledge & Kegan Paul.

Beswick, N. W. (1967). 'The "Library College" – the "true university"?' *Library Assocn. Record* 69 (6): 198–202.

—— (1970). 'The Certain Standards in context: A study of the American School Library Materials Centre concept', *Journal of Librarianship* 2 (3), July: 160–74.

—— (1971). 'Certain and after: from School Library to Media Centre', *Journal of Librarianship* 3 (2), April: 120–35.

—— (1972). *School resource centres*, Schools Council Working Paper 43, Evans/Methuen.

—— (1975). *Organizing resources: Six case studies*, Heinemann Educational Books.

Black Papers see Cox, C. B. and Dyson, H. E. (eds) (1969).

Bloom, B. S. (1956). *Taxonomy of educational objectives: the classification of educational goals. Handbook 1: Cognitive domain*, Longman.

Branscomb, Harvie (1940). *Teaching with books: a study of college libraries*, Chicago: American Library Assocn.

Bridges, S. A. (1969). *Gifted children and the Brentwood experiment*, Pitman.

—— (1975). *Gifted children and the Millfield experiment*, Pitman.

Briggs, Leslie *et al.* (1967). *Instructional media: a procedure for the design of multi-media instruction: a critical review of research and suggestions for future research*, Pittsburgh: American Institutes for Research.

Bruner, Jerome S. (1963). *The process of education*, New York: Vintage.

—— (1971). 'The process of education revisited', *Phi Delta Kappan* 53 (1), Sept.: 18–21.

—— (1972). *The relevance of education*, Allen & Unwin.

Bullock, *Sir* Alan, *see* Great Britain: Dept. Education and Science (1975).

Burstall, Claire (1968). *French from eight: a national experiment*, Slough: National Foundation for Educational Research; New York: Fernhill House Ltd.

—— (1970). 'French in the primary school: some early findings', *Journal of Curriculum Studies* 2 (1): 48–58.

Campeau, Peggy (1965). *Level of anxiety and presence or absence of feedback in programmed instruction*, Palo Alto, Calif: American Institutes for Research.

Carey, R. J. P. (1964). 'A technical information course for engineering and science students at Hatfield College of Technology', *Library Assocn. Record* 66 (1), Jan.: 14–20.

Cartier, Francis A. (1964). 'After the programming fad fades – then what?' *Visual Education*, April: 2–5.

Cattell, Raymond B. (1965). *The scientific analysis of personality*, Penguin.

Centre for Educational Research and Innovation (CERI) (1972). *The nature of the curriculum for the eighties and onwards: report of a workshop . . . from 29th. June to 4th. July 1970*, Paris: OECD (edited by George Taylor).

Certain, C. C. (1920) *see* National Education Association and North Central Association . . . Committee on Library Organization (1920).

Chamberlin, Leslie J. (1969). *Team teaching: Organization and Administration*, Columbus, Ohio: Charles Merrill.

Chibnall, Bernard (1976). *The organization of media*, Bingley.

Collis, Paul (1974). '8mm film-making in an ESN school', *Project. Newham Teachers Centre* series 2, v. 12, July: 10–12.

Connell, Stephanie (1973). 'Audio-visual aids in the infants school', *Trends in Education*, Jan.: 23–26.

Coulson, Ernest H. and Nyholm, R. S. (1966). 'Aims and ideals of the Nuffield Chemistry Project', *Education in Chemistry* 3 (5), Sept.: 229–32.

Council for Educational Technology (CET) (1975). *Learning resources in teacher education: Report of a seminar on the availability, management and application of learning resources in teacher education held at Windermere, Feb. 19–21 1975*, CET.

Cox, C. B. & Dyson, D. E. (eds) (1969a). *Fight for education: a black paper*; (1969b) *Black paper two: the crisis in education*, Critical Quarterly Society.

Cunningham, Hugh (1971). 'A most sophisticated white elephant replies ... to "Multi-media resource centres: a cautionary note" [by K. Evans q.v.]', *Secondary Educn.* 2(1), Autumn: 21, 25–6.

Davies, I. K. and Hartley, J. M. (eds) (1972). *Contributions to an educational technology*, Butterworths.

Davies, T. N. and Leith, G. O. M. (1967), 'Some determinants of attitude and achievement in a programmed learning task', *Aspects of Educnl. Technology*, Methuen: 446–67.

Dewey, Melvil (1906). 'Library pictures', *Public Library* 11: 10–11.

Dow, Peter B. (1971). '"Man: A course of study" in retrospect: a primer for curriculum in the 70s', *Theory into Practice* 10 (3), June: 168–77.

Drucker, Peter (1959). 'The educational revolution', *in* Halsey, A. H., Floud, Jean, and Anderson, C. Arnold (eds) (1965). *Education, economy and society: a reader in the sociology of education*, London: Collier-Macmillan; New York: Free Press (1961).

Dyer, C., Brown, R. and Goldstein, E. D. (1970). *School libraries: theory and practice*, Bingley.

Edison, Thomas Alva *in* Saettler, P. (1968). *A history of instructional technology*, New York: McGraw Hill.

Edwards, R. P. A. (1969). 'The resource centre in a flexible school', *Library Assocn. Record* 71 (8), August: 237–40.

—— (1973). *Resources in schools*, Evans.

Esland, Geoffrey M. 'Teaching and learning as the organization of knowledge', *in* Young, M. F. D. (1971), *Knowledge and control*, Collier-Macmillan.

Evans, Keith (1971). 'Multi-media resource centres: a cautionary note', *Secondary Educn.* 1 (3), Summer: 3–5.

Fairfax, O. and others (1976). *Audio-visual materials: development of a national cataloguing and information service*, Council for Educational Technology, (Working Paper 12).

Farndon, R. F. 'The role of the educational designer', *in* Walton, J. and Ruck J. (1975). *Resources and resource centres*, Ward Lock Educational.

Foskett, D. J. (1962). *The creed of a librarian: no politics, no religion, no morals*, Library Assocn. Reference, Special and Information Section, North-Western Group (Occasional Papers 3).

Foskett, D. J. and Foskett, Joy (1974). *The London Education Classification: a thesaurus/classification of British educational terms*, Education Libraries Bulletin Supplement six, 2e. London University, Institute of Education Library.

Fothergill, Richard (1973). *Resource centres in colleges of education*, Working Paper 10, Nat. Council Educnl. Technol.

Freeman, John (1969). *Team teaching in Britain*, Ward Lock Educational.

Friedlander, B. Z. (1965). 'A psychologist's second thoughts on concepts, curiosity and discovery in teaching and learning', *Harvard Educnl. Review* 35(1), Winter: 18–38.
Gallagher, James J. (ed.) (1965). *Teaching gifted students: a book of readings*, Boston: Allyn & Bacon Inc.
Garnett, E. (1970) *see* Leicestershire Curriculum Development Project (1970).
Garnett, E. (1972). *Area resource centres*, Arnold.
General studies project, York *see* Schools Council General Studies Project York (1970).
Getzels, J. W. and Jackson, B. W. (1962). *Creativity and intelligence*, New York: Wiley.
Goodman, Paul (1971). *Compulsory miseducation*, Penguin.
Gossage, Wayne (1975). 'The American Library College movement to 1968: the library as curriculum, and teaching with books', *Education Libraries Bulletin* 18(2), Summer 1975: 1–21.
Gould, Ronald (1950). 'Local film libraries', *Visual Education* 1(2), Feb.: 4–5.
Great Britain: Board of Education (1944). *Teachers and Youth Leaders: Report of Committee . . . to consider supply, recruitment and training of teachers and youth leaders* (Chairman: Sir Arnold McNair), HMSO.
—— Dept. of Education and Science (1964). *The use of books*, Educational Pamphlet No. 45, HMSO.
—— (1975). *A language for life: Report of the Committee of enquiry . . . chairmanship of Sir Alan Bullock FBA*, HMSO.
—— Ministry of Education (1957). *Circular 323. Liberal education in technical colleges*, May, HMSO.
Gribble, J. H. (1970). *Introduction to the philosophy of education*, Allyn & Bacon.
Guilford, J. P. (1959). *Personality*, McGraw Hill.
Halsey, A. H., Floud, Jean, and Anderson, C. Arnold (eds) (1961). *Education, economy and society: a reader in the sociology of education*, New York: Free Press; London: Collier-Macmillan (1965).
Haney, J. B. and Ulmer, H. J. (1970). *Educational media and the teacher*, Dubuque, Iowa: Brown.
Hanson, John (1975). *The use of resources*, Unwin Education Books.
Hartley, J. A. (1974). 'Programmed instruction 1954–1974: a review', *Programmed Learning and Educational Technology* 11 (6), Nov: 278–91.
Heeks, Peggy (1967). *Administration of children's libraries*, Library Assocn. Pamphlet No. 30, Library Association.
Henderson, R. P. (1972) *in Automated Education Letter*, December.
Hilliard, Robert *in* Toffler, Alvin (1970), *Future shock*, Pan.
Hines, Barry (1968). *A kestrel for a knave*, Michael Joseph; or *Kes*, Penguin 1969.
Hirst, Paul (1973). 'Towards the logic of curriculum development', *in* 'Standing Conference on Curriculum Studies', *The curriculum: Research innovation and change*, Philip Taylor and Jack Walton (eds), Ward Lock Educational: 9–26.
Holder, Malcolm and Mitson, R. (1974). *Resource centres*, Methuen.
Holly, Douglas (1971). 'Preparing teachers for the resources approach', *Forum for discussion of new trends in education*, 14(1), Autumn: 8–10.
Holly, Douglas (1974). *Beyond curriculum: changing secondary education*, Paladin; Hart-Davis, McGibbon 1973.

Holt, John (1964). *How children fail*, Pitman.

Hostrop, R. W. (1973). *Education inside the library-media center*, Hamden, Conn: Shoestring Press.

Howson, Geoffrey (ed.) (1970). *Developing a new curriculum*, Heinemann for Centre for Curriculum Renewal and Educational Development Overseas.

Hudson, Liam (1966). *Contrary imaginations*, Methuen; Penguin 1967.

Hudson, V. C. (1963). *O ye jigs and juleps!* Joseph.

Humanities Curriculum Project *see* Nuffield Schools Council Humanities Curriculum Project (1970).

Illich, Ivan (1971). *De-schooling society*, Calder & Boyars.

Jackson, Philip W. (1968). *Life in classrooms*, New York: Holt Rinehart & Winston.

Jamison, Dean, Suppes, Patrick and Wells, Stuart (1974). 'The effectiveness of alternative instructional media', *Review of Educational Research* 44(1), Winter: 1–67.

Jones, Sir Brynmor (1968). 'The development of visual aids and their place in schools', *Photographic Journal*, Sept.: 281–5.

Judge, Harry (1974). *School is not yet dead*, Longman.

Kes, see Hines, Barry (1968).

Knapp, Patricia B. (1966). *The Monteith College Library Experiment*, New York: Scarecrow Press.

Knapp School Libraries Project *see* Sullivan, Peggy (ed.) (1968).

Knudson, Richard (1971). 'The effect of pupil-prepared videotaped dramas upon the language development of selected rural children', *Research in the teaching of English* 5(1), Spring: 60–6.

Labov, W. (1972), 'The logic of nonstandard English', *in* Giglioli, P. P. (ed.) (1972). *Language and social contract*, Penguin.

Lathrop, Edith A. (1934). *A study of rural school library practices and services*, Chicago: US Office of Education, Dept. of the Interior.

Leicestershire. Curriculum Development Project (1970). *Creation: handbook* (duplicated typescript).

—— Curriculum notebooks (1970). No. 1. *Belgrave: study of a parish church* (duplicated typescript).

Leith, G. O. M. (1969). 'Learning and personality', *Aspects of Educational Technology II*, Methuen: 101–9.

Library Association (1967). *College of Education libraries: recommended standards for their development*, Association of Teachers in Colleges and Depts. of Education and Library Assocn.

—— (1970 and 1972). *School library resource centres: recommended standards for policy and provision. 1970. A supplement on non-book materials 1972*, Library Assocn.

—— (1971). *College libraries: Recommended standards of library provision in colleges of technology and other establishments of further education*, Library Assocn.

—— Media Cataloguing Rules Committee (1973). *Non-book materials cataloguing rules*, Working Paper 11, National Council for Educational Technology with Library Assocn.

Linden, R. O. (1967). 'Tutor–Librarianship: a personal view', *Library Assocn. Record* 69(1), Oct.: 351–5, 357.

Locke, Michael (1974). 'The technological frontiers', *Education* 144(4), 26 July: 120–1

MacDonald-Ross, Michael *quoted in* Locke, Michael (1974).

McLuhan, Marshall (1962). *The Gutenberg galaxy: the making of typographic man*, Routledge.

—— (1964). *Understanding media: the extensions of man*, New York: New American Library (Signet books).

—— and Fiore, Quentin (1967). *The medium is the massage*, New York: Bantam.

—— (1968). *War and peace in the global village*, New York, London, Toronto: Bantam.

McNair Report (1944) *see* Great Britain: Board of Education (1944).

Mager, R. F. (1962). *Preparing objectives for programmed instruction*, San Francisco: Fearon.

Marburger, C. L. (1963). 'Considerations for educational planning', *in* Passow, A. H. (ed.) *Education in depressed areas*, Teachers College Press: 298–321.

Mews, Hazel (1972). *Reader instruction in colleges and universities: an introductory handbook*, Bingley.

Mitson, R. (1972). 'A view of resource centres', *Ideas* no. 22, June: 45–9.

Morris, C. W. *et al.* (1972). *Libraries in secondary schools*, School Library Assocn.

National Conference of Professors of Educational Administration (1971). *Educational futurism 1985*, Berkeley, Calif: McCutchen.

National Council for Educational Technology (NCET). *Progress and promise, 1967–73*, NCET, 1974.

National Education Association and North Central Association of Colleges and Secondary Schools (1920). *Standard library organization and equipment for secondary schools of different sizes: Report of the Committee on Library and Equipment of the NEA and NCACSS. Chairman: C. C. Certain*, Approved by American Library Assocn.: Committee on Education. Amer. Lib. Assocn.

National Society for Study of Education (NSSE) (1943). *Yearbook* 42nd, Part Two, *The library in general education*, Chicago: Univ. of Chicago Dept. of Educn.

Needham, C. D. (1971). *Organizing knowledge in libraries*, Deutsch.

Netscher, Paddy (1973). 'Five schools and an estate', *Forum for discussion of new trends in education*, 16(1), Autumn: 25–6.

Nuffield/Schools Council Humanities curriculum project (1970). *The humanities project*, Heinemann Educational Books.

Oettinger, Anthony G. (1969). *Run, computer, run: the mythology of educational innovation*, Camb. Mass: Harvard Univ. Press.

Peterson, A. D. C. (1972). 'Secondary education as a phase in life-long education', *Comparative Education* 8(1), April: 1–5.

Phenix, Philip H. (1964). *Realms of meaning: a philosophy of the curriculum for general education*, McGraw Hill.

Pidgeon, A. A. (1970). *Expectation and pupil performance*, Slough: National Foundn. for Educational Research; New York: Fernhill House Ltd.

Platt, Peter (ed.) (1972), *Libraries in colleges of education*, 2e. Library Assocn.

Postlethwait, Samuel *et al.* (1969). *The audio-tutorial approach to learning through independent study and integrated experiences*, Minneapolis: Burgess.

Postman, N. and Weingartner, C. (1971). *Teaching as a subversive activity*, Penguin.

Programmed Learning and Educational Technology (1967). Editorial.

Reimer, Everett (1971). *School is dead*, Penguin.

Riddle, Jean *el al.* (1970). *Nonbook materials: the organization of integrated collections*, Ottawa: Canadian Library Assocn.

Rowntree, Derek (1974), *Educational technology in curriculum development*, Harper & Row.

Rubinstein, D. and Simon B. (1969). *The evolution of the comprehensive school, 1926–1966*, Routledge & Kegan Paul.

Ruddock, Jean (1973). 'Dissemination in practice', *Cambridge Journal of Education* 3: 143–58.

Ryder, Leslie (1972). 'Curriculum planning should come first', *Times Educnl. Supplement*, 21 July: 30.

Saettler, P. (1968). *A history of instructional technology*, New York: McGraw Hill.

Sayers, W. C. Berwick (1926). *Manual of classification*, Grafton.

Schools Council General Studies Project, York, (1969). *Resource centres*, Schools Council.

Schools Council/Nuffield Humanities Curriculum Project *see* Nuffield/ Schools Council.

Schools Council, Working Papers, 43 (1972) *see* Beswick, N. W. (1972).

Sharp, H. A. (1922). 'Some further uses of gramophones in public libraries', *Library World* 25: 297–9.

Shifrin, Malcolm (1973). *Information in the school library*, Bingley.

Shores, Louis (1935). The Library Arts College, a possibility in 1954? *School and Society* XLI, 26 Jan., 110–14. Also reprinted in *The Library College* Philadelphia, Penn: Drexel Press, 1966: 3–9.

—— (1955). 'Enter the materials center', *American Library Assocn. Bulletin* June: 285–8.

—— (1970). *Library-College USA: essays on a prototype for an American higher education*, Tallahassee, Florida: South Pass Press.

—— *et al.* (1966). *The Library College*, Philadelphia, Penn: Drexel Press.

Sigel, I., Jarman, P. and Hanesian, H. (1967). 'Styles of categorization and their intellectual and personality correlates in young children', *Human Development* 10(1): 1–17.

Skinner, B. F. (1954), 'The science of learning and the art of teaching', *Harvard Educnl. Review* 24(2), Spring: 86–97.

Snow, R. E. and Saloman, G. (1968). 'Aptitudes and instructional media', *Audiovisual Communications Review* 16(4), Winter: 341–357.

Snow, R. E., Tiffin, J. and Seibert, W. F. (1965). 'Individual differences and instructional film effects', *Journal of Educational Psychology* 56(6), December, 315–326.

Stenhouse, Lawrence (1970–1). 'Some limitations of the use of objectives in curriculum research and planning', *Paedagogica Europea*: 78–83.

—— (1975). *An introduction to curriculum research and development*, Heinemann Educational Books.

Sullivan, Peggy (ed.) (1968), *Realization: the final report of the Knapp School Libraries Project*, Chicago: American Library Assocn.

Taylor, Harold (1960). *Art and intellect*, New York: Doubleday.

Taylor, L. C. (1972). *Resources for learning*, 2e. Penguin (1e. 1971).

Thelen, Herbert A. (1972). *Education and the human quest*, University of Chicago Press.

Toffler, Alvin (1971). *Future shock*, Pan; Bodley Head (1970).

Torrance, E. P. (1962). *Guiding creative talent*, Englewood Cliffs, New Jersey: Prentice Hall.
—— (1963). *Education and the creative potential*, University of Minnesota Press.
—— (1965). *Rewarding creative behavior*, Englewood Cliffs, New Jersey: Prentice Hall.
Trump, J. L. (1959). *Images of the future*, Washington DC: National Assocn. Secondary School Principals.
—— (1966). 'Team teaching', *Visual Educn*. Nov.: 26–35.
Unwin, D. (ed.) (1969). *Media and methods: Instructional technology in higher education*, McGraw Hill.
Vernon, Philip E. (ed.) (1957). *Secondary school selection: British Psychological Society enquiry*, Methuen.
—— (1964). *Personality assessment: a critical survey*, Methuen.
Waite, C. A. and Colebourn, R. (eds) (1975). *Not by books alone*, School Library Assocn.
Walton, J. and Ruck, J. (eds) (1975). *Resources and resource centres*, Ward Lock Educational.
Warwick, David (1971). *Team teaching*, University of London Press.
Weihs, J. R., Lewis, S. and Macdonald, J. (1973). *Non-book materials: the organization of integrated collections*, Ottawa: Canadian Library Assocn. (distributed in UK by White Lion Publishers Ltd).
Whitfield, Richard (1971). 'Curriculum in crisis', *in* Whitfield, Richard (ed.), *Disciplines of the curriculum*, McGraw Hill.
Williams, Lester A. (1939). 'What the school expects of the school librarian', *Library Journal* 64, 15 Sept.: 678–80.
Woodruff, A. B. *et al.* (1966). 'Effects of learner characteristics on programmed learning performance', *Psychology in the schools* 3, Jan.: 72–77.
Wright, Gordon H. (1961). Letter, *Library Assocn. Record* 63(9), Sept.
Yates, A. and Pidgeon, D. A. (1957). *Admission to grammar schools: Third interim report on the allocation of primary school leavers to courses of secondary education*, National Foundation Educational Research.
Young, Michael F. D. (1971). 'An approach to the study of curricula as socially organized knowledge', *in* Young, Michael F. D. *Knowledge and control: new directions for the sociology of knowledge*, Collier-Macmillan, 19–46.
—— (1973). 'Taking sides against the probable: problems of relativism and commitment in teaching and the sociology of knowledge', *Educational Review* 25, June: 210–22.

Bibliographic sources

(See Chapter 5, 'The sources of selection'.)

Books in Print (annual). New York and London: Bowker.
British Books in Print: the reference catalogue of current literature, (annual). London: Whitaker.
British Education Index (1954–). London: Library Association.
British National Bibliography (1950–). London: British Library, Bibliographic Service Division.
British National Film Catalogue (1963–). London: British Film Institute.
Cumulative Book Index (1898–). New York: H. W. Wilson.
Education Index (1929–). New York: H. W. Wilson.
ERIC (Education Resources Information Center) (1964–). US National Institute of Education, Washington DC 20202 (for more detail *see* Humby, Michael (1975).
Humby, Michael (1975). *A guide to the literature of education*, Education Libraries Bulletin Supplement one, 3rd. edn, University of London Institute of Education Library.
Library of Congress Catalogs (various). These catalogs can be consulted in major libraries.
Visual Education National Information Service for Schools (VENISS) including their catalogues, *viz*:
Audio-visual aids: films, filmstrips, transparencies, wallsheets and recorded sound. London: Educnl. Foundn. for Visual Aids (EFVA).
Part 1: religious education, English, modern languages (1971).
Part 2: history, social history, social studies (1971).
Part 3: economics; general, physical and economic geography (1971).
Part 4: (i): regional geography 1: general and Europe (1971).
Part 4 (ii): regional geography 2: the Americas, Africa, Asia, Australasia (1971).
Part 5: mathematics, astronomy, physics, chemistry (1973).
Part 6 (i): palaeontology, biology, botany, zoology (1973).
Part 6 (ii): human biology, hygiene and health, teacher education (1973).
Part 7: engineering and technology, agriculture, business studies (1973).
Part 8: arts and crafts, domestic science, sport (1975).

Additional reading

Innovation

Ackoff, Russell L. (1974). *Redesigning the future: a systems approach to societal problems*, New York and London: Wiley (Chapter 5, Education: 71–95).

Bennis, W. G., Benne, K. D., and Chin, R. (1969). *The planning of change*, Holt, Rinehart & Winston.

*Bolam, R. (1974). *Teachers as innovators: the types of environment most likely to favour the active and effective participation of teachers in educational innovation*, Supplementary paper for OECD Conference on Teacher Policies, Nov.

Goodlad, John I. (1963). *Planning and organizing for teaching*, Washington: National Education Assocn.

Gross, N. *et al.* (1971). *Implementing organizational innovations*, Harper & Row.

Havelock, R. G. (1969). *Planning for innovation through dissemination and utilization of knowledge*, Ann Arbor, Mich: Centre for Research on Utilization of Scientific Knowledge, Inst. for Social Research.

Havelock, R. G. and Havelock, M. C. (1973). *Training for change agents*, Univ. Michigan Institute for Social Research.

Hoyle, E. (1970). 'Planned organizational change', *Research in education* 3: 1–22.

Lippitt, R. *et al.* (1958). *The dynamics of planned change*, Harcourt Brace & World.

Parlett, Malcolm and Hamilton, David (1972). *Evaluation as illumination: a new approach to the study of innovatory programs*, Univ. Edinburgh, Centre for Research in the educational sciences, Occasional Paper 9, Oct.

Smith, L. and Keith, P. (1971). *Anatomy of educational innovation: an organizational analysis of an elementary school*, Wiley.

Spackman, R. C. (1971). *A consideration of the role of the teachers centre warden as an external change agent with reference to sixth form general studies project*, M. Ed. Bristol Institute of Education.

Curriculum and methodology

Dearden, R. F. 'Instruction and learning by discovery', *in* Peters, R. S. (1967). *The concept of education*, Routledge & Kegan Paul: 135–55.

Eisner, Elliot W. (1971). 'Media, expression and the arts', *Studies in Art Education* 13 (1), Fall: 4–12.

Hooper, Richard (ed.) (1971). *The curriculum: context, design and development*, Edinburgh: Oliver & Boyd.

James, Charity M. (1968). *Young lives at stake: a reappraisal of secondary schools*, Collins.

Maclure, Stuart (1972). *Styles of curriculum development*, conference held at Allerton Park, Monticello, Illinois, USA, 19–23 Sept. 1971, organized jointly by CERI and University of Illinois, Paris: OECD.

Pring, Richard (1972). 'Knowledge out of control', *Education for Teaching* 89, Autumn: 19–28.

—— (1973). 'Curriculum integration: the need for clarification', *New Era* 54 (3), April: 59–64.

Richmond, W. Kenneth (1971). *The school curriculum*, Methuen.

—— (1972–3). 'Are alternatives to schooling necessary?' *Scottish Educn. Journal* 55(46), 29 Dec. 1972/5 Jan. 1973: 977–8.

—— (1973). 'The "hidden curriculum" in education', *Scottish Educn. Journal* 56(1), 12 Jan.: 8–9.

Rudd, W. G. A. (1969). *Curriculum innovation: regional and local efforts in curriculum innovation in practice*, (ed. M. R. Bar) Edge Hill College of Educn.

Schelsky, H. (1961). 'Technical change and educational consequences', *in* Halsey, A. H., Floud, J. and Anderson, C. Arnold (eds). *Education, economy and society: a reader in the sociology of education*, New York: Free Press; London: Collier-Macmillan: 31–6.

Shulman, Lee S. and Keislar, Evan R. (eds) (1966). *Learning by discovery: a critical appraisal*, Proceedings of a conference (under the sponsorship of Stanford University and the Committee on Learning and the Educational Process of the Social Science Research Council) Chicago: Rand McNally.

Educational technology

Chu, G. C. and Schramm, W. (1967). *Learning from television: what the research says*, Institute for Communications Research, Stanford University.

Centre for Educational Research and Innovation (1971). *Educational technology; the design and implementation of learning systems*, Paris: OECD.

Coles, Colin (1969). 'Educational television and educational technology', *National Educational Closed Circuit Television Association Bulletin* 2, Spring: 19–22.

Feeley, Joan T. (1974). 'Interest patterns and media preferences of middle grade children', *Reading World* 8(3), March: 224–37.

Hartley, J. R. and Lovell, K. (1974). 'Computer based learning: a perspective,' *Social Science Research Council Newsletter* 21, Jan.: 8–10.

Layard, Richard (1973). 'The cost-effectiveness of the new media in higher education', *British Journal Educational Technology* 3(4), Oct.: 158–76.

Libraries and resources

Alice Josephine, Sister (1971). 'A library-media school', *Journal of Education* (Halifax, Nova Scotia) 21(1), Fall: 14–18.

Blandford, S. (1969). The role of the professional librarian in the school, *Library Assocn. Record* 71(7), July: 207–9.

Bradbury, Dennis (1974). 'The resource centre in further education', *National Educational Closed Circuit Television Assocn. Bulletin* 10: 25–6.

Briault, Eric (1974). *Allocation and management of resources in schools*, Council for Educational Technology, Occasional Paper 6, Councils and Educn. Press.

Brick, E. Michael (1967). 'Learning centers: the key to personalized instruction', *Audiovisual Instruction* 12(8), Oct.: 786–92.

Commonwealth Secondary School Libraries Research Project (1972) *Secondary school libraries in Australia: a report on the evaluation of the Commonwealth Secondary Schools Libraries Program*, Brisbane: Univ. of Queensland Dept. of Education.

Davies, W. J. K. (1975). *Learning resources: an argument for schools*, CET.

Enright, B. J. (1972). *New media and the library in education*, Bingley.

Fothergill, R. (1971). *A challenge for librarians?* (National Council Educational Technology Working Paper 4), Councils and Educn. Press for NCET.

Gaver, M. V. (1969). *Patterns of development in elementary school libraries today: a five year report on emerging media centers*, 3rd. ed. Chicago: Encyclopedia Britannica Inc.

—— (1963). *Effectiveness of centralized library service in elementary schools*, 2nd. ed., New Brunswick, New Jersey: Rutgers Univ. Press.

Hallworth, F. (1972). 'Public libraries and resource centres', *Library Assocn. Record* 74(3), March, 39–41.

Hare, G. (1971). 'Resource centres: a challenge to the library service', *Library Assocn. Public Libraries Conference 1971: Proceedings*; 24–9.

Hill, Janet (1973). *Children are people: the librarian in the community*, Hamilton.

Holly, J. F. and Carnahan, D. J. (1971). 'Creating a multimedia library: a case study', *Library Trends* 19(4), April: 419–36.

McCart, Kathryn B. (1971). 'Inter-professional links in education', *Scottish Library Assocn. News* 106, Nov.: 383–8.

Powell, Len S. (1974). 'Learning resource centres', *BACIE Journal* 28(4), April: 42–4.

Resources and their management: a working party report (1972). Oxfordshire Education Committee.

Swarthout, Charlene R. (1967). *The school library as a part of the instructional system*, Metuchen, New Jersey: Scarecrow Press.

Weiss, Peter (1974). 'The work of Inner London Education Authority's (ILEA) Media Resources Centre – a personal view by its director', *Ideas* 27. Feb.: 4–8.

Retrieval

Balmforth, C. K. and Cox, N. S. M. (eds) (1971). *Interface: library automation with special reference to computing activity*, Cambridge, Mass: Mass. Inst. Technol. Press.

Croghan, Antony (1972). *A code of rules for, with an exposition of integrated cataloguing of, nonbook media*, Coburgh Press.

Jolley, J. L. (1974). 'Retrieval systems theory and resource centres', *Ideas* 29, Oct. 154–61.

National Education Association. Dept. of Audio-Visual Instruction (1968). *Standards for cataloguing, coding and scheduling educational media*, Washington DC: NEA.

Ofiesh, G. D. (1968). *Dial access information retrieval systems: guidelines handbook for educators*, Washington DC: US Dept. Health, Education and Welfare, Office of Educn., Bureau of Research, July.

Sedgley, Anne and Merrett, Bronwen (1974). 'Cataloguing slide collections: art and architecture slides at Royal Melbourne Institute of Technology', *Australian Library Journal* 23(4), May: 146–52.

Squires, Geoffrey (1971). 'Information retrieval at sub-document level', *British Journal of Educnl. Technology* 2(3), Oct.: 212–15.

Index